Fodor's

FIFTH New EDITION

Acapulco, Ixtapa, Zihuatanejo

Parts of this book appear in *Fodor's Mexico*

Fodor's Travel Publications, Inc.
New York • London • Toronto

ISBN 0-679-02251-1

Fodor's Acapulco, Ixtapa, Zihuatanejo

Editor: Craig Seligman
Contributors: Anya Schiffrin, Wendy Ortiz de Montellano, Marcy Pritchard, Linda K. Schmidt
Creative Director: Fabrizio La Rocca
Cartographer: David Lindroth
Illustrator: Karl Tanner
Cover Photograph: Peter Guttman

Design: Vignelli Associates

About the Authors

Anya Schiffrin, a well-traveled freelance writer, has been published in the *Village Voice*, and various British publications. Wendy Ortiz de Montellano, an American writer, has lived in Mexico and worked in tourism there for more than 20 years.

Special Sales

Fodor's Travel Publications are available at special discounts for bulk purchases (100 copies or more) for sales promotions or premiums. Special editions, including personalized covers, excerpts of existing guides, and corporate imprints, can be created in large quantities for special needs. For more information, write to Special Marketing, Fodor's Travel Publications, 201 E. 50th Street, New York, NY 10022. Inquiries from Canada should be sent to Random House of Canada, Ltd., Marketing Dept., 1265 Aerowood Dr., Mississauga, Ontario L4W 1B9. Inquiries from the United Kingdom should be sent to Fodor's Travel Publications, 20 Vauxhall Bridge Road, London, England SW1V 2SA.

MANUFACTURED IN THE UNITED STATES OF AMERICA
10 9 8 7 6 5 4 3 2 1

Contents

Maps

Foreword

"Nirvana by the Sea," "Miami on the Pacific," and "Queen of the Mexican Resorts" are among the names that have, at one time or another, been applied to Acapulco, the archetypal beachgoer's destination. Legendary haven for the jet-set, politicians, and literary greats, Acapulco today attracts those of more modest means seeking almost-guaranteed sunshine; bargains in silver, leather, and Mexican handicrafts; and the frenzied nightlife of lore.

Three and a half hours up the coast, the newer resort towns of Ixtapa and Zihuatanejo offer equally splendid sun and sand, far cleaner bays, and even better prices. The pace of the nightlife can't compare with the year-round party in Acapulco, but travelers in search of beauty and serenity will find it up here, and the two towns offer lodging, dining, and shopping of a sophistication to rival Acapulco's.

The sliding peso and the so-called Mexican Riviera's proximity to the United States make these resorts even more attractive as a vacation option to those north of the border, especially in winter. This guide presents the widest range of sights, activities, restaurants, and accommodations and, within that range, selections that are worthwhile and of the best value. The descriptions provided are just enough for you to make your own informed choices from among our selections.

While every care has been taken to ensure the accuracy of the information in this guide, the passage of time will always bring change, and, consequently, the publisher cannot accept responsibility for errors that may occur.

All prices and opening times quoted here are based on information supplied to us at press time. Hours and admission fees may change, however, and the prudent traveler will avoid inconvenience by calling ahead.

Fodor's wants to hear about your travel experiences, both pleasant and unpleasant. When a hotel or restaurant fails to live up to its billing, let us know and we will investigate the complaint and revise our entries when the facts warrant it.

Send your letters to the editors of Fodor's Travel Publications, 201 E. 50th Street, New York, NY 10022.

Highlights and Fodor's Choice

Highlights

Acapulco is a survivor. Although Fonatur, Mexico's tourism department, continues to build a string of new coastal resorts, Acapulco still grows and draws visitors from around the world.

With the **change in presidents** in late 1988, Acapulco—and Mexican tourism in general—entered an era of enthusiasm typical of the start of the new leader's six-year term.

This administration's economic program permits **100% investment by foreigners** in tourism projects, which is an abrupt change from the former carved-in-stone mandate allowing less than 50% investment by foreigners.

In late 1990 the government-imposed "floating" of the peso was reduced from one peso to 40 centavos a day; then, in 1991, it was reduced again another 20 centavos. (At press time one peso was worth US$ .00035.) The long-rumored currency change from peso to **azteca** remains just another rumor. The peso's relative weakness against the U.S. dollar makes Mexico one of the world's best travel values.

Airlines, the transport for most travelers to Mexico, appear to be settling down as well. **Aeroméxico,** the former government-owned airline, went bankrupt in 1988 but has been resurrected as a private enterprise. Though it has one-third fewer planes than before, the airline is steadily rebuilding the routes it serves south of the border. **Foreign bus companies** have finally been given permission to operate within Mexico, though service is still limited.

In Acapulco, work continues on developing the **Punta Diamante** area, and the **Camino Real Acapulco** was scheduled to open in late 1992. And there are still more T-shirt shops than any sane city should have.

Work on refurbishing hotels throughout **Acapulco Tradicional,** the older area of the city, continues. The area, which retains the flavor of Mexico, is still rough around the edges. But it offers a gentle respite from the generic glitz of the string of hotels lining The Strip.

Construction of a marina on the site of the former Club de Pesca hotel (one of the first luxury hotels in Acapulco) continues in stops and starts.

The governments—municipal, state, and national—are working on the resort's infrastructure with the usual initial enthusiasm so characteristic of governments in general. Time only will tell if they see completion. Work is almost completed on a new highway between Acapulco and Mexico City that will cut the driving time to 3½ hours (a good portion is already open), more stoplights and telephone booths have been installed along the Costera Miguel Alemán, and the streets seem to be cleaner. The city and state governments have also built several large garages and parking lots in town to handle the expected increase in tourists arriving by automobile.

Long-distance calls can be made from many of the phones—some of them even take credit cards. In an effort to get the hawkers off the streets and beaches, the government has built open-air markets at strategic points throughout the city. The municipal beaches look a lot cleaner and new restrooms and showers have been installed, but pollution in Acapulco Bay remains a sore point. Swimmers should stick to the hotel pool.

Fodor's Choice

No two people will agree on what makes a perfect vacation, but it's fun and helpful to know what others think. Here, then, is a very personal list of Fodor's Choices. We hope you'll have a chance to experience some of them yourself while visiting Acapulco, Ixtapa, and Zihuatanejo. For detailed information about each entry, refer to the appropriate chapters within this guidebook.

Special Moments

Dancing under the stars at Discobeach

Fireworks at Fantasy Disco

Holy Week services at Santa Prisca in Taxco

Riding the cable car up to the Monte Taxco hotel

The view of the bay from Miramar or Extravaganzza

A boat trip on the Coyuca Lagoon

Taste Treats

Cheeseburgers at Mimi's Chili Saloon

Yogurt fruit shakes at 100% Natural

The succulent breakfast buffet at the Princess

Grilled *huachinango* (red snapper) at beach restaurants

Chilled summery soups at Madeiras

Cold beer and chips at Zorrito's

After Hours

A night cruise on the *Aca Tiki*

Euphoria Disco to see the "volcano" erupt

Mexican fiesta and mariachis at the Centro Internacional

Sunset at Pie de la Cuesta

Champagne boat ride to see the cliff divers

Off the Beaten Track

Breakfast at the Zócalo

Horseback riding on the beach in Ixtapa

Mass at Nuestra Señora de la Soledad

Exploring the market downtown

People-watching from the balcony of Paco's bar in Taxco

Best Restaurants

Coyuca 22 (Acapulco, *Very Expensive*)
Villa de la Selva (Ixtapa, *Expensive*)
La Taberna (Taxco, *Moderate*)
La Ventana de Taxco (Taxco, *Moderate*)
Madeiras (Acapulco, *Moderate*)
Beto's Barra Vieja (Acapulco, *Inexpensive*)
Tlaquepaque (Acapulco, *Inexpensive*)
Zorrito's (Acapulco, *Inexpensive*)

Best Hotels

Acapulco Princess (Acapulco, *Very Expensive*)
Las Brisas (Acapulco, *Very Expensive*)
Pierre Marqués (Acapulco, *Very Expensive*)
Villa del Sol (Zihuatanejo, *Very Expensive*)
Villa Vera (Acapulco, *Very Expensive*)
Camino Real (Ixtapa, *Expensive*)
Fiesta Americana Condesa (Acapulco, *Expensive*)
Boca Chica (Acapulco, *Moderate*)
Hacienda del Solar (Taxco, *Moderate*)
Playa Hermosa (Acapulco, *Inexpensive*)
Ukae Kim (Acapulco, *Inexpensive*)

Acapulco to Mexico City

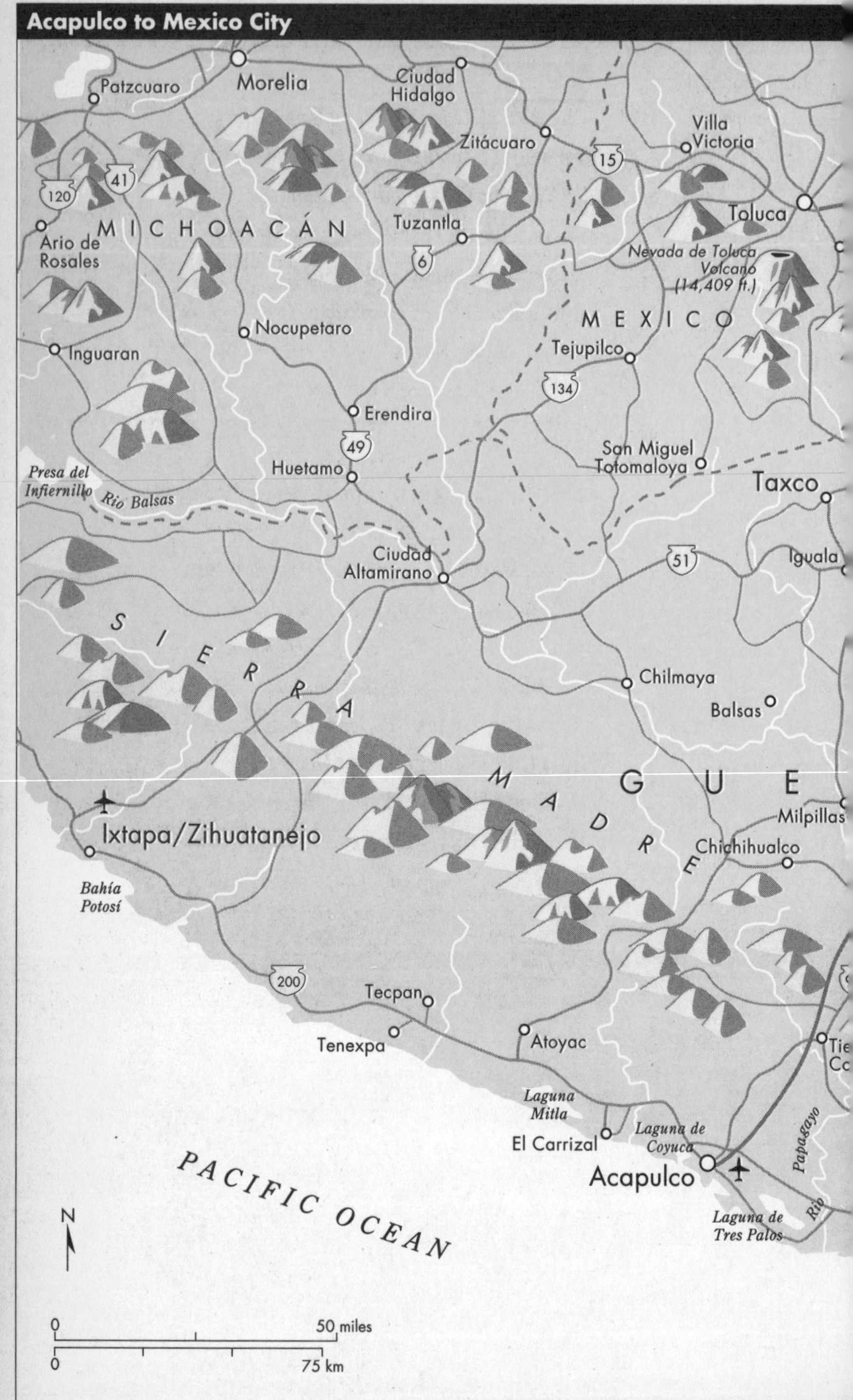

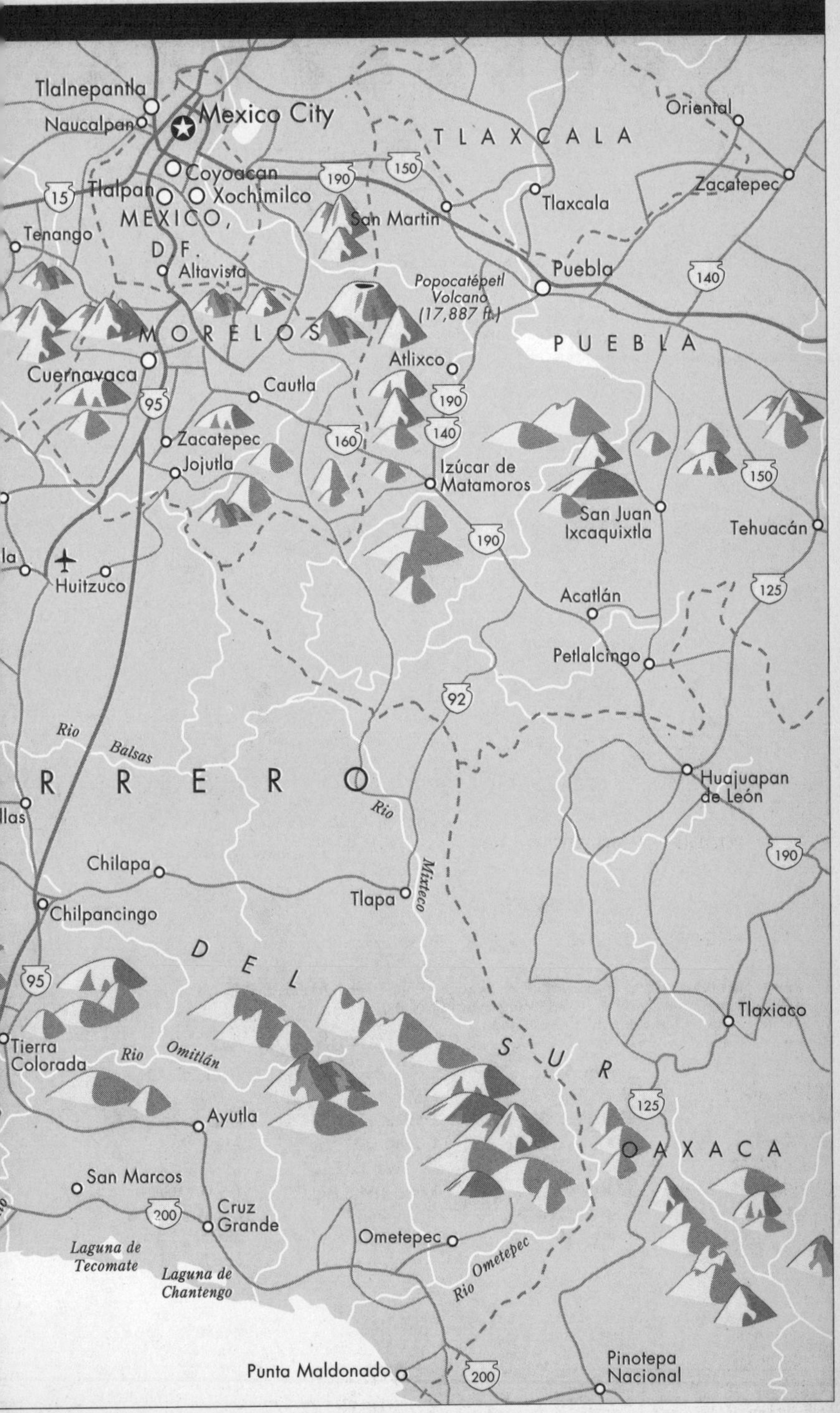

Tlalnepantla
Naucalpan
Mexico City
TLAXCALA
Oriental
Coyoacan
150
190
Zacatepec
15
Tlalpan
Xochimilco
Tlaxcala
MEXICO,
D.F.
San Martin
Tenango
Altavista
Puebla
140
Popocatépetl
Volcano
(17,887 ft.)
MORELOS
PUEBLA
Atlixco
Cuernavaca
Cautla
190
95
140
Zacatepec
160
Jojutla
Izúcar de
Matamoros
150
San Juan
Ixcaquixtla
Tehuacán
190
Huitzuco
125
Acatlán
Petlalcingo
92
Rio
Balsas
RRERO
Huajuapan
de León
Rio
Mixteco
190
Chilapa
Tlapa
Chilpancingo
DEL
95
Tlaxiaco
Tierra
Colorada
Rio
Omitlán
SUR
125
Ayutla
OAXACA
San Marcos
Cruz
Grande
200
Ometepec
Laguna de
Tecomate
Laguna de
Chantengo
Rio
Ometepec
Punta Maldonado
200
Pinotepa
Nacional

World Time Zones

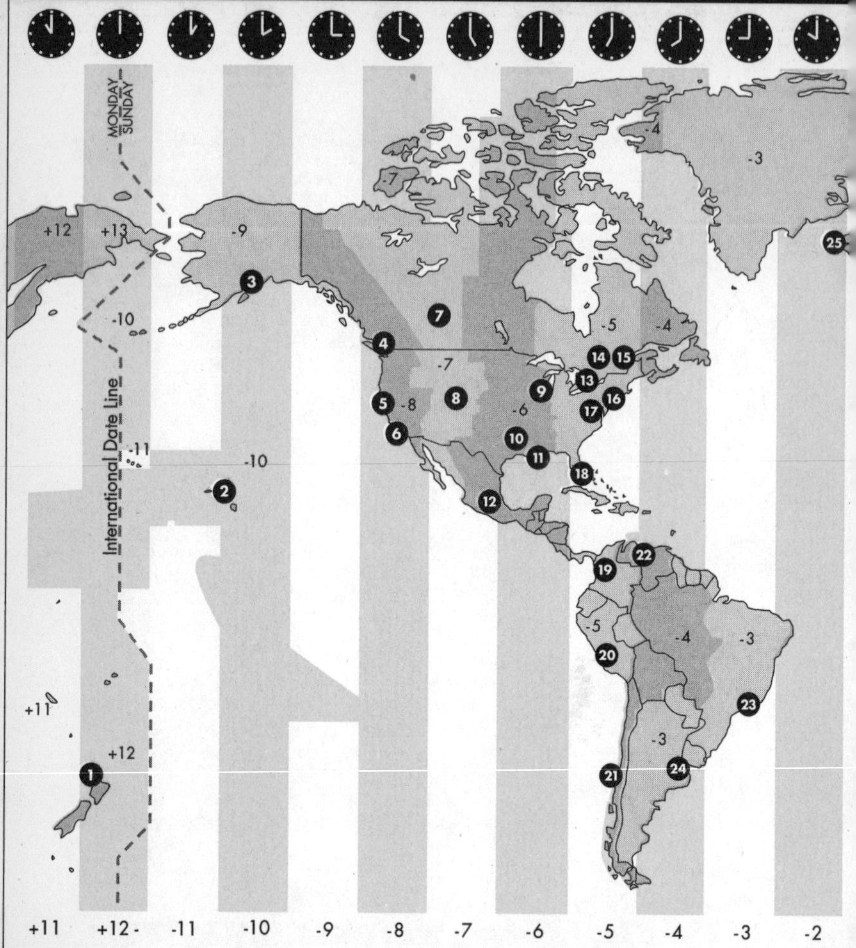

+11 +12 -11 -10 -9 -8 -7 -6 -5 -4 -3 -2

Numbers below vertical bands relate each zone to Greenwich Mean Time (0 hrs.).
Local times frequently differ from these general indications,
as indicated by light-face numbers on map.

Algiers, **29**
Anchorage, **3**
Athens, **41**
Auckland, **1**
Baghdad, **46**
Bangkok, **50**
Beijing, **54**
Berlin, **34**
Bogotá, **19**
Budapest, **37**
Buenos Aires, **24**
Caracas, **22**
Chicago, **9**
Copenhagen, **33**
Dallas, **10**
Delhi, **48**
Denver, **8**
Djakarta, **53**
Dublin, **26**
Edmonton, **7**
Hong Kong, **56**
Honolulu, **2**
Istanbul, **40**
Jerusalem, **42**
Johannesburg, **44**
Lima, **20**
Lisbon, **28**
London (Greenwich), **27**
Los Angeles, **6**
Madrid, **38**
Manila, **57**

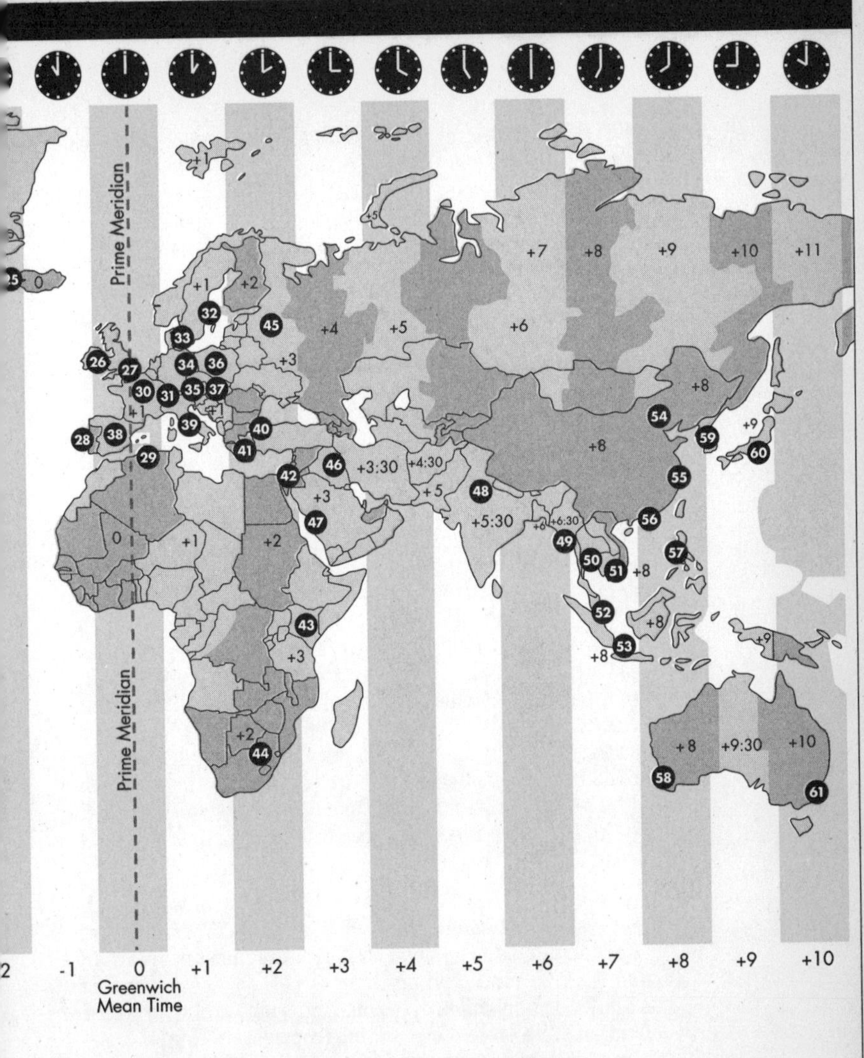

Mecca, **47**
Mexico City, **12**
Miami, **18**
Montréal, **15**
Moscow, **45**
Nairobi, **43**
New Orleans, **11**
New York City, **16**

Ottawa, **14**
Paris, **30**
Perth, **58**
Reykjavík, **25**
Rio de Janeiro, **23**
Rome, **39**
Saigon (Ho Chi Minh City), **51**

San Francisco, **5**
Santiago, **21**
Seoul, **59**
Shanghai, **55**
Singapore, **52**
Stockholm, **32**
Sydney, **61**
Tokyo, **60**

Toronto, **13**
Vancouver, **4**
Vienna, **35**
Warsaw, **36**
Washington, D.C., **17**
Yangon, **49**
Zürich, **31**

Introduction

For sun lovers, beach bums, and other hedonists, Acapulco is the ideal holiday resort. Don't expect high culture, historic monuments, or haute cuisine. Anyone who ventures to this Pacific resort 260 miles south of Mexico City does so to relax. Translate that as swimming, shopping, and nightlife.

Everything takes place against a staggeringly beautiful natural backdrop. Acapulco Bay is one of the world's best natural harbors, and it is the city's centerpiece. By day the water looks clean and temptingly deep blue; at night it flashes and sparkles with the city lights. Just drinking margaritas by the bay becomes a glamorous experience simply because the setting is so stunning.

Added to Acapulco's attraction is the exchange rate. Mexico is one of the few countries in the world where the dollar has not taken a beating in the past year. Although the Mexican government claims to have reduced inflation substantially by entering into a "solidarity pact" with businessmen (i.e., price controls), the truth is that prices continue to rise, salaries remain low, interest on savings has dropped, and the peso continues to weaken, making life difficult for the Mexicans. Visitors, however, will find that a little hard currency goes pretty far. Acapulco is an ideal destination for the budget-minded. There are plenty of hotels in which a double room is less than $50 and dozens of small eateries, usually family run, where three courses and drinks rarely exceed $10.

The weather is Acapulco's major draw—warm waters, almost constant sunshine, and year-round temperatures in the 80s. It comes as no surprise, then, that most people plan their day around laying their towel on some part of Acapulco's many miles of beach. Both tame and wild water sports are available—everything from waterskiing to snorkeling, diving, and the thrill of parasailing. Less-strenuous possibilities are motorboat rides and fishing trips. Championship golf courses, tennis courts, and the food/crafts markets also occasionally lure some visitors away from the beach, but not out of the sun.

Apart from these options, most people rouse themselves from their hammocks, deck chairs, or towels only when it is feeding time. Eating is one of Acapulco's great pleasures. You will find that in most dishes the ingredients are very fresh. Seafood is caught locally, and restaurateurs go to the *mercado* (market) daily to select the produce, meats, and fish for that night's meals. There are many good no-frills, down-home Mexican restaurants. Prices are reasonable and the food in these family-run places is prepared with care—spiced soups filled with red snapper (and red snapper heads), baskets filled with hot corn tortillas instead of bread. Eating at one of these spots gives you a glimpse into the real Mexico: office workers breaking for lunch, groups of men socializing over a cup of coffee. Even at a little *fonda* you can eat well for $5. Those with strong stomachs will discover, if they are willing to take the risk, that it is usually possible to eat a $1 plate of tacos from a street vendor without being rushed immediately to the hospital.

At night, Acapulco is transformed as the city rouses itself from the day's torpor and prepares for the long hours ahead. Even though Acapulco's heyday is past, its nightlife is legendary. This is true despite the fact that many of the city's discos look like they were designed in the early '70s by an architect who bought mirrors and strobe lights wholesale. Perpetually crowded, the discos are grouped in twos and threes, so most people go to several places in one night. Last year's disco hits and huge fruity cocktails are trademarks of the Acapulco disco experience.

Acapulco was originally an important port for the Spanish, who used it to trade with countries in the Far East. The Spanish built Fuerte de San Diego (Fort San Diego) to protect the city from pirates, and today the fort houses a historical museum with exhibits about Acapulco's past.

The name of the late Teddy Stauffer, an entrepreneurial Swiss, is practically synonymous with that of modern Acapulco. He hired the first cliff divers at La Quebrada in Old Acapulco, and founded the Boom Boom Room, the town's first dance hall, and Tequila A Go-Go, its first discotheque. The Hotel Mirador at La Quebrada and the area stretching from Caleta to Hornos beaches, near today's Old Acapulco, were the center of activity in the 1950s, when Acapulco was a town of 20,000 with an economy based largely on fishing.

Former President Miguel Alemán Valdés bought up miles of the coast just before the road and the airport were built. The Avenida Costera Miguel Alemán bears his name today. Since the late 1940s, Acapulco has expanded eastward so that today it is one of Mexico's largest cities, with a population of approximately 2 million.

Currently under development is a 3,000-acre expanse known as Acapulco Diamante. It stretches east from the Las Brisas area and Guitarron Peninsula (where the Sheraton Acapulco is located) through Puerto Marqués, Playa Revolcadero, and Playa Diamante, and up to the airport. It is an area of great beauty, where some of Acapulco's most luxurious villas, condos, and hotels (including Las Brisas, the Princess, the Pierre Marqués, and the Sheraton) are already located. Plans for the areas known as Punta Diamante and Playa Diamante call for additional hotels (a new Westin Camino Real should have opened by the time you read this), as well as condominiums, villas, shopping centers, a golf course (in addition to the two at the Princess and the Pierre Marqués), tennis and beach clubs, and parks.

Acapulco is laid out very neatly. Almost everything takes place on the Avenida Costera Miguel Alemán, the wide boulevard that hugs the shoreline. From the airport going west, you come first to the developing Acapulco Diamante area. Extravaganzza—the newest and most elegant disco—is here, on the highway to Las Brisas, as are the prestigious Madeiras and Miramar restaurants. Going down the scenic highway to the East Bay, you come to the naval base and the Hyatt Regency. This marks the beginning of the Costera Miguel Alemán, and specifically the stretch of it known as The Strip, which is the touristy area of town.

Several luxury hotels, most of the restaurants that are popular with Americans and Canadians, and the luxury stores and discos are here, as are all the airline offices and car rental agencies. The area around the Fiesta Americana Condesa Hotel is at the thick of things. Once you get to the American Express office, things slow down until you reach the Diana Glorieta (traffic circle). The Acapulco Plaza and Ritz hotels and a cluster of five discos stretch between the Diana and Papagayo Park. The park signals the end of The Strip. From there you pass a few hotels and beach restaurants and Fuerte de San Diego. On the right is the Central Post Office and the Zócalo (the main plaza). This marks the heart of Old Acapulco. Woolworth's, small tailors, inexpensive seafood restaurants, several markets, and the doctors' offices are here. Cruise ships and fishing boats leave from the dock near the Zócalo. Five minutes southwest of the Zócalo is La Quebrada, where the cliff divers daily perform their daring leaps. A few minutes more down the Costera is Caleta Beach, where you catch the boat to Roqueta Island.

A relaxed, holiday atmosphere pervades Acapulco; shorts and T-shirts are the standard dress, and many visitors go home with a full address book. People strike up conversations on the beach, in bars, and with whoever is eating dinner at the next table. The Mexicans you meet are friendly and will always help out with directions on the street or in the post office. Many travelers return to Acapulco every year to catch up on friendships begun on a previous vacation. The only drawback to this laid-back air is that things aren't done on a fixed schedule. Everything, from car rentals to purchases, takes much longer than you might expect. But there is no point in getting annoyed—just sit back and relax while you wait.

1 Essential Information

Before You Go

Government Tourist Offices

Contact the Mexican Government Tourism Office for brochures, lists of special events, and transportation schedules.

In the United States. 405 Park Ave., Suite 1401, New York, NY 10022, tel. 212/755–7261, 212/421–6655, or 800/262–8900; 1911 Pennsylvania Ave., Washington, DC 20006, tel. 202/728–1792; 70 E. Lake St., Suite 1413, Chicago, IL 60601, tel. 312/606–9015; 2707 N. Loop West, Suite 450, Houston, TX 77008, tel. 713/880–5153; 10100 Santa Monica Blvd., Suite 224, Los Angeles, CA 90067, tel. 213/203–8328; 128 Aragon Ave., Coral Gables, FL 33134, tel. 305/443–9160; 45 N.E. Loppe 410, Suite 125, San Antonio, TX 78216, tel. 512/366–3242.

In Canada. 1 Place Ville Marie, Suite 2409, Montreal, Quebec H3B 3M9, tel. 514/871–1052; 2 Bloor St. West, Suite 1801, Toronto, Ont. M4W 3E2, tel. 416/925–0704.

In the United Kingdom. 60/61 Trafalgar Sq., 3rd floor, London WC2N 5DS, tel. 4471/839–3177.

Tour Groups

Mexico remains one of the few real travel bargains available these days. The weak peso and the buying power of tour operators combine to create some very attractively priced packages. Independent packages are the typical way to tour the coastal resorts because everything is pretty much in one place and getting to sights is relatively easy. Group tours are more common for interior and special-interest programs. Tours linking Mexico City and Acapulco may start out as a group program in Mexico City and then offer free time on the coast. Below is a sampling of tour operators with packages in the region. For additional resources, contact your travel agent and/or the Mexican Government Tourism Office.

Before booking a tour, find out exactly what expenses are included (particularly tips, taxes, side trips, additional meals, and entertainment); government ratings of all hotels on the itinerary and the facilities they offer; cancellation policies for both you and the tour operator; and, if you are traveling alone, the cost of a single supplement. Most tour operators request that bookings be made through a travel agent—there is no additional charge.

General-interest Tours

American Express Vacations (300 Pinnacle Way, Norcross, GA 30093, tel. 800/241–1700 or 800/421–5785 in GA) is a veritable supermarket of tours.

Friendly Holidays (1983 Marcus Ave., Lake Success, NY, tel. 516/358–1200 or 800/221–9748) has been planning Mexican vacations for more than 20 years and has tours to beach and inland resorts throughout the country. It also arranges special itineraries.

GoGo Tours (69 Spring St., Ramsey, NJ 07446, tel. 800/821–3731), with 74 offices nationwide, offers a wide selection of tours at prices from budget to bonanza.

Gadabout Tours (700 E. Tahquitz Way, Palm Springs, CA 92262–6761, tel. 619/325–5556 or 800/952–5068) has an eight-day Copper Canyon tour. Trips to Veracruz and the Yucatan peninsula, as well as a Mexican Riviera cruise, are also available.

Ibero Travel (Box 758, Forest Hills, NY 11375, tel. 800/882–6678 in New York State, 800/654–2376 elsewhere in the United States) has three-to-seven-night packages to Acapulco and other destinations in Mexico.

Mexico Travel Advisors (1717 N. Highland Ave., Suite 1100, Los Angeles, CA 90028, tel. 213/462–6444 or 800/876–6824) has been leading tours to Mexico for 60 years.

Sun Holidays (26 6th St., Suite 603, Stamford, CT 06905, tel. 203/323–1166 or 800/243–2057) offers a four-day/three-night tour that includes Acapulco, Puerto Vallarta, and Cancún, as well as a seven-night Mexico Fiesta tour to Mexico City, Taxco, and Acapulco.

Other popular operators include **American Leisure** (9800 Center Pkwy., Suite 800, Houston, TX 77036, tel. 713/988–6098 or 800/777–1980) and **ASTI Tours** (21 E. 40th St., New York, NY 10016, tel. 212/684–3040).

Special-interest Tours

The **Acapulco Princess** runs a Mexican cooking school featuring the techniques of executive chef George Olah, who teaches dishes from the Aztecs right up to *nouvelle* Mexican. The school is limited to 20 participants per session; there are two five-day/four-night sessions a year. Contact the Princess Hotel (tel. 800/223–1818).

Package Deals for Independent Travelers

All the tour operators listed above offer air/hotel packages. There are dozens of nearly identical ones to Mexico City, Acapulco, or both. Your travel agent can steer you to those using reliable airlines and respectable hotels.

When to Go

The weather in Acapulco, Ixtapa, and Zihuatanejo is basically the same all year, with an average temperature of 80°F (or 27°C). The hottest months are June, July, and August; the coolest is January. During high season, December 15 to Easter, it rarely rains. The summer is more humid, August and October being the rainiest months. Whatever the time of year, you never need a jacket or a wrap, and the water is always warm. Low season (July to October) offers the advantage of lower prices and fewer people, though some restaurants and hotels close for vacation or to make repairs.

November is considered a "shoulder" month; prices will be midway between those in effect in high and low seasons. But even in low season, tour operators fill up the biggest hotels. The peak time for crowds is December 25 to January 3, when you may have trouble booking a hotel room. *Semana Santa*, the week before Easter, is very popular with Mexicans; schools are in recess and families come to Acapulco for their children's vacation. Budget hotels get very noisy and many tourists party all night and sleep on the beaches. Remember, no matter when you want to visit, book ahead to avoid disappointment.

Climate The following are the average daily maximum and minimum temperatures for Acapulco.

Jan.	88F	31C	**May**	90F	32C	**Sept.**	90F	32C
	72	22		77	25		75	24
Feb.	88F	31C	**June**	91F	33C	**Oct.**	90F	32C
	72	22		77	25		75	24
Mar.	88F	31C	**July**	90F	32C	**Nov.**	90F	32C
	72	22		77	25		73	23
Apr.	90F	32C	**Aug.**	91F	33C	**Dec.**	88F	31C
	73	23		77	25		72	22

Current weather information for foreign and domestic cities may be obtained by calling the **Weather Channel Connection** at 900/WEATHER from a touch-tone phone. In addition to the weather report, the service offers the local time, helpful travel tips, and hurricane, foliage, and ski reports. Calls cost 95¢ per minute.

Festivals and Seasonal Events

The following is a sampling of the top festivals held annually in the region. For additional information, contact the **Mexican Government Tourism Office,** 405 Park Ave., Suite 1002, New York, NY 10022, tel. 212/755–7261 or 421–6657.

Jan. 1: New Year's Day is celebrated throughout Mexico. In the provinces, many agricultural and livestock fairs take place.
Jan. 6: Feast of Epiphany is the day the Three Kings bring gifts to children throughout Mexico.
Feb. 2: Candlemas Day, or the Blessing of Candles, is celebrated nationwide, with fiestas, fairs, and lantern-decorated streets.
Feb. 5: Constitution Day is a national holiday commemorating the National Charter, which officially ended the Revolution of 1910, giving birth to modern Mexico.
Feb. 17–23: Carnival week is celebrated throughout the country with colorful parades and fiestas.
Mar. 21: Benito Juárez's Birthday is a national holiday.
April 4–11: Holy Week (Semana Santa) means processions, services, and other events, culminating on Easter.
May 1: Labor Day is a national holiday with workers' parades.
May 3: Holy Cross Day is observed nationwide by construction workers, who place decorated crosses atop unfinished buildings.
May 5: Cinco de Mayo is the anniversary of the French defeat at Puebla in 1862.
May 15: Feast of San Isidro Labrador is celebrated nationwide with the blessing of new seeds and animals.
June 1: Navy Day is commemorated in all seaports in Mexico and is especially colorful in Acapulco.
June 24: Saint John the Baptist Day is a national holiday.
July 16: Feast of the Virgin del Carmen is a holiday celebrated across Mexico with fiestas, pilgrimages, and religious rites.
July 25: Feast of Santiago is a national holiday that features Mexican-style rodeos.
Aug. 15: Feast of the Assumption of the Blessed Virgin Mary is celebrated nationwide with religious processions.
Sept. 15–16: Independence Day is when all Mexico reaffirms independence. The biggest celebrations are held in Mexico City.

Oct. 4: Feast of St. Francis of Assisi is commemorated nationwide with processions and parties.
Oct. 12: Columbus Day is observed throughout Mexico.
Nov. 1: All Saints Day includes religious rites and processions throughout the country. This is also the date on which the president of Mexico gives his State of the Nation address.
Nov. 2: All Souls Day is a time to honor the dead nationwide.
Nov. 20: Anniversary of the Mexican Revolution is observed as a national holiday.
Dec.: Sailfish Tournamet is held in Ixtapa/Zihuatanejo.
Dec. 12: Feast Day of the Virgin of Guadalupe is when the patron saint of the nation is honored.
Dec. 16–25: Christmas season is highlighted with nightly processions and *piñatas*. Christmas Eve and Christmas Day are family holidays.

What to Pack

Pack lightly, because the bargains are hard to resist. If you're like most tourists to Mexico, your luggage will be considerably heavier on your trip home. The luggage restrictions on flights from the United States to Mexico are the same as for domestic United States flights. You are allowed either two pieces of check-in luggage and two pieces of carry-on, or three pieces of check-in and one carry-on.

Clothing Acapulco, Ixtapa, and Zihuatanejo are very informal. Pack as you would for any beach resort that has extremely hot, humid weather. Leave suits, ties, and fancy clothes at home. Concentrate on light cotton clothes and a bathing suit. Shorts, T-shirts, and separates are what most people wear. At night, men turn up in slacks and shirts, and women dress up a bit more, usually in cotton dresses or skirts and blouses. But except for what's fashionable at the discos and the better restaurants, the Mexican Riviera look is very casual; not even at the top places does anyone wear a tie or anything that could be termed "formal." Women should pack just a couple of simple accessories to jazz up their day wear, which will provide a quick conversion from casual to casual-but-elegant. With the exclusion of shoes and lingerie, you can buy anything you need in Acapulco, often dirt-cheap.

Miscellaneous Women should take along all their favorite **cosmetics,** including nail polish and shampoo; you can't be sure you'll find your brand or your shade. Forget **hair spray, mousse,** and **gel;** they get sticky in the heat and are magnets for mosquitoes. A **small calculator** helps to figure out prices on the spot. Many department stores sell currency converter calculators. If you are staying in a modest hotel with a small staff, a **travel alarm** can be useful in case you need to get up early for an excursion. Small packets of **facial tissue** are a good idea because many small restaurants run out of toilet paper. Also take along lots of **suntan lotion** and **sunscreen;** resort prices are high. Bring a supply of **film**—the selection is limited and expensive. Bring plenty of **reading matter;** the selection of English-language books is limited and prices are higher than in the United States. Bring **sneakers, sandals,** and **shoes.** Mexican shoes aren't available in larger sizes and come in only one width. Take **dental floss,** since the Mexican variety comes apart in your mouth. **Sunglasses** are expensive down here and styles are limited. A **collapsible umbrella** is handy if you are traveling between May and October. A strong **change purse** will be useful for storing all those heavy Mexican coins. A **cheap tote bag** should be used on the beach so you don't risk losing your favorite purse. The electrical current is the same as in the United States, 110 volts and 60 cycles, so an **adapter** is not necessary.

If you are taking any foreign-made equipment from home, such as cameras, it's wise to carry the original receipt with you or register it with U.S. Customs before you leave (Form 4457). Otherwise you may end up paying duty on your return.

Taking Money Abroad

Traveler's checks and major U.S. credit cards are accepted almost everywhere in Acapulco, Ixtapa, and Zihuatanejo. You'll need cash for some of the smaller restaurants and shops. Although you won't get as good an exchange rate at home as in Mexico, it's wise to change a small amount of money into Mexican pesos so you won't have to face long lines at airport currency exchange booths. Most U.S. banks will convert dollars into pesos. If your local bank does not provide this service, you can exchange money through Thomas Cook Currency Service. To find the office nearest you, contact Thomas Cook Currency Service at 630 Fifth Ave., New York, NY 10111, tel. 212/757-6915.

For safety and convenience, traveler's checks are preferable to cash. The most recognized traveler's checks are those issued by American Express, Barclay's, Thomas Cook, and major commercial banks such as Citibank and Bank of America. Some banks will issue the checks free to established customers, but most charge a 1% commission. AAA offers free traveler's checks to its members. Buy part of the traveler's checks in small denominations for use toward the end of your trip. This will save you from having to cash a large check and ending up with more pesos than you need. You can also buy traveler's checks in Mexican pesos, a good idea if the U.S. dollar is falling and you want to lock in the current rate (although at press time this seems unlikely, since the Mexican peso has fallen steadily over the past few years and has been devalued several times). Remember to take the addresses of offices where you can get refunds for lost or stolen traveler's checks.

Banks and *casas de cambio* (literally, exchange houses) are the best places to change money. Hotels offer a significantly lower rate of exchange.

Getting Money from Home

There are at least three ways to get money from home: (1) Have it sent through a large commercial bank that has a relationship with a corresponding bank in Acapulco, Ixtapa, or Zihuatanejo. The only drawback is that you must have an account with the bank; if not, you'll have to go through your own bank, and the process will be slower and more costly. (2) Have it sent through American Express. If you are a cardholder, you can cash a personal check or a counter check at an American Express office for up to $1,000; $200 will be in pesos and $800 in traveler's checks. There is a 1% commission on the traveler's checks. You can also receive money through an American Express MoneyGram, which enables you to obtain up to $10,000 in cash. It works this way: You call home and ask someone to go to an American Express office—or an American Express MoneyGram agent located in a retail outlet—and fill out an American Express MoneyGram. It can be paid for with cash or with Visa, MasterCard, Discover, or the American Express Optima Card. (An American Express green, corporate, gold, or platinum card cannot be used unless the cardholder has a line of credit.) The person making the payment is given a reference number and telephones you with that number. The American Express MoneyGram agent calls an 800 number and authorizes the transfer of funds to the American Express office or participating agency in Acapulco or Ixtapa. In most cases, the money is available immediately on a 24-hour basis. You pick it up by showing identification and giving the reference number. Fees vary with the amount of money sent. For $300 the fee is $35; for $5,000, the fee is $175. For the American Express MoneyGram location nearest your home and to find out the Mexican locations, call 800/543–4080. You do not have to be a cardholder to use this service. (3) Have money sent through Western Union, whose U.S. number is 800/325–6000. If you have a MasterCard or Visa, you can have money sent for any amount up to your credit limit. If not, have someone take cash or a certified cashier's check to a Western Union office. The money will be delivered to a Mexican bank. Fees vary with the amount of money sent. For $1,000 the fee is $48; for $500, the fee is $34.

Cash Machines

Banamex is affiliated with the Cirrus network (and a few branches with the PLUS network), and automated teller machines (ATMs) can be found in many branch banks.

Mexican Currency

The unit of currency in Mexico is the peso. The bills come in denominations of 100,000, 50,000, 20,000, 10,000, 5,000, and 2,000. Coins are 5,000, 1,000, 500, 200, 100, and 50. At press time the peso was being devalued at a rate of 20 centavos (.0006 cents) per day, at a rate of about 2,817 pesos to the U.S. dollar.

What It Will Cost

Travel almost anywhere in Mexico is a bargain. This is true in Acapulco, where the dollar buys more than in years past and the not-too-picky traveler can easily spend less than $70 per day for all meals, accommodations, and sightseeing. Taxis are an especially good bargain (around $2 for a two-mile ride). Prices are always less if you make transactions in Spanish.

Taxes A 10% sales tax (called an IVA) is added to most purchases, although some stores include it in the price (*con IVA*). To be sure, always ask.

Sample Prices 1993: cup of coffee, 75¢ to $1.50; bottle of beer, $1.25 to $3.00; milkshake, $1.50; taco from street vendor, 50¢; cocktail, $3 to $5. Double room (inexpensive): under $65; (moderate): $65 to $110; (expensive): $100 to $185; (very expensive): $185 and up.

Passports and Visas

American Passports and visas are not formally required for entry into Mexico by U.S. citizens, though Mexican tourist cards are required. They are issued free upon proof of U.S. citizenship (valid U.S. passport, birth certificate with a driver's license, or certified copy of a birth certificate). Tourist cards can be obtained from Mexican consulates, the Mexican Government Tourism Office, Mexican Immigration Offices at entry points, most airlines serving Mexico, or travel agents.

Canadian Canadian citizens can enter Mexico with a tourist card—which can be obtained from travel agents, airlines, or local Mexican consulates—and proof of citizenship. The only acceptable proof is a valid passport or your original birth certificate plus a photo ID.

British *See* Tips for British Travelers, *below*.

Customs and Duties

On Arrival You are allowed to take into Mexico duty-free: 400 cigarettes or 2 boxes of cigars (50 cigars); 1 still and 1 movie camera and 12 rolls of film; a reasonable amount of perfume; 3 liter bottles of liquor or wine, for personal use; prescription medicines, also for personal use; and gift items not exceeding a combined value of $300. No plant material is allowed; permits are required for firearms, and pets require a visa (contact the Mexican Embassy for details). Before clearing Mexican Customs, air travelers must complete a baggage declaration, which is distributed on all airlines entering Mexico. There are no restrictions or limitations on the amount of cash, foreign currencies, checks, or drafts that can be imported or exported by visitors, though amounts over $4,000 must be declared.

On Departure Visitors are required to pay a $12 departure tax, either in dollars or pesos, before boarding their plane.

U.S. residents who have been out of the country for at least 48 hours and have not made an international trip in 30 days may bring home duty-free up to $400 worth of foreign goods. Each member of the family, regardless of age, is entitled to the same exemption, and exemptions can be pooled. For the next $1,000 worth of goods, a flat 10% rate is assessed; duties vary with the merchandise for anything over $1,400. The exemption for travelers 21 or older can include one liter of alcohol, 100 cigars (non-Cuban), and 200 cigarettes. Only one bottle of perfume trademarked in the United States may be brought in. There is no duty on antiques or art more than 100 years old. Anything exceeding these limits will be taxed at the port of entry and may be taxed additionally or prohibited in the traveler's home state. Mexico has been designated a "developing" or GSP country, which means that under the Generalized System of Preferences, unlimited amounts of certain goods can be brought home duty-free; check with the U.S. Customs Service, Box 7407, Washington, DC 20044. Gifts valued at less than $50 may be mailed duty-free to friends or relatives at home, but not more than one package per day to any one addressee and not to include perfumes costing more than $5, tobacco, or liquor.

Exemptions for returning **Canadian residents** range from $20 to $300, depending on length of stay out of the country. For the

$300 exemption, you must have been out of the country for one week. In any given year, you are only allowed one $300 exemption. You may bring in duty-free up to 50 cigars, 200 cigarettes, 2.2 pounds of tobacco, and 40 ounces of liquor, provided these are declared in writing to customs on arrival and accompany you in hand or checked-through baggage. Personal gifts should be mailed labeled "Unsolicited Gift—Value under $40." Obtain a copy of the Canadian Customs brochure *I Declare* for further details.

Tips for British Travelers

Passports and Visas British subjects need a valid passport and a Mexican tourist card. Passport-application forms are available from most travel agents and major post offices and from the Passport Office (Clive House, 70 Petty France, London SW1H 9BR, tel. 071/279–3434 for recorded information, or 071/279–4000.) A passport costs £15 and is valid for 10 years. The Mexican tourist card is available from airlines or from the Mexican Embassy (8 Halkin St., London SW1X 7DW, tel. 071/235–6393) or from your travel agent or if you are already abroad, from any Mexican Embassy or national airline office. Business travelers and students wishing to study in Mexico must inquire at the consulate for additiońal requirements. A passport or other proof of citizenship must be presented to reenter Great Britain.

Customs You are allowed to take into Mexico duty-free: 200 cigarettes or 50 cigars or 250 grams of tobacco; 1 still and 1 8mm film or video camera and 12 rolls of film for each; a reasonable amount of perfume; 2 liter bottles of liquor or wine, for personal use; prescription medicines, also for personal use; and gift items not exceeding a combined value of $300 (£156). No plant material is allowed. Permits are required for firearms, and pets require a visa (contact the Mexican Embassy for details). Before clearing Mexican Customs, air travelers must complete a baggage declaration, which is distributed on all airlines entering Mexico. On your return to Britain you may bring home: (1) 200 cigarettes or 100 cigarillos or 50 cigars or 250 grams of tobacco; (2) two liters of table wine with additional allowances for (a) one liter of alcohol over 22% by volume (38.8 proof, most spirits), (b) two liters of alcohol under 22% by volume, or (c) two more liters of table wine; (3) 60cc of perfume and 250 ml of toilet water; and (4) other goods up to a value of £32, but no more than 50 liters of beer or 25 mechanical lighters.

Insurance We recommend that to cover health and motoring mishaps, you insure yourself. One company worth trying is **Europ Assistance** (252 High St., Croydon, Surrey CRO 1NF, tel. 081/680–1234). It is also wise to take out insurance to cover loss of luggage (check, though, that this isn't already covered in an existing homeowner's policy). Trip-cancellation insurance is another wise buy. **The Association of British Insurers** (51 Gresham St., London EC2V 7HQ, tel. 071/600–3333) gives comprehensive advice on all aspects of vacation insurance.

Tour Operators Companies offering packages to Acapulco and other parts of Mexico include the following:

Mexican Holidays (23 Eccleston St., London SW1W 9LX, tel. 071/730–8640) can custom design an itinerary to any part of Mexico.

Sunset Travel Ltd. (306 Clapham Rd., London SW9 9AE, tel. 071/622–5466) offers packages to luxury and resort hotels overlooking Acapulco Bay.

Electricity Usually 110 volts; it will be helpful to bring an adapter because appliance outlets are primarily American-style and take flat, two-pronged plugs.

Traveling with Film

Never pack unprocessed film in check-in luggage; if your bags get X-rayed, you can say good-bye to your pictures. Carry the undeveloped film with you through security and have it inspected by hand. It helps if you keep your film in a separate plastic bag, ready for quick inspection. Inspectors at U.S. airports are required by law to honor requests for hand inspection; abroad, you'll have to depend on the kindness of strangers. The old airport scanning machines—still in use in some Third World countries—use heavy doses of radiation that can turn a family portrait into an early morning fog. The newer models—used in all U.S. airports—are safe for anything from five to 500 scans, depending on the speed of your film.

Language

English is more prevalent in Acapulco, Taxco, and Ixtapa/Zihuatanejo than in less touristy parts of Mexico. Hotel and restaurant staffs, taxi drivers, store clerks, and most street vendors speak English, but they will appreciate any attempt to converse with them in their native tongue. Those who speak Spanish are generally charged less by taxi drivers and vendors.

Staying Healthy

Many visitors to Mexico are eventually hit with a diarrheal intestinal ailment. Although uncomfortable, it generally is not serious and disappears in three or four days without medication. Drink only bottled water, and eat no raw food except fruit you can peel yourself.

The Centers for Disease Control (CDC) in Atlanta recommends swimming in chlorinated swimming pools only—unless you are absolutely certain that the beaches and freshwater lakes are not polluted. If you are fair-skinned, be sure to bring sunscreen with a high SPF factor (10 or above).

If you have a health problem that might require purchasing a prescription drug while in Mexico, have your doctor write a prescription using the drug's generic name. Brand names vary widely from country to country.

The **International Association for Medical Assistance to Travelers** *(IAMAT)* is a worldwide association offering a list of approved, English-speaking doctors whose training meets British and American standards. For a list of Mexican physicians and clinics that are part of this network, contact IAMAT, 417 Center St., Lewiston, NY 14092. In Canada: 40 Regal Rd., Guelph, Ontario N1K 1B5. In Europe: 57 Voirets, 1212 Grand-Lancy, Geneva, Switzerland. Membership is free.

Shots and Medication Persons entering Mexico from areas infected with yellow fever must have a certificate of vaccination. For a list of those areas, contact your local health department or the nearest Mexican consulate.

The American Medical Association (AMA) recommends Pepto-Bismol for traveler's diarrhea.

The CDC reports that malaria exists in the Acapulco area although the risk to visitors staying in resort hotels is low. The CDC recommends malaria-preventive drugs if you plan to go off the beaten path. Because malaria is carried by a mosquito that feeds at night, be certain your hotel room has screens, spray yourself liberally with insect repellent after sunset, and wear protective clothing. If you do go off the beaten path, you may also want to take precautions against dengue fever.

Insurance

Travelers may seek insurance coverage in four areas: health and accident, lost luggage, trip cancellation, and flight. Your first step is to review your existing health and homeowner policies; some health insurance plans cover health expenses incurred while traveling, some major medical plans cover emergency transportation, and some homeowner policies cover the theft of luggage.

Health and Accident Several companies offer coverage designed to supplement existing health insurance for travelers:

Carefree Travel Insurance (Box 310, 120 Mineola Blvd., Mineola, NY 11501, tel. 516/294–0220 or 800/323–3149) provides coverage for emergency medical evacuation and accidental death and dismemberment. It also offers 24-hour medical advice by phone.

International SOS Assistance (Box 11568, Philadelphia, PA 19116, tel. 215/244–1500 or 800/523–8930), a medical assistance company, provides emergency evacuation services, worldwide medical referrals, and optional medical insurance.

Travel Guard International (1145 Clark St., Stevens Point, WI 54481, tel. 715/345–0505 or 800/782–5151), underwritten by Transamerica Occidental Life Companies, offers emergency evacuation and reimbursement for medical expenses with no deductibles or daily limits.

Wallach and Company, Inc. (107 W. Federal St., Box 480, Middleburg, VA 22117–0480, tel. 703/687–3166 or 800/237–6615) offers comprehensive medical coverage, including emergency evacuation services worldwide.

Lost Luggage Airlines are responsible for lost or damaged property only up to $1,250 per passenger on domestic flights, $9.07 per pound (or $20 per kilo) for checked baggage on international flights, and up to $400 per passenger for unchecked baggage on international flights. If you're carrying valuables, either take them with you on the airplane or purchase additional insurance for lost luggage. Some airlines will issue additional luggage insurance when you check in, but many do not. Hand luggage is not included.

Insurance for lost, damaged, or stolen luggage is available through travel agents or directly through various insurance companies. Two of these are **Tele-Trip** (Box 31685, 3201 Farnam St., Omaha, NE 68131–0618, tel. 800/228–9792), a subsidiary of Mutual of Omaha, and **The Travelers Insurance Corporation** (Ticket and Travel Dept., 1 Tower Sq., Hartford, CT 06183-5040, tel. 203/277-0111 or 800/243-3174). Tele-Trip operates sales booths at airports and issues insurance through travel agents. Rates vary according to the length of the trip. Travelers will insure checked or hand luggage for $500-$2,000 valuation per person, for a maximum of 180 days. Rates for 1-5 days for $500 valuation are $10; for 180 days, $85. Neither company makes a distinction between domestic and international flights. Check the travel pages of your Sunday newspaper for the names of other companies that insure luggage. Before you go, itemize the contents of each bag in case you need to file an insurance claim. Be certain to put your address on and inside each piece of luggage, including carry-on bags. (A business address is recommended, so thieves don't have directions to your empty house.) If your luggage is stolen and later recovered, the airline will deliver the luggage to your home free of charge.

Luggage loss coverage is usually part of a comprehensive travel insurance package that includes personal accident, trip cancellation, and sometimes default and bankruptcy. Several companies offer broad policies:

Access America, Inc., a subsidiary of Blue Cross-Blue Shield, Box 11188, Richmond, VA 23230, tel. 800/334-7525 for claims, 800/284-8300 for sales.

Near Services, 450 Prairie Ave., Suite 101, Calumet City, IL 60409, tel. 708/868-6700 or 800/654-6700.

Travel Guard International (*see above*).

Carefree Travel Insurance (*see above*).

Trip Cancellation Consider purchasing trip-cancellation insurance, which covers you if an emergency causes you to cancel or postpone your trip, especially if you are traveling on a promotional or discounted ticket that does not allow changes or cancellations. It is usually included in the combination travel insurance packages available from most tour operators, travel agents, and insurance agents.

Flight Flight insurance, which covers passengers in the case of death or dismemberment, is often included in the price of a ticket when paid for with American Express, MasterCard, or other major credit cards.

Student and Youth Travel

The **International Student Identity Card (ISIC)** entitles students to youth rail passes, special fares on local transportation, and discounts at museums, theaters, sports events, and many other attractions. If purchased in the United States, the $14 cost of the ISIC also includes $3,000 in emergency medical insurance, plus $100 a day for up to 60 days of hospital coverage, as well as a collect phone number to call in case of emergency. Apply to the Council on International Educational Exchange (CIEE), 205 E. 42nd St., New York, NY 10017, tel. 212/661-1414. In Canada, the ISIC is available from Travel Cuts (187 College St., Toronto, Ont. M5T 1P7, tel. 416/979-2406) for CN$13. In the UK, students enrolled in university programs can purchase the ISIC at any student union or student travel company.

Council Travel, a CIEE subsidiary, is the foremost U.S. student travel agency, specializing in low-cost charters and serving as the exclusive U.S. agent for many student airfare bargains and student tours. CIEE's 72-page *Student Travel Catalog* and "Council Charter" brochure are available free from any Council Travel office in the United States (enclose $1 postage if ordering by mail). In addition to the CIEE headquarters at 205 E. 42nd Street and a branch office at 35 W. 8th Street in New York City, there are Council Travel offices in Tempe, AZ; Berkeley, La Jolla, Long Beach, Los Angeles, San Diego, San Francisco, and Sherman Oaks, CA; Boulder, CO; New Haven, CT; Washington, DC; Atlanta, GA; Chicago and Evanston, IL; New Orleans, LA; Amherst, Boston, and Cambridge, MA; Ann Arbor, MI; Minneapolis, MN; Durham, NC; Columbus, OH; Portland, OR; Philadelphia, PA; Providence, RI; Austin and Dallas, TX; Seattle, WA; and Milwaukee, WI.

The Information Center at the **Institute of International Education,** IIE (809 UN Plaza, New York, NY 10017, tel. 212/883–8200), has reference books, foreign university catalogues, study-abroad brochures, and other materials, which may be consulted by students and nonstudents alike, free of charge. The Information Center is open weekdays from 10 to 4.

IIE administers a variety of grant and study programs offered by U.S. and foreign organizations and publishes a well-known annual series of study-abroad guides, including *Academic Year Abroad* and *Vacation Study Abroad.* For a current list of IIE publications, prices, and ordering information, write to Publications Service, Institute of International Education, 809 UN Plaza, New York, NY 10017. Books must be purchased by mail or in person; telephone orders are not accepted.

General information on IIE programs and services is available from its regional offices in Chicago, Denver, Houston, San Francisco, and Washington, DC.

Traveling with Children

Publications ***Family Travel Times,*** an 8- to 12-page newsletter, is published 10 times a year by TWYCH (Travel with Your Children, 45 W. 18th St., 7th Floor Tower, New York, NY 10011, tel. 212/206–0688). A subscription for $35 includes access to back issues and weekly opportunities to call in for specific information.

Villa Rentals **At Home Abroad, Inc.,** 405 E. 56th St., Suite 6H, New York, NY 10022, tel. 212/421–9165. **Villas International,** 605 Market St., Suite 510, San Francisco, CA 94105, tel. 415/281–0910 or 800/221–2260. **Hideaways, Inc.,** Box 1270, Littleton, MA 01460, tel. 800/843–4433. **Villas and Apartments Abroad,** 420 Madison Ave., Suite 1105, New York, NY 10017, tel. 212/759–1025 or 800/433–3020.

Getting There On international flights, children under two not occupying a seat pay 10% of adult fare. Various discounts apply to children 2–12. Reserve a seat behind the bulkhead of the plane, which offers more leg room and can usually fit a bassinet (supplied by the airline). At the same time, inquire about special children's meals or snacks, offered by most airlines. (See "TWYCH's Airline Guide," in the February 1990 and 1992 issues of *Family*

Travel Times, for a rundown on children's services furnished by 46 airlines.) Ask your airline in advance if you can bring aboard your child's car seat. (For the booklet "Child/Infant Safety Seats Acceptable for Use in Aircraft," write to the Federal Aviation Administration, APA-200, 800 Independence Ave. SW, Washington, DC 20591, tel. 202/267-3479.)

Baby-sitting Services Arrangements for child care are easily made through your hotel concierge.

Hints for Disabled Travelers

The **Information Center for Individuals with Disabilities** (Fort Point Pl., 1st floor, 27–43 Wormwood St., Boston, MA 02210-1606, tel. 617/727-5540 or 800/462-5015 in Massachusetts, voice and TDD) offers general information about travel, including two fact sheets: "Tour Operators and Travel Agents for People with Disabilities" and "Tips for Travelers" ($5 each for Massachusetts nonresidents).

Moss Rehabilitation Hospital Travel Information Service (1200 West Tabor Rd., Philadelphia, PA 19141-3099, tel. 215/456-9600; TDD 215/456-9602) provides information on tourist sights, transportation, and accommodations in destinations around the world. Free by phone; $5 by mail for up to three destinations. Allow one month for delivery.

Mobility International USA (Box 3551, Eugene, OR 97403, tel. 503/343-1284, voice and TDD) is an international organization with 500 affiliated members. For a $20 annual fee, it coordinates exchange programs for disabled people around the world and offers information on accommodations and organized study programs.

Nautilus Tours (5435 Donna Ave., Tarzana, CA 91356, tel. 818/343-6339) has for nine years operated international trips and cruises for the disabled. **Travel Industry and Disabled Exchange** (TIDE, at the same address, tel. 818/368-5648), an industry-based organization with a $15 annual membership fee, provides a quarterly newsletter and information on travel agencies and tours.

The **Society for the Advancement of Travel for the Handicapped** (SATH, 347 5th Ave., Suite 610, New York, NY 10016, tel. 212/447-7284, fax 212/725-8253) offers access information. Annual membership is $45, or $25 for senior travelers and students. For specific information send $2 and a self-addressed envelope.

The Itinerary (Box 2012, Bayonne, NJ 07002, tel. 908/858-3400) is a bimonthly travel magazine for the disabled.

Hints for Older Travelers

The **American Association of Retired Persons** (AARP, 601 E St. NW, Washington, DC 20049, tel. 202/434-2277) has two programs for independent travelers: (1) the Purchase Privilege Program, which offers discounts on hotels, airfare, car and RV rentals, and sightseeing, and (2) the AARP Motoring Plan, provided by Amoco, which furnishes emergency aid and trip routing information for an annual fee of $33.95 per couple. AARP members must be 50 or older. Annual dues are $5 per person or per couple.

To use an AARP or other identification card, ask for a reduced hotel rate at the time you make your reservation rather than when you check out. At restaurants, show your card to the maître d' before you're seated because discounts may be limited to certain set menus, days, or hours. When renting a car, remember that special promotional rates may offer greater savings than those available with your ID card.

National Council of Senior Citizens (1331 F St. NW, Washington, DC 20004, tel. 202/347–8800) is a nonprofit advocacy group with some 5,000 local clubs across the country. Annual membership is $12 per person or per couple. Members receive a monthly newspaper with travel information and an ID card for reduced-rate hotels and car rentals.

Mature Outlook (6001 N. Clark St., Chicago, IL 60660, tel. 800/336–6330), a subsidiary of Sears, Roebuck & Co., is a travel club for people over 50, with hotel and motel discounts and a bimonthly newsletter. Annual membership is $9.95 per couple.

Arriving and Departing

From the North by Plane

There are three types of flights to Acapulco: nonstop—no changes, no stops; direct—no changes, but one or more stops; and connecting—two or more planes, one or more stops.

Airlines From the United States: **American** (tel. 800/433–7300) has nonstops from Dallas; connections from Chicago and New York through Dallas. **Continental** (tel. 800/525–0280) has nonstop service from Houston. **Delta's** (tel. 800/843–9378) nonstop service is from Dallas and Los Angeles. **Mexicana** (tel. 800/531–7921) has nonstop service from Chicago and connecting service from New York, Miami, Denver, Dallas, Los Angeles, San Francisco, and San Jose, California, all via Mexico City. **Aeromexico's** (tel. 800/237–6639) flight from New York to Acapulco stops in Mexico City. Other major carriers fly into Mexico City, where you can make a connection to Acapulco.

From Canada: At press time **Sunquest** (tel. 800/776–3000) had charter service from Toronto on a biweekly basis using La Tur airlines; **Delta** has flights from most major Canadian cities via Los Angeles to Acapulco; **Canadian Holidays** (tel. 800/387–7663) has nonstop charter flights from Toronto to Acapulco.

Flying Time From New York via Dallas, 4½ hours; from Chicago, 4¼ hours; from Los Angeles, 3½ hours.

Luggage Regulations

Checked Luggage U.S. airlines generally allow passengers to check in two suitcases whose total dimensions (length + width + height) do not exceed 62 inches and whose weight does not exceed 70 pounds per bag.

Rules governing foreign airlines vary from airline to airline, so check with your travel agent or the airline itself before you go. All airlines allow passengers to check in two bags. In general, expect the weight restriction on the two bags to be not more than 70 pounds each, and the size restriction for each to be 62 inches total dimensions.

Carry-on Luggage Passengers aboard major U.S. carriers are usually limited to two carry-on bags. For a bag you wish to store under the seat, the maximum dimensions are 9″ × 14″ × 22″, a total of 45″. For bags that can be hung in a closet or on a luggage rack, the maximum dimensions are 4″ × 23″ × 45″, a total of 72″. For bags you wish to store in an overhead bin, the maximum dimensions are 10″ × 14″ × 36″, a total of 60″. Your two carryons must each fit one of these sets of dimensions, and any item that exceeds the specified dimensions will generally be rejected as a carryon, and handled as checked baggage. Keep in mind that an airline can adapt these rules to circumstances, so on an especially crowded flight, don't be surprised if you are allowed only one carry-on bag.

In addition to the two carryons, the rules list seven items that may also be brought aboard: a handbag (pocketbook or purse); an overcoat or wrap; an umbrella; a camera; a reasonable amount of reading material; an infant bag; and crutches, a cane, braces, or other prosthetic devices upon which the passenger is dependent. Infant/child safety seats can also be brought aboard if parents have purchased a ticket for the child or if there is space in the cabin.

Note that these regulations are for U.S. airlines only. Foreign airlines generally allow one piece of carry-on luggage in tourist class, in addition to handbags and bags filled with duty-free goods. It is best to check with your airline ahead of time to find out the exact rules regarding carry-on luggage.

Discount Flights

The major airlines offer a range of tickets that can make the price of any given flight vary by more than 300%, depending on the day of purchase. As a rule, the further in advance you buy the ticket, the less expensive it is and the greater the penalty (up to 100%) for canceling. Check with airlines for details.

It's important to distinguish between companies that sell seats on charter flights and companies that sell one of a block of tickets on scheduled airlines. Charter flights are the least expensive and the least reliable—with chronically late departures and not infrequent cancellations. They also tend to depart less frequently (usually once a week) than regularly scheduled flights. A wise alternative is a ticket on a scheduled flight bought from a wholesaler or ticket broker. It's an unbeatable deal, at up to 50% off the APEX fare. Tickets are subject to availability, however, so passengers must generally have flexible travel schedules.

Another option is to join a travel club that offers special discounts to its members. You might consider **Moment's Notice** (425 Madison Ave., New York, NY 10017, tel. 212/486–0500), **Travelers Advantage** (CUC Travel Service, 49 Music Square West, Nashville, TN 37203, tel. 800/548–1116); or **Worldwide Discount Travel Club** (1674 Meridian Ave., Suite 300, Miami Beach, FL 33139, tel. 305/534–2082).

Travelers willing to put up with some restrictions and inconvenience, in exchange for substantially reduced airfares, may be interested in flying as air couriers to accompany shipments between designated points.

For a telephone listing of courier companies by the cities to which they fly, send $5 and a self-addressed, stamped business-size envelope to Pacific Data Sales Publishing (2554 Lincoln Blvd., Suite 275-I, Marina del Rey, CA 90291). For "A Simple Guide to Courier Travel" send $15.95 postpaid by check, Visa, or MasterCard to Box 2394, Lake Oswego, OR 97035. Call (tel. 800/344–9375) for more information.

Enjoying the Flight If you're lucky enough to be able to sleep on a plane, it makes sense to fly at night. Unless you are flying from Europe, jet lag won't be a problem. There is little or no time difference between the Mexican Riviera and the United States and Canada. Sleepers usually prefer window seats to curl up against; those who like to move about the cabin should request an aisle seat. Bulkhead seats (located in the front row of each cabin) have more legroom, but seat trays are attached rather awkwardly to the arms of your seat rather than to the back of the seat ahead.

Smoking If smoking bothers you, ask for a seat far away from the smoking section. If the airline tells you there are no nonsmoking seats, insist on one: Department of Transportation regulations require airlines to find seats for all nonsmokers on the day of the flight, provided they follow check-in-time regulations. This requirement applies to all international flights on domestic carriers, but the DOT does not have jurisdiction over foreign carriers flying out of or into the United States.

Between the Airport and City Center Private taxis are not permitted to carry passengers from the airport to town, so most people rely on **Transportes Terrestres,** a special airport taxi service. The bus system looks confusing, but there are dozens of helpful English-speaking staff to help you figure out which bus to take.

Look for the name of your hotel and the number of its zone on the overhead sign on the walkway in front of the terminal. Go to the desk for your zone and buy a ticket for an airport taxi that goes to your zone. The ride from the airport to the hotel zone on the trip costs about $8. The drivers are usually helpful and will often take you to hotels not on their list. Tips are optional. The journey into town takes 20 to 30 minutes.

From the North by Car

A car can be handy in these parts, but we don't recommend you drive from either the United States or Canada. Except for major highways, the roads are not well maintained and distances from the border are great. If you prefer to see the sights by car, we suggest renting a car once you're there (*see* Car Rentals, below).

Whether you drive from the United States or Canada or rent a car in Acapulco, bear in mind that Mexico is a developing country and things are much different than in North America or Western Europe.

Unleaded gasoline is now available at the green-and-white Pemex stations along major tourist routes, but sometimes you'll find the supply has been depleted. It's a good idea to fill up your tank whenever possible, especially before starting out on long stretches of road.

Spare parts are another worry. Parts for a Ford or Chevy are plentiful, but getting a new transmission for a Toyota or Mercedes is not easy.

The best highway, although two lanes most of the way, is Route 85 from Laredo to Monterrey and Route 57 on to Mexico City. Driving time is about 16 hours.

The trip to Acapulco from Mexico City takes about six hours, but many people opt for going via Taxco and spending at least one night there.

Practical Tips There are two absolutely essential things to remember about driving in Mexico. First and foremost is to carry Mexican car insurance. If you injure anyone in an accident, you could well be jailed—whether it was your fault or not—unless you have insurance. This is part of the country's Napoleonic Code: guilty until proved innocent.

The second item is that if you enter Mexico with a car, you must leave with it. The fact that you drove in with a car is stamped on your tourist card, which you must give to immigration authorities at departure. If an emergency arises and you must fly home, it is now fairly simple to get permission from the immigration office if you can give a day's notice. With this permit, you do not have to leave your car in bond when leaving the country, but you must show a round-trip ticket as proof that you will be returning.

The reason is that cars are much cheaper in the United States, and you are not allowed to sell your vehicle in Mexico. The authorities at the airport assume that unless you have a customs release, you have sold your car for a hefty profit. If such a situation should arise, contact the customs officials at the airport to see if you may leave your car in their special parking lot.

Mileage and speed limits are given in kilometers; 100 kph and 80 kph (62 and 50 mph, respectively) are the most common maximum speeds. A few of the newer toll roads allow 110 kph (68.4 mph). Cities and towns may have posted speed limits of 40 kph (25 mph), sometimes even 30 kph (18 mph), and it's best to observe them (*see* Conversion Tables, *at end of book*).

Streets can be one- or two-way. Your guide is an arrow posted on the sides of corner buildings, its point indicating the direction of traffic flow. A two-pointed arrow means two-way traffic. The arrow may have the words *tránsito* or *circulación* printed on it.

In town, a sign with a large *E* inside a circle stands for *estacionamiento*, or parking. Much more frequently seen is the same sign with a strong bar diagonally through the *E* and maybe the word *NO* underneath—no parking!

When you approach one end of a narrow bridge *(puente angosto)* at the same time that another car approaches the opposite end, the first one to flick his lights has the right of way.

Don't drive at night unless absolutely necessary, and even then only on the superhighways. The hazards are too many—you can't see roaming animals soon enough; large rocks may have been left on the pavement by some motorist who had car trouble and braced his wheels with them; a pedestrian or cyclist appears around a sudden curve; new rock slides occur in mountain areas during the rainy season; potholes abound—the list is a long one and the risk not worth the mileage gained.

During the day be alert to cattle crossings. Free-grazing animals may decide to amble across the highway just as you approach. Domestic animals frequently graze along the shoulders, and the sight or sound of an approaching car could cause one or more to bolt—not always away from the pavement. Older animals are wise to the dangers of the highway and will seldom move fast, but watch for the young ones, like calves. They're nervous and easily frightened into bolting.

There are several toll roads in Mexico, and tolls are much higher than for comparable stretches in the United States. Some of these roads are two-lane affairs, but most are four-lane with a divider strip. These highways have toll-free roads running roughly parallel to them. The toll roads have signs that say *cuota* (literally, dues) and give the destination (usually *México*, meaning Mexico City, and perhaps an intermediary city) while the parallel routes have signs saying *libre* (free) with the destination. These two signs, with arrows pointing in different directions, are usually posted before the road splits. Remember that because of the mountainous nature of central and southern Mexico and the many trucks on the highways, driving times are longer than for comparable distances in the United States. There are also toll bridges in various parts of the country.

When you buy insurance, you will probably receive a folder showing Mexican road signs. Here are a few words on the road signs that you should know: *alto*—stop; *no rebase*—do not pass; *ceda el paso*—yield right of way; *conserve su derecha*—keep to the right; *curva peligrosa*—dangerous curve; *derrumbes*—landslide zone; *despacio* (sometimes also *disminuya su velocidad*)—slow down; *tramo en reparación*—road work ahead; *no hay paso*—road closed; *desviación*—detour.

Topes, meaning bumps, are indicated by a sign showing a series of bumps. Since many highways—sometimes even major ones—cut through towns and villages, these bumps are an effective way of slowing down the speeding traffic to protect life and livestock. Take it easy when approaching any village—at times the bumps are there but the signs are not.

As you climb into the highlands of central Mexico, your car might not feel quite right because of the altitude. This could be a result of the lower-octane gasoline or your carburetor's needing adjustment.

Road maps are handy for those traveling by car in Mexico. In Mexico, try Guía Roji's *Atlas de Carreteras*.

Aid to Motorists

The Green Angels. The Mexican Tourism Secretariat operates a fleet of special pickup trucks on all the nation's major highways to render assistance to motorists. Though known officially as the Tourist Assistance Service, everyone calls them, with affection, the *Angeles Verdes* (Green Angels). The bilingual drivers are equipped to offer mechanical first aid to your car, medical first aid to you, communication through a two-way radiotelephone network, basic supplies of all types, towing if needed, adjustment and changing of tires, tourist information, and protection. The trucks are painted two shades of green and have a flashing red light atop the cab. The doors carry printed identification in English and Spanish. The number of Green Angels has been increased to about 300 in recent years.

How to hail one in case of need? Pull off the road as far as possible and lift the hood of your car. If you're on an isolated section of highway, hail the first passing car in either direction and ask the driver to notify the patrol of your trouble. Bus drivers and drivers of heavy trucks will also be helpful in this respect.

The patrol's services are rendered free of charge. Tips, however, are not refused. Some parts, fuel, and lubricants are provided at cost.

The Green Angels patrol fixed sections of highway, passing a given spot several times a day. The service is provided from 8 AM to around 8 PM every day on major highways.

Insurance Remember that your foreign car insurance coverage is no good in Mexico. Purchase enough Mexican automobile insurance at the border to cover the length of your trip. It's sold by the day, and if your trip is shorter than your original estimate, a prorated refund for the unused time will be issued to you upon application after you leave the country. Dan Sanborn's Insurance and Seguros Atlántico (Allstate reps) have offices in most border cities. Also, you might try Instant Mexico Auto Insurance in San Ysidro and Chula Vista, CA, and Nogales, AZ. All three are experienced and reliable. (At press time, the regulations were in flux, so if you're planning to drive in, check with the nearest Mexican tourist office or consulate for up-to-date information.)

Always lock your car securely in Mexico when no one's in it. *Never* leave valuable items in the body of the car; either lock them in the trunk or carry them with you into your hotel or motel at night.

Service Stations Your American gasoline charge cards won't work in Mexico. All service stations are Pemex—the national gas company. Stations are fairly few and far between. Always fill up once the gauge hits the half-empty mark.

Regular gasoline, around 80 octane, was selling for US$1 a gallon at press time. Regular gas is sold out of blue pumps. Nonleaded *Magna Sin,* around 90 octane, is sold out of silver-colored pumps. It was going for 1,400 pesos a liter or roughly $1.75 a gallon. (The red pumps are for diesel fuel.) Pumps measure gas not by the gallon but by the liter (*see* Conversion Tables, *at end of book*).

Oil: Pemex's *Faja de Oro* (black and gold can), Esso, Shell, Quaker State, and Mobiloil are the best brands of motor oil. Pemex products usually cost less. Mexican-made tires are of good quality but are more expensive than those made in the United States and Canada.

Rest rooms have been modernized and are periodically inspected for cleanliness and serviceability. In between inspections, however, some station operators neglect them, while others, to assure their proper maintenance, keep them under lock and key. If you must ask for the key to a locked women's room, say *"la llave para damas, por favor"* (la YAH-vay pah-rah DAH-mahs, pohr fah-VOHR); for a men's room key, say *"caballeros"* (cah-bah-YEHR-ohs).

Tell the attendant *"Lleno, por favor"* (YAY-noh)—that is, "Fill'er up." Point out the pump you want. Most Mexican cars built prior to 1991 do well on the *Nova* (blue pump), but if yours is a late Mexican or U.S. model, you'll need the *Magna Sin* (unleaded, in the silver pump), which is sold only at the Pemex stations painted green and white. Check to be sure the pump gauge is turned back to zero before the attendant starts pumping your gas; as soon as the tank is filled, write down the amount of pesos shown as due. In a busy station—and most highway stations are—a second attendant may turn the gauge back to zero to service another car and your amount due may be forgotten (or escalated).

A tip, the equivalent of a quarter or so for extra services, such as having your windshield cleaned or your oil checked, is customary and expected. The gas stations do not have mechanics.

Automobile Repair You may have heard tales about how Mexican mechanics put motors back together with bobby pins and glue. True, many mechanics are resourceful and capable, as evidenced by the large number of vintage automobiles still plying the streets. However, finding U.S.-made spare parts can be a major problem, as is trying to locate an English-speaking mechanic. We suggest that you ask for help at your hotel if you need mechanical work done on your car.

Parking If you can't find a legal place to park, we recommend parking in a pay lot, usually labeled *estacionamiento,* because towing away illegally parked cars is becoming common.

Missing License Plates Mexican police have always employed a most effective means for punishing those who park their automobiles in prohibited areas—they remove one license plate or simply tow the car away to the pound. Redeeming it requires a trip to the local *tránsito* headquarters and the payment of a fine.

Witnessing an Accident If you see an accident or an injured person, think twice before stopping to help. As a rule, it is best to notify the first policeman you see or, if on the highway, the first Green Angel Tourism Secretariat truck or highway patrol car. Not helping an injured person may be contrary to your instincts and training, but doing so can get you seriously involved, even thrown in jail. You can be accused of *mal medicina,* for instance, if you move an injured person. He, or the police, can later charge that you made things worse. If he dies you could even be implicated in the death.

Police The color and cut of police uniforms vary throughout the Mexican Republic. Acapulco tourism police wear white pants and blue shirts; civil police wear blue. The uniforms in Ixtapa and Zihuatanejo are dark blue.

Car Rentals

If you're flying into Acapulco or Ixtapa/Zihuatanejo and plan to spend some time there, you can save money on a rental by arranging to pick up your car in town the day you need it, or you can pick up and return your car at the airport. You'll have to weigh the added expense of renting a car from a major company with an airport office against the savings on a car from a budget company with offices in town. You could waste precious hours trying to locate the budget company in return for only a small saving. Be prepared to pay more for a car with an automatic transmission, and since they are not readily available, reserve it in advance. Rental rates vary widely, depending on size and model, number of days you use the car, insurance coverage, and whether special drop-off fees are imposed. In most cases, rates quoted include unlimited free mileage and standard liability protection. Collision damage waiver (CDW), which eliminates your deductible should you have an accident, is recommended in Mexico. Not included are personal-injury insurance, gasoline, and a local 10% sales tax.

You must be 21 or older to rent a car in Mexico. Driver's licenses issued in the United States and Canada are valid. You might also take out an International Driving Permit before you leave, not only to smooth out difficulties if you have an accident but to serve as an additional piece of identification should you need it. Permits are available for a small fee through local offices of the American Automobile Association (AAA) and the Canadian Automobile Association (CAA), or from their main offices: AAA, 12600 Fair Lakes Cr., Fairfax, VA 22033, tel. 703/222-6000; or CAA, 2 Carlton St., Toronto, Ontario M5B 1K4, tel. 416/964-3111.

It's best to arrange a car rental before you leave. You won't save money by waiting until you arrive, and you may find that the type of car you want is not available at the last minute. Rental companies usually charge according to the exchange rate of the dollar at the time the car is returned or when the credit card payment is processed. Companies that serve Acapulco include **Budget** (tel. 800/472-3325 in the United States and Canada), **Avis** (tel. 800/331-1084 in the United States, 800/879-2847 in Canada), **Hertz** (tel. 800/654-3001 in the continental United States, 800/654-3131 in Alaska and Hawaii, 800/263-0600 in Canada), and **National** (tel. 800/227-7368). Hertz and Avis also have offices in Ixtapa/Zihuatanejo.

From the North by Ship

Many cruises include Acapulco as part of their itinerary. Most originate from Los Angeles. Cruise operators include *Carnival Cruise Lines* (tel. 800/327-9501); *Clipper Cruise Line* (tel. 800/325-0010); *Cunard Line* (tel. 800/221-4770); *EuropAmerica Cruises* (tel. 800/221-1666); *Holland America Lines* (tel. 800/426-0327); *Krystal Cruises* (tel. 213/785-9300); *Norwegian Cruise Line* (tel. 800/327-3070); *Paquet French Cruises* (tel. 800/556-8850); *Princess Cruises* (tel. 800/421-0522); *Royal Caribbean Cruise Line* (tel. 365/539-6000); *Royal Cruise Line* (tel. 800/227-4534); *Royal Viking Line* (tel. 800/422-8000); and *Seaborn Cruise Line* (tel. 415/391-7444). Bookings are generally handled through a travel agent.

Cruise lines that visit Zihuatanejo include *EuropAmerica Cruises, Princess Cruises, Royal Cruise Line,* and *Royal Viking Line.*

For details on freighter travel to or from Mexico, consult *Pearl's Travel Tips* (9903 Oaks La., Seminole, FL 34642, tel. 813/393-2919, fax 813/392-2580).

From the North by Train and Bus

There is no train service to Acapulco, Ixtapa, or Zihuatanejo from anywhere in the United States or Canada. Buses to Acapulco can be boarded on the U.S. side of the border, but the trip is not recommended; even the most experienced travelers find the trip exhausting and uncomfortable. Bus service from Mexico City to Acapulco, however, is worth trying, especially if you want to see some of the Mexican countryside. Buses are comfortable and in good condition, and the trip takes six hours. They leave three times a day from Tasqueña station. A first-class ticket costs about $15. You check your baggage and collect it from the baggage window at the Estrella de Oro bus station in Acapulco when you arrive.

Bus service from Mexico City to Ixtapa and Zihuatanejo is through Acapulco.

From the United Kingdom by Plane

There are no direct flights to Acapulco from the United Kingdom, though the following airlines have service via Mexico City or major U.S. or European cities: **Air France** (tel. 081/759-2311); **Iberia** (tel. 071/437-5622); and **KLM** (tel. 081/568-9144). The flying time will vary, depending on the point of departure.

Staying in Acapulco

Important Addresses and Numbers

Tourist Information The State of Guerrero Department of Tourism (SEFOTUR) will help you find your way around and answer questions. The office is in the Centro Internacional, tel. 74/84-70-50. It is open Monday through Saturday from 9 to 3 and 6 to 9. Much more helpful is the Secretaría de Turismo, across from the Super-Super, Costera Miguel Alemán 187, which is open weekdays 8-8, Saturday and Sunday 10-6. The staff speaks English, has brochures and maps on other parts of Mexico, and can help you find a hotel room. Tel. 74/85-12-49 or 74/85-13-04.

Consulates The consular representative for the United States is Bonny Urbaneck. Her office is in the Club del Sol Hotel on the Costera, tel. 74/85-72-07. The Canadian representative is Diane McLean de Huerta, and her office is on the mezzanine level of the Club del Sol Hotel, tel. 74/85-66-21.

Emergencies **Police,** tel. 74/85-08-62.

The **Red Cross** can be reached at tel. 74/85-41-00 or 74/85-41-01. Two reliable hospitals are **Hospital Privado Magallanes,** Wilfrido Massiue 2, tel. 74/85-65-44, and **Hospital Centro Médico,** J. Arevalo 99, tel. 74/82-46-92.

Doctors and Dentists Your hotel and the Secretaría de Turismo can locate an English-speaking doctor. But English-speaking doctors don't come cheap—house calls are about $50. The Secretaría de Turismo has a list of dentists and suggests Dr. Guadalupe Carmona, Costera Miguel Alemán 220-101, tel. 74/85-71-76, or Dr. Arturo Carmona, Costera Miguel Alemán 220, Suite 110, tel. 74/85-72-86.

English-language Bookstores English-language books and periodicals can be found at Sanborns, a reputable American-style department store chain, and at the newsstands in some of the larger hotels. Most reading material costs more than at home. Many small newsstands and the Super-Super carry the *Mexico City News*, an English-language daily newspaper with a large Sunday edition carrying reports from many cities, including Acapulco and Ixtapa/Zihuatanejo. Social events and evening activities in the area are often covered. Every day several pages are devoted to foreign news drawn from the wire services with reprints of articles from the *Washington Post*, *New York Times*, and *Los Angeles Times*. *The Sun*, an English-language weekly sold at newsstands on Sundays, usually includes a report from Acapulco and Ixtapa/Zihuatanejo. *Time* and *Newsweek* magazines are also available.

Travel Agencies **American Express,** at Costera Miguel Alemán 709, tel. 74/84-60-60, and **Viajes Wagon-Lits,** at Scenic Highway 5255 (Las Brisas Hotel), tel. 74/82-28-64.

Staying in Touch

Telephone The area code for Acapulco is 74. Due to constant development in Acapulco and other parts of Mexico, phone numbers are constantly being added and changed. This is a fact of life in Mexico.

Local Calls A working pay phone is as rare as a cloudy day in Acapulco. If you find one that works, use it immediately. You may never see one again. Seriously, pay phones are in short supply, though you can find some in the Zócalo and along the Costera Miguel Alemán. Just look for the lines of bored Mexicans, and prepare for a wait of up to 15 minutes. Operators take a long time to answer, especially in the afternoon and on weekends. You may have to make several attempts. There are now two other types of phones, both for making long-distance calls. One of them takes change (mountains of it) and you need a basic knowledge of Spanish in order to follow the instructions. The other, which is much simpler, takes major credit cards. The best places to make long-distance calls are from the pay phones in Sanborns, which almost always seem to be in working order.

International Calls At your hotel, the operator can put calls through. Surcharges vary, but a good rule of thumb is that the more expensive the hotel, the more expensive the call. Surcharges for placing the call will range from 35% to 56% of the total cost, even if you are calling collect. Long-distance charges are exorbitant. To call the United States costs about $5 a minute; to call Europe costs more than $7 a minute. The cheapest way to phone is collect. Just go to a phone booth and dial 09. English-speaking operators take a while to answer but put calls through immediately.

Mail
Postal Rates The main post office is on the Costera in Old Acapulco, one block west of Sanborns. Weekdays it is open 9 AM–7 PM, weekends 9–1. You can also send telegrams from this post office. A letter to the United States takes about 10 days, about two weeks to Europe. Rates for postcards and letters are the same: Up to 10 grams to the United States or Canada runs about 35¢, to Europe about 40¢. You can buy postcards and envelopes in all sizes from vendors outside the post office. If the postcards you are mailing are small, put them in an envelope, or the stamps will cover the address. We recommend that you don't mail anything other than a postcard or letter from Mexico. It may never reach its destination.

Receiving Mail If you aren't sure where you will be staying, you can receive mail at the general post office (Lista de Correos, Oficina Central, Costera Miguel Alemán 215, Acapulco 39301, Gro., Mexico). If you have an American Express card or traveler's checks, you can receive mail at the American Express office (Costera Miguel Alemán 709, Acapulco, Gro., Mexico).

If officials can't find your letter, ask them to look under your first name or middle initial because Mexicans often have two last names and so have a different system for filing letters.

Tipping

Restaurants: 15%

Waiters in discos: 15%

Porters: $1 per suitcase

Doormen in luxury hotel: 50¢ for carrying suitcases to front desk

Doormen in moderate hotel: Optional, but usually 50¢ for carrying bags to front desk

Bellhops in moderate or luxury hotel: $1 per suitcase

Getting Around

Getting around in Acapulco is quite simple. You can walk to many places and the bus costs only 20¢. Taxis cost less than in the United States, so most tourists quickly become avid taxi takers.

By Bus The buses tourists use the most are those that go from Puerto Marqués to Caleta and stop at the fairly conspicuous metal bus stops along the way. If you want to go from the Zócalo to The Strip, catch the bus that says "*La Base*" (the naval base near the Exelaris Hyatt Regency). This bus detours through Old Acapulco and returns to the Costera just east of the Ritz Hotel. If you want to follow the Costera for the entire route, take the bus marked "Hornos." The price is about 20¢. Buses to Pie de la Cuesta or Puerto Marqués say so on the front. The Puerto Marqués bus runs about every half hour and is always crowded.

By Taxi We could write an entire guide on taxis in Acapulco, since there are so many different kinds with various prices. The first thing to understand is that you will never pay as little as the Acapulqueños; the most expensive fare for them is no more than $3 in town. That is another fact of life in Mexico. On the bright side, taxis are still cheaper than at home. How much you pay depends on what type of taxi you get.

The most expensive are hotel taxis. A price list that all drivers adhere to is posted in hotel lobbies. Fares in town are usually about $1.50 to $5; to go from downtown to the Princess Hotel or Caleta beach is about $10 to $15. Hotel taxis are by far the plushest and are kept in the best condition.

Cabs that cruise with their roof light off occasionally carry a price list. But don't expect to find a running meter because they are all mysteriously "broken." You need to reach an agreement with these drivers, but the fare should be less than at a hotel. There is a minimum charge of $1. Some taxis that cruise have hotel or restaurant names stenciled on the side, but are not affiliated with any establishment. Before you go anywhere by cab, find out what the price should be and agree with the driver on a price. You can usually persuade one to overcharge you by only 50¢ to $1. Alternatively, you can hand him the correct fare when you arrive, but that can lead to a nasty scene where the driver is disappointed to receive the correct fare and argues with you for more.

The cheapest taxis are the little Volkswagens. Officially there is a $1 minimum charge, but many cab drivers don't stick to it. A normal, i.e., Mexican-priced, fare is $1 to go from the Zócalo to American Express, but lots of luck getting a taxi driver to accept that from a tourist. Rates are about 50% higher at night and though tipping is not expected, Mexicans usually leave small change.

You can also hire a taxi by the hour or the day, which means that you can have one take you to Pie de la Cuesta or wait while you do your shopping. Prices vary from about $12 an hour for a hotel taxi to $8 an hour for a street taxi. Never let a taxi driver decide where you should eat or shop, since many get kickbacks from some of the smaller stores and restaurants. In fact if you look carefully, you can see people waiting outside various destinations; their job is to note down the cabs' license plate numbers and pay them a 10% commission when they return later.

By Motorscooter Little Honda motorscooters can be rented from a stand outside CiCi, the children's water park on the Costera. They are also available at the Plaza Hotel. Cost: $15 to $20 for up to four hours, depending on the size, or $30 to $40 per day.

By Horse and Carriage Buggy rides up and down The Strip are available on weekends. Bargain before you get in—they cost about $20 a half hour.

Guided Tours

Orientation Tours There are organized tours everywhere in Acapulco, from the red-light district to the lagoon. Tours to Mexican fiestas in the evenings or the markets in the daytime are easy to arrange. Tour operators have offices around town and desks in many of the large hotels. If your hotel can't arrange a tour, contact **Consejeros de Viajes** at the Torre de Acapulco, Costera Miguel Alemán 1252, tel. 74/84–74–00, or **Acuario,** Costera Miguel Alemán, opposite the Plaza Hotel, tel. 74/85–61–00; and *see* Chapter 9.

Special-interest Tours The Acapulco Princess runs a Mexican cooking school featuring the techniques of executive chef George Olah, who teaches dishes from the Aztec time to nouvelle Mexican. The school is limited to 20 participants per session, and there are two 5-day/4-night sessions a year. Contact the Acapulco Princess hotel, tel. 800/223–1818.

Credit Cards

The following credit-card abbreviations are used: AE, American Express; DC, Diners Club; MC, MasterCard; V, Visa.

2 Portraits of Acapulco

Host to the World

by Erica Meltzer

A writer and translator whose specialty is Mexico, Erica has been a frequent visitor there since 1967, and has lived in Mexico City for three years.

The story of Acapulco begins with a Romeo-and-Juliet-like myth of the Yope Indians, who had been driven to Acapulco from the north by the Nahuas, forerunners of the Aztecs. Acatl (his name means "reed"), firstborn son of the tribal chief, heard a voice telling him that in order to perpetuate his race, he should seek the love of Quiahuitl ("rain"), daughter of an enemy chieftain. But after the two fell in love, her father refused to allow the marriage. Grief-stricken, Acatl returned to his home in the foothills of the Sierra Madre above the Bay of Acapulco, intent on being devoured by the animals. But Acatl missed the sweet warbling of the *zenzontle* bird and returned to the bay to lie beneath the mesquite tree, where he wept so hard that his body dissolved into a puddle of mud, which spread across the coastal plain. From the mud sprang little reeds, yellowish green tinged with red: These were the sons of Acatl, bearing the colors of the mesquite and the zenzontle. Quiahuitl, in turn, was transformed into an immense cloud and floated toward the bay where, finding her lost love, she dissolved in tears. The teardrops fell on the reeds, and Quiahuitl was united forever with Acatl. This is said to be the origin of the name Acapulco, which means "in the place where the reeds were destroyed." The legend holds that whenever the bay is threatened by clouds, Quiahuitl, remembering her love, is returning.

Acapulco has been inhabited since at least 3000 BC; the oldest Nahua artifacts in the region date from 2,000 years ago. These artifacts—clay heads, known as the "Pretty Ladies of Acapulco"—were discovered in the lost city of La Sabana, in the hills outside Acapulco. Because of earthquakes, the region contains few other archaeological remains.

From 1486 to 1502, after centuries under Toltec rule, Acapulco became part of the Aztec empire. It was then taken over by the Tarascans, another Indian tribe, along with the rest of the province of Zacatula. It was such power struggles among the Indians that eventually led to Acapulco's conquest by the Spaniards under Hernán Cortés. Montezuma II, the Aztec emperor, told Cortés that more gold came from Zacatula than from anywhere else so that Cortés would conquer Montezuma's rivals, the Tarascans, and leave his realm alone.

Acapulco was discovered by Francisco Chico on December 13, 1521, and has been a magnet for seekers of wealth ever since. Chico had been sent by Cortés to find sites for ports, since Cortés was obsessed with locating a route to the Spice Islands. Acapulco has a great natural harbor, twice as deep as either San Francisco or New York, and so was a perfect choice. In accordance with a custom of Spanish explorers, Chico named the bay after the saint whose feast day coincided with the day of his landing: Santa Lucía. Cortés then built a mule path from Mexico City to Acapulco—his Spanish overlords forbade the use of Indians to transport cargo —and used the settlement to build ships for his explorations of the South Pacific. In 1532, the town officially became a domain of the Spanish crown, known as the *Ciudad de los Reyes*, or City of the Kings. Cortés went frequently to Acapulco, staying at Puerto Marqués Bay, which was named for him (Cortés was the marquis, or Marqués, of the Valley of Oaxaca).

By 1579, Acapulco was booming, and King Philip II decreed it the only official port for trade between America and Asia—primarily the Philippines, which had been discovered by Spaniards sailing from Acapulco. (In the Spanish spoken in the Philippines, *acapulco* is the name of a plant, the *Cassia alata*, introduced to the Philippines by traders from Mexico.) For centuries afterward, the port played a crucial role in the history of the New World: In 1537, Cortés sent ships to Francisco Pizarro to help his conquest of Peru, and two years later he launched an expedition to discover the Seven Cities of Cíbola. Ships from Acapulco explored Cape Mendocino, California, in 1602.

But it was the Manila galleons—the *naos de China*—that brought Acapulco its early fame. The first vessel, the *San Pablo*, sailed in 1565, and for the next 250 years the Spanish crown maintained a stranglehold on trade with the Orient. The naos carried the richest cargo of their day: silks, porcelain, cottons, rugs, jade, ivory, incense, spices, and slaves. When goods from the East reached Acapulco, they were then carried overland—a 20-day journey along the six-foot-wide Road to Asia trail—to Veracruz on the Gulf of Mexico, where other ships then bore the cargo to Europe. On their return voyages to the East, the galleons transported silver from Mexico and Peru. The Spaniards limited the traffic to one arrival a year, usually at Christmas, and this event was heralded by the great Acapulco Fair of the Americas. Traders and merchants came from all over New Spain to buy the goods, and the malaria-ridden village, normally home to 4,000 people (mostly blacks and mulattoes), was suddenly host to 12,000. Thus, from its early days, Acapulco became well versed in the arts of hospitality. Because accommodations were insufficient to lodge the flood of visitors, locals developed a lucrative business by renting out houses, patios, corrals, and even doorways. They made fortunes as entertainers, quack doctors, porters, food vendors, and water carriers. Visitors amused themselves with bullfights, cockfights, and horse races. So much Peruvian gold and silver changed hands that the mules were literally laden with coins, and the Spanish crown was obliged to remint the precious metals and exploit the Mexican silver mines.

All this wealth had several unfortunate consequences for Acapulco and New Spain. One was that the monopolies enjoyed by the guilds of Acapulco and Veracruz kept prices high and the demand for locally produced goods low. Eventually the Spaniards allowed two overland journeys a year and established other ports to relieve the trade bottleneck.

The other outcome was the arrival of pirates. Until Sir Francis Drake's *Golden Hind* first sailed into Acapulco Bay in his exploration of the Pacific, the riches of the Manila galleons were a Spanish secret. Drake, whose ship was shot at by panicking Spaniards, boarded their ship, stole the map to Manila, and a few days later intercepted one of the galleons. Drake informed Queen Elizabeth of his windfall, and from that day on, Acapulco was under constant siege by the likes of British pirates Thomas Cavendish, Henry Morgan, and William Dampier. (Treasure is still said to be buried off Roqueta Island.) The galleon crews arriving from Manila, exhausted from their journey and from malnutrition (food generally rotted during the long sea voyages), were never a match for the corsairs (English pirates), well fed from the excellent fishing in the Gulf of California. The first fort, the Castillo de San Diego, was built in 1616, and even it could not stave off the Dutch Prince of Nassau, who pillaged the city in 1624.

An earthquake destroyed the fort in 1776; its replacement, the Fuerte de San Diego, dates from 1783. In 1799, King Carlos IV declared Acapulco an official city, but shortly thereafter, its decline set in. With the independence movement in 1810, the fair was suspended; the arriving nao found the beaches deserted, and the captain was told to take his ship to San Blas. That same year insurgent leader José Maria Morelos attacked Acapulco, and a long and bloody siege ensued. The Acapulqueños, who were not particularly enthused by the prospect of losing the source of their livelihood, preferred continued allegiance with the Spanish empire to the dubitable gains of independence. Acapulco, an important source of revenue for Spain, was a natural target for the rebels, and Morelos burned it in 1814 to destroy its value.

Despite a devastating cholera outbreak in 1850, Acapulco enjoyed a brief revival in the 1850s, an outcome of the California gold rush. Ships stopped in Acapulco on their way to the Isthmus of Panama and returned to San Francisco carrying Mexican textiles. (Coincidentally, the great-grandson of "49er" John Sutter, Ricardo Morlet Sutter, was Acapulco's municipal president in the 1960s.) And in 1855 Benito Juárez, widely considered the father of modern Mexico, was sent to Acapulco to help bring down the dictator Antonio Santa Anna. A few years later, the city was bombarded by a French squadron during

Juárez's fight against Emperor Maximilian, who had recognized Acapulco's strategic importance.

Acapulco resumed its fitful slumber through most of the 19th and early 20th centuries. An earthquake nearly razed the city in 1909; two years later it was invaded by some rebellious *lobos*—Afro-Indians from the neighboring Costa Chica region descended from escaped slaves—who threw off the yoke of a tyrant, Johann Schmidt, during the early years of the Mexican Revolution. Modern Acapulco dates from the 1920s, when wealthy Mexicans—and adventurous gringos—began frequenting the somnolent village. With the opening of the first highway along Cortés's mule trail in 1928 and initial air service from the capital in 1929, Acapulco began to attract the Hollywood crowd and international statesmen. President Lázaro Cárdenas (1934–40) started public works; the first telephone service began in 1936.

Ironically, it was Cárdenas's nationalism that modernized Mexico's hotel industry, thereby paving the way for the early foreign hotel entrepreneurs who would later dominate that sector of the economy. Cárdenas prohibited foreigners both from owning property within 50 kilometers of the Mexican coastline and from buying hotels. Foreigners circumvented the law either by becoming Mexican citizens or by setting up dummy corporations.

Thus it was a Texan, Albert B. Pullen, who first formed a company in the 1930s to develop the beautiful Peninsula de las Playas—now known as Old Acapulco—where many of Acapulco's first hotels rose. Pullen became a millionaire in the process, and a real estate boom soon followed. J. Paul Getty was alleged to have purchased 900 acres of land at 3 cents an acre, some of which he used to build the Pierre Marqués ("Pierre" after his New York hotel of that name, "Marqués" after Cortés). In 1933, Carlos Barnard erected his first bungalows at El Mirador, atop the cliffs at La Quebrada, and other hotels followed suit.

But despite the growing tourist traffic, Acapulco still had the look, and appeal, of a humble town. Writers flocked to it: the reclusive B. Traven, author of *Treasure of the Sierra Madre,* ran a restaurant there from 1929 to 1947. Malcolm Lowry (*Under the Volcano*) first saw Mexico from his Acapulco-bound ship on November 2, 1936; that four-month sojourn was spent sampling the charms of tequila, pulque, mezcal, and Mexican beer. The playwright Sherwood Anderson visited Acapulco in 1938, and Tennessee Williams spent the summer of 1940 there. (Acapulco is, in fact, the setting for *The Night of the Iguana,* his celebrated play that John Huston later filmed in Puerto Vallarta.) That same year, Jane and Paul Bowles, the bohemian writer-couple, rented a house there, complete with avocado and lemon trees, a hammock, and their own tropical menagerie. At that time Acapulco boasted dirt roads, a wooden pier, no electricity, and a lot of mosquitoes.

Well-heeled foreigners first became interested in Acapulco during World War II, when most other pleasure spots were off-limits. In 1947, a two-lane highway improved accessibility, cutting travel time from Mexico City to a day and a half. By then there were 28,000 residents, compared to just 3,000 in 1931.

It was President Miguel Alemán Valdés (1946–52) who is credited with turning Acapulco into a tourist destination. Alemán ordered roads paved, streets laid out, water piped in, and public buildings erected. Even after his presidency, when he directed the newly formed National Tourism Council, Alemán was instrumental in the town's development. He was responsible for the new four-lane super-highway, which in 1955 made it possible to reach Acapulco from Mexico City in just six hours.

The jet-setters' invasion of Acapulco reached its peak in the 1940s and '50s. While many of them owned homes there, they still liked to congregate primarily at two hotels. Las Brisas was built in 1954 as a small cottage colony, Bermuda-style, by Juan March, on the former site of the fortress. The other watering hole was the Villa Vera Racquet Club. Originally a private residence for an Omaha businessman, it was later managed by Ernest Henri ("Teddy") Stauffer, a Swiss swing bandleader who had fled the Nazis and settled in Acapulco, where he became affectionately known as "Mr. Acapulco." Stauffer also put up Acapulco's first discotheque, Tequila A Go-Go, and took over the popular La Perla restaurant at La Quebrada, home to the cliff divers. The Villa Vera boasted one of Acapulco's many innovations, the first swim-up bar, and its first tennis club. (Another Acapulco first was parasailing.)

Lana Turner used to frequent the Villa Vera's piano bar. Elizabeth Taylor married Mike Todd there, with Debbie Reynolds and Eddie Fisher as witnesses. JFK honeymooned in Acapulco, as did Brigitte Bardot and, many years later, Henry Kissinger. Yugoslav President Tito stayed there for 38 days, in one of 76 private homes owned by Las Brisas. President Eisenhower's visit in 1959 brought Acapulco even more publicity, as did an international film festival that debuted that year. Acapulco's guest list filled the society pages and gossip columns of America and Europe: Frank Sinatra, Johnny Weissmuller, New York Mayor Robert Wagner, Harry Belafonte, Douglas Fairbanks, Jr., Judy Garland, Sir Anthony Eden, John Wayne, Gina Lollobrigida, Gary Cooper, Edgar Bronfman, Jimmy Stewart, the Guinness family, Richard Widmark, Baron de Rothschild. . . .

By the late 1950s and early '60s, Acapulco, which had also acquired the sobriquet "Nirvana by the Sea," was being called "Miami on the Pacific." It had long since ceased to be the exclusive haven for the rich and famous: Hotel construction had mushroomed, and the city's infrastructure could not keep pace with the growing resident population, then 100,000. La Laja, a seedy cluster of tenements outside town lacking sewers, drinking water, and electricity, swelled with 8,000 minimum-wage hotel workers known as *paracaidistas* (parachutists), or squatters. The government tried discreetly to squelch the city's social problems by selling the land at La Laja to the squatters, but also feared that move would encourage even more migration and aggravate unemployment. Hundreds of locals—mostly Indians from the surrounding region—were reduced to roaming the beaches, peddling kitschy folk art, tie-dyed beachwear, suntan oil, and soda.

By the mid-1960s, the government was eyeing the Port of Acapulco with renewed interest as a way to balance the economy and offset the seasonality of tourism. Acapulco was again trading, primarily with the Orient, and in 1963 some 180 freighters arrived, laden with Japanese appliances and automobiles. Each year, 60,000 tons of copra—dried coconut meat, used for making soap and margarine—left port; the copra industry was second to tourism in the region. The government wanted to capitalize on Acapulco's revived trade status by building a new port and opening a railroad to convey all the imports and locally produced copra, rubber, and wood pulp to Mexico City. But the projects never got off the ground.

So tourism—which generated $50 million a year in direct spending—remained the key to Acapulco. With the advent of international jet travel in 1964, and the start-up of nonstop service from the United States in 1966, Acapulco's ascendancy became even more spectacular. The once lowly airport was dressed up in marble, and countless foreigners arrived to set up fashion boutiques and restaurants and indulge in the lucrative trade of marijuana and cocaine. Media stories continued to appear with great regularity, focusing largely on Merle Oberon Pagliai, the queen of Acapulco society, who spent six months a year in Acapulco in her Moorish-style villa, El Ghalal. Needless to say, that abode was as lavish as the nightly parties thrown about town by her fellow travelers, where socks were prohibited and themed events varied from disco nights (accompanied by the sounds of the Beach Boys) to costume frolics (all invitees dressed as Charles Addams's characters). *Coco locos*—a mouthful of coconut juice with a generous serving of rum, gin, or tequila, inevitably presented in a coconut shell—were all the rage.

But Acapulco's clients in the '60s—and today still—were not only the Beautiful People. The majority were actually Mexicans, to whom Acapulco was the equivalent of Atlantic City. In addition, there were vacationing college students—frequently indulging in midnight surf-dancing—seamen, and middle-class Americans who felt comfortable with the American-brand fast-food outlets lining the Costera Alemán, a south-of-the-border Coney Island.

Commercialization and unbridled growth took their toll on Acapulco in the 1970s. Belatedly, the government planned a $14 million project to pipe the city's sewage out to sea; prior to that the sewage had simply been carried in an open canal, and the hotels had installed their own services. Having reached the mature stage of its development, Acapulco found its glamour and popularity waning. That may have been a godsend for its 300,000 residents, crowded to the breaking point, as rural unrest in the surrounding countryside led increasingly to outbursts of violence. In the early 1970s, guerrillas assassinated Acapulco's police chief, kidnapped the state senator, and occasionally took hostages in Acapulco itself before most of the group was killed in gun battles.

As Acapulco waned, Mexico began looking elsewhere to practice its magic. In Ixtapa, Cancún, Los Cabos, and now Huatulco, the government is attempting to avoid the mistakes it made in Acapulco through careful planning, while duplicating its formula of sea, sand, and sex. Several of those destinations now siphon off the tourism business. Whereas in the 1960s foreigners represented 45% of Acapulco's tourist revenue, by the mid-1980s that figure had slipped to 32%.

But Acapulqueños, who for centuries have derived their livelihood from commerce with foreigners, are intent on keeping their city afloat. In 1988, the public and private sectors banded together to refurbish the area known as Traditional (or Old) Acapulco, centered on Caleta Beach and the Zócalo. Hotels are being spruced up, street vendors are being paid to relocate to public markets, and the streets are undergoing a face-lift. And although one-third of Acapulco's one million residents still live in slums, that fact seldom intrudes on the tourist's conscience. In terms of sheer size, Acapulco is still the biggest of Mexico's tourist destinations. To many, it continues to epitomize the glamour and vitality for which it has long been celebrated. And though it will go through more permutations, Acapulco holds a secure place in Mexico's future.

The Cliff Dive

by Craig Vetter

Chicago is home for freelance writer Craig Vetter.

Just before the divers at La Quebrada in Acapulco take the long fall from the cliff into the surf, they kneel at a little shrine to Our Lady of Guadalupe and say their prayers. It's not hard to imagine what they ask her—I used to know the prayers they know—probably something like, "Remember, O most gracious Virgin, that never was it known that anyone who fled to thy protection, implored thy help or sought thy intercession was left unaided. Inspired by this confidence, I fly to thee, O Virgin of Virgins, my Mother. To thee I come, before thee I stand, sinful and sorrowful. O Mother of the word incarnate, despise not my petitions but in thy mercy hear and answer me: Let the water be deep enough, let the current be gentle, save me from garbage on the water, from the rocks, from blindness, from death, and may the *turistas* drop at least ten pesos apiece into the hat before they haul their fat white bodies back onto the buses."

I watched them dive half a dozen times one day. I sat on the terrace of the Mirador Hotel that overlooks the cliff with tequila and beer in front of me, telling myself I was trying to decide whether or not I would do this thing. I knew that the power of prayer wouldn't get me into the air off that rock. I've dived from heights before, but never that high, never out over rocks like those, never into a slash of water as narrow as that. Still, the only reason I was down there in the good tropical sun was to dive or to come up with an eloquent string of reasons why I hadn't. As it was, every time a Mexican dived, I was adding a because to my list of why nots.

One of them would walk out onto the rock and look down at the surf 130 feet below him. Then he'd kneel at the shrine, cross himself and pray. When he got up, he'd wander out of sight for a moment behind the little statue of Mary, then come back and stand for another five minutes on the edge while the tourists crowded the railings of the hotel terrace and filled the vantage points on the rocks below. Then he'd put both arms out straight in front of him, drop them to his sides, cock his legs, roll forward, and then spring with what looked like all his strength into a perfect flying arch. Foam boils up where the divers go in and the sound when they hit the water is like an old cannon going off. Then, a few seconds later, he'd be up, waving one arm and treading water against the white surge that was trying to slap him up onto the rocks.

After a couple of divers and a couple of tequilas, I was telling myself I could live through it. I'd probably get hurt real bad, but it wouldn't kill me. I could get out past those rocks, all right, then it would just be a matter of going into the water as straight and skinny and strong as I could. I figured the worst I could get would be a broken back. Or else . . . or else I could sit right there on that terrace, have another shot of Cuervo, maybe six, lay back on my laurels and review the risks already taken. The worst I could get would be a hangover.

One of the divers came around to collect 50 cents. I gave him a dollar and when he said that was too much, I told him no, it wasn't. His name was Fidel and he had a broad face and a paunch that hung out over his tight red trunks. He looked about 40 years old. I asked him what kind of injuries the *clavadistas* got when they didn't hit the water right. Broken bones, he told me, when the arms sometimes collapse into the head on impact. And the eyes, he said, if you break the water eyes first instead of with the top of your head, you go blind. But they have an association, he said, and the 26 divers in it have a fund, so that if one of them is hurt or killed, his family is taken care of. I didn't ask him if there was a fund for half-wit gringos with a history of foolish moments and a little too much sauce in them. There are no funds for people like that, people like me. Just simple services when the time comes.

Fidel moved off through the crowd, looking for more peso notes, and pretty much left me thinking there was no way in hell I was going to make that dive. The idea that I'd probably survive the plunge didn't mean nearly as much after he told me about the arms snapping over the head on entry. Somehow, I could *hear* that one. Even from 40 or 45 feet, which is the highest I've ever dived, you hit the water hard enough to make a moron out of yourself if you do it wrong. It *hurts* even when you do it right.

Finally, that afternoon, I figured out exactly what that cliff was to me. It wasn't a test of guts, or coordination, or strength, or Zen oneness with this imaginary existence. It was an intelligence test, the most fundamental kind of intelligence test: If you're intelligent, you don't *take* the test. Still, to sit there and think it through was one thing. I knew I had to let the animal make the final decision; take the meat up there onto that rock and let it look down the throat of this thing, let it *feel* the edge. There'd be no more maybes after that.

You actually have to climb down the rocks from the hotel to the spot from which they dive. On my way, I kept waiting for someone to stop me, tell me it was divers only out there, but no one did and there were no warning signs. I jumped a low stone wall and crept down some rock steps overhung with trees that made it feel like a tunnel out the end of which I could see the backside of the little shrine. It was cement, painted silver, and behind it, stacked like cordwood—as if to say that even among religious people liquor takes up where prayer leaves off—were two dozen empty tequila bottles. Two steps beyond that and I was out from under the green overhead and on the small flat pad from which they do it, and the scene opened before me: to my left, the hotel. I could see people tapping each other and pointing at me, as if to say, "Here goes another one, Edith." To my right, the flat blue Pacific stretched out to a sharp tropical horizon, and then turned into sky. I stepped up and hung my toes over the edge, and then looked down at the rocks below me, then at the rocks on the other side, then at the skinny finger of water between them, rising and falling, foaming in and out. There were Styrofoam cups on the tide, pieces of cardboard and other trash I couldn't make out. I remembered my mother, who was a champion swimmer in the '30s, telling me about a woman high diver who'd gone off a 100-foot tower in Atlantic City and hit an orange peel on the water. She lived, but the image of their hauling her limp from the water has stayed with me, and it was never more vivid than at that moment at La Quebrada. Looking down from that cliff, your perspective is so hopelessly distorted it seems that, to miss the rocks on your side of the channel, you'd have to throw yourself onto the rocks on the other side. I tried to imagine myself through it. Get steady, feet together, arms down, roll, push, arch . . . but I couldn't take the fantasy any further than that. "No," I said out loud. "Just turn around and say goodbye to the Lady, Craig."

A couple of hours later, the defeat of the thing didn't seem very profound at all. If I'd kept drinking tequila, I just might have gone screaming off that cliff. Tequila, after all, talks to the animal in you and *he* thinks he can do anything when he's drunk.

After all, you gotta stop somewhere.

3 Cruising on the Mexican Riviera

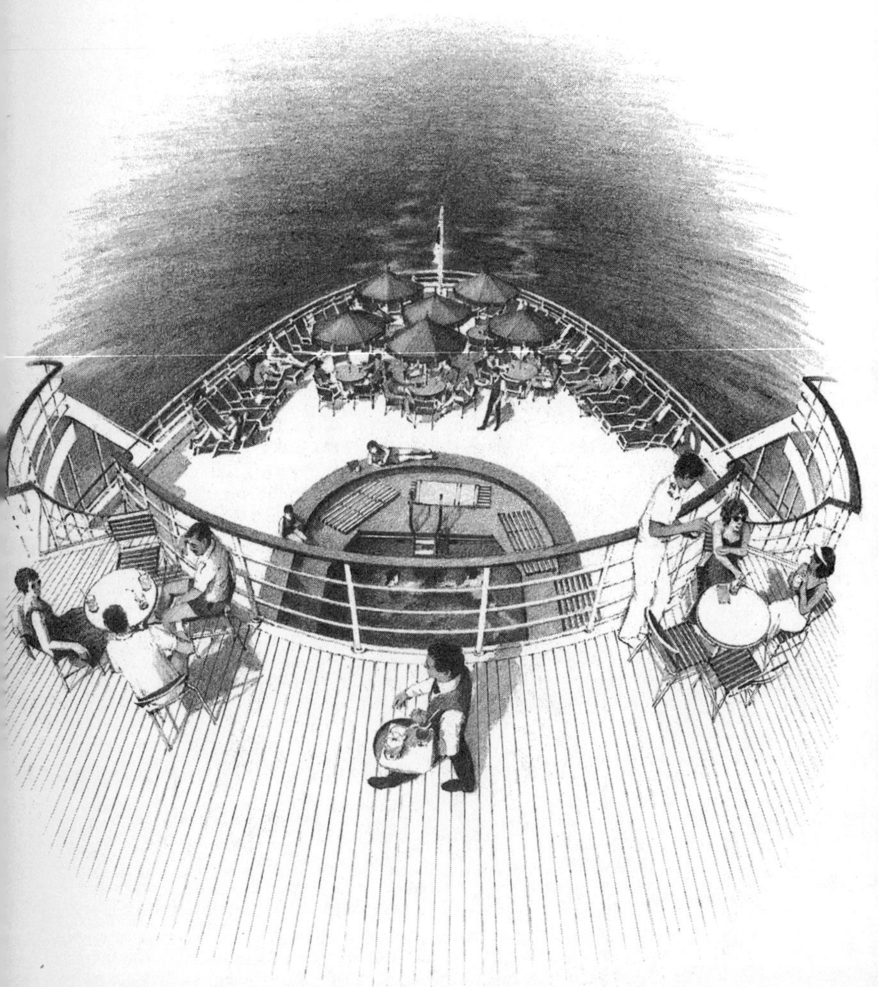

Choosing Your Cruise

Cruise Information

Cruise Travel Magazine, published every two months, has photos and features on ships and ports of call. Subscriptions are $9.97 for six issues (Box 342, Mt. Morris, IL 61054).

Ocean & Cruise News is a newsletter that profiles a different ship each month (World Ocean & Cruise Liner Society, Box 92, Stamford, CT 06901).

The **Center for Environmental Health and Injury Control** performs regular sanitation inspections on all cruise ships sailing in American waters. Ships are given a rating between 1 and 100, with scores under 85 considered Not Satisfactory. The latest sanitation summary is available free from the Department of Health and Human Services (Public Health Service, Centers for Disease Control, Atlanta, GA 30333).

Types of Ships

A bigger ship can offer a greater number of activities, public rooms, and dining options, and a broader range of entertainment. Large ships invariably hold more people, which is a plus for gregarious individuals. Also, rates on these ships may be lower because larger, newer ships are less expensive per passenger to operate. Some ships, though, are too big to dock in port, and you may have to wait in line to take a tender.

Smaller cruise ships offer a level of intimacy virtually unheard of on larger vessels; the crew may be more informal, and the level of activity is usually less intense. Small ships can often slip into tiny, shallow harbors and dock right at quayside. A small ship, however, may not have as many amenities.

When considering a ship's size, don't forget to factor in other variables, such as the passenger/crew ratio (or service ratio), which is an indication of how many passengers each crew member must serve. If all things are equal between two ships, the one with the lower service ratio will probably offer more personal service. Space ratio, which indicates relative size of cabins and public areas, is also very important. To calculate it, divide the ship's gross tonnage by its passenger capacity.

Mainstream Ships A mainstream cruise ship carries between 400 and 2,000 passengers and is similar to a self-contained, all-inclusive resort. Vast quantities of food are served, and guests can enjoy swimming pools, spas and saunas, movie theaters, exercise rooms, Las Vegas–style entertainment, a casino, and shore excursions, not to mention plenty of planned group activities.

Mainstream ships charge on average from $150 to $600 per diem (the daily rate, per passengers, when two people occupy a cabin), although economy ships—generally older and smaller mainstream ships—offer lower per diem prices, ranging from under $100 for the smallest inside cabins to about $400 for top-of-the-line suites. Upscale ships justify higher prices—from $150 to $620—by offering a level of service, accommodation and cuisine that's a cut above average; their passengers tend to be older and more sedate.

Luxury ships have more spacious staterooms, and most are outside cabins. This is complemented by white-glove service, formal or semi-formal dining, and a low passenger-to-crew ratio. Per diem prices range from $200 to $750 and up.

The **megaship** is 60,000 tons or larger, carrying 1,500 or more passengers. An increasing number of these big ships now exist because the economics of cruising make them far more profitable. The only difference between these and other mainstream ships is that they offer more of everything.

Cost

For one all-inclusive price (plus tips, shopping, bar bills, and other incidentals), you can cover your entire trip. The axiom "the more you pay, the more you get" doesn't always hold true; most mainstream ships are one-class vessels on which the passenger in the cheapest inside cabin eats the same food, sees the same shows, and shares the same amenities as the passenger paying up to $700 per day for the top suite. Paying for a larger cabin may not be important because the average cruise passenger uses it only for sleeping and showering. Where price does make a difference is in the choice of ship. It helps to compare the per diem cost—the price of a cruise on a daily basis per passenger, when two people occupy a cabin. If a seven-day cruise costs $700 per person, the per diem for each person is $100.

Pre- and post-cruise arrangements: If you plan to arrive a day or two early at the port of embarkation, or linger a few days for sightseeing after the cruise is over, estimate the cost of your hotel, meals, car rental, and other expenditures. Cruise lines sell packages for pre- and post-cruise stays that can cover many of these costs. These packages usually save you money.

Airfare: Airfare and transfers are often included in the price of a cruise; however, the cruise line chooses your airline and flight. There is usually a reduction of $50–$200 for passengers not using the whole transportation package. Per diem rates are for the cruise only and do not include transportation packages.

Pre-trip incidentals: These may include trip insurance, flight insurance, the cost of boarding your pets, airport or port parking, departure tax, visas, long distance calls home, cruise clothing, film, and other miscellaneous expenses.

Shore excursions: Estimate an average of $70–$100 per passenger on a seven-day cruise. Port tax on the Mexican Riviera is typically $60 to $70 per person.

Amusement and gambling allowance: Losses in the casino, on bingo, or on other forms of gambling average about $400 per family.

On-board incidentals: According to the Cruise Lines International Association (CLIA), the typical tip total works out to $7–$11 per passenger per day. Daily on-board expenditures, including bar tabs, wine with meals, laundry, beauty parlor services, and gift shop purchases, average $22.50 per person.

Accommodations

Where you sleep matters only if you enjoy extra creature comforts and are willing to pay for them; on most of today's one-class cruise ships no particular status or stigma is attached to your choice of cabin. Having said that, there's certainly an advantage to selecting personally the best cabin within your budget, rather than allowing your travel agent or cruise line representative to book you into the next available accommodation. The earlier you book, the better the selection will be: The best cabins are often reserved a year or more in advance.

Cabin Size On most ships the terms "cabin" and "stateroom" are nearly interchangeable. The price of a cabin is proportional to how large it is, and the overwhelming majority of ship cabins are *tiny*—certainly far smaller than the average American bedroom.

Suites are the roomiest and best-equipped accommodations, although there may be a considerable difference in size, facilities, and prices among those on each ship. Most have a sitting room or area, and they may receive better steward service. The top suites on some ships are even assigned private butlers. Some have two bathrooms, possibly with a Jacuzzi. The most expensive suites may be priced as complete packages, regardless of how many passengers occupy them.

Sharing The great majority of cabins are designed for two people. Smaller, one-person cabins usually carry a premium price. If more than two people share a cabin, often there can be a substantial saving for the third or fourth person. Children sharing a cabin with their parents often get an extra discount. When no single cabins are available, passengers traveling on their own must pay a single supplement, which usually ranges from 125% to 200% of the double-occupancy rate.

Location On all ships, regardless of size or design, the bow (front) and stern (back) bounce up and down on the waves far more than amidships (middle). Similarly, the closer your deck is to the true center of the ship—about halfway between the bottom of the hull and the highest deck—the less you will feel the ship's movement. Some cruise lines charge more for cabins amidships; most charge more for the higher decks.

Outside cabins have portholes or windows (which, often as not, cannot be opened); on the upper decks, the view from outside cabins may be partially obstructed by lifeboats or look out onto a public deck. Because outside cabins are more desirable, many newer luxury ships are configured with outside cabins only.

Inside cabins often are smaller and oddly shaped to fit around the ship's particular configuration. On newer ships inside cabins are virtually identical to outside cabins except they have no porthole. If sleeping in windowless, inside cabins doesn't make you feel claustrophobic, it's a great way to save money.

Booking Your Cruise

Most cruise ships sail at or near capacity, especially during the high season, so consider making reservations as much as two years in advance. On the other hand, you may be able to save hundreds of dollars by booking close to the sailing date, especially if you go through a cruise specialist or a discounter.

Getting the Best Cruise for Your Dollar

It used to be an article of faith that one travel agent would give you cruise rates identical to those offered by any other. In fact, until airline deregulation in 1978, it was illegal for travel agents to discount, or charge lower than the set price, for airline tickets. And by custom, most other bookings—from cruise ships to hotels to car rentals—were also sold at the same price, regardless of the agency. The rare discount or rebate was kept discreetly under the table. In recent years, however, this practice among travel agencies has gradually declined—and cruise travelers benefit.

Like any piece of retail merchandise, a cruise brochure has a *list* price. However, the actual selling price can vary tremendously: These days, if you ask any 10 passengers on almost any given ship what they're paying per diem, they'll give you 10 sharply different answers. Discounts on the same accommodation can range from 5% to 60%!

Though a single, sure-fire path to whopping savings may not exist, you can maximize your chances in several ways:

Full-Service Travel Agents Consider booking with a full-service travel agent. He or she can make your arrangements and deal directly with airlines, cruise companies, car rental agencies, hotels, and resorts. You won't be charged a service fee—agents make money on commissions from the cruise lines and other suppliers—and you'll eliminate such expenses as long distance phone calls and postage.

However, don't rely solely on your agent when selecting your cruise. Since most travel agencies book everything from cruises to business flights to theme park vacations, your local agent probably hasn't sailed on the ships and visited the ports that interest you—and has learned everything s/he knows about cruises from the same booklets and brochures available to the public. Because agents work on commission, there is some potential conflict of interest. Fortunately, disreputable agents remain relatively few.

Cruise-Only Travel Agencies "Cruise-only" travel agencies constitute one of the fastest growing segments of the industry, and most major towns or cities have at least one or two. Their knowledgeable employees may have sailed on many of these ships themselves. But that's only one of their strengths. Working in conjunction with specific cruise lines, cruise-only agencies obtain discounts by agreeing to sell large blocs of tickets. To make their quotas, they pass along savings to their clients. The discount depends on agency, cruise line, season, ship popularity, and current demand. Nationally run agencies offer the best discounts.

However, though many cruise-only agencies can book you on any cruise, others represent specific cruise lines. If you're interested in Seabourn when your agency can market only Princess, you may have to look elsewhere.

Cruise Travel Clubs Some cruise-only agencies operate as private clubs, and for an annual fee of $25 to $50 offer members a newsletter, free gifts, top cabin selection, and sometimes, if the agency negotiates a group charter with the cruise line, better rates.

Last-minute Booking When cruise companies have cancellations or unsold cabins, they use cruise-only agencies and cruise specialists to recoup revenue. The closer it is to the sailing date, the bigger the savings. Typically, discounts range from 25% to more than 60%. You can't book very far in advance—usually only from two weeks to a month—to obtain the best discount, you have to be flexible, and ideally be prepared to leave on as little as 24 hours notice. You might end up spending your vacation at home, or you might luck into the travel bargain of a lifetime.

Choosing the Right Agency or Club

How do you find an honest, competent travel agent? Word of mouth is always a safe bet—get recommendations from friends, family, and colleagues, especially those who have cruised before. Or look in the *Yellow Pages* for agents identified as members of "CLIA" (Cruise Lines International Association) or "ASTA" (American Society of Travel Agents). In theory, there's little difference between the level of service you'll receive from a tiny mom-and-pop agency and a national chain. In practice, however, larger, well-established agencies are more likely to employ experienced cruisers, and smaller agencies may give you more personal attention. Check around and weigh your options carefully. Then phone for an appointment to interview a few prospects. Choose the agent who takes a personal interest in finding the right cruise line for you.

Major cruise publications such as *Cruise Travel Magazine* also list agencies that handle cruises. Here are a few of the better ones:

Cruise Headquarters, 4225 Executive Square #1200, La Jolla, CA 92037; tel. 800/424-6111, in California 619/453-1201.

Cruise Pro, 99 Long Court, Suite 200, Thousand Oaks, CA 91360; tel. 800/222-7447, in California 800/258-7447, in Canada 800/433-8747.

Cruise Quarters of America, 1241 E. Dyer Rd., Suite 110, Santa Ana, CA 92705; tel. 800/648-2444 or 714/549-3445.

Crui$e Value, 16 Digital Dr., Suite 100, Box 6115, Novato, CA 94948; tel. 800/551-1000, in California 415/382-8900.

CruiseMasters, 3415 Sepulveda Blvd., Suite 645, Los Angeles, CA 90034; tel. 800/242-9444, in California 800/242-9000.

Cruises Only, 1801 East Colonial Dr., Orlando, FL 32803; tel. 800/683-7447, in Florida 407/898-5353.

Cruises Inc., 5000 Campuswood Dr., East Syracuse, NY 13057; tel. 800/854-0500, in New York 315/463-9695.

Kelly Cruises, 2001 Midwest Rd., Suite 108, Oak Park, IL 60521; tel. 800/837-7447, in Illinois 708/932-8300.

Landry and Kling East, Inc. Cruise Specialists, 1390 S. Dixie Hwy, Suite 1207, Coral Gables, FL 33148; tel. 800/431-4007.

MVP Cruise Club ($30 annual membership), 917 N. Broadway, North Massapequa, NY 11758; tel. 800/253-4242, in New York 516/541-7782.

Personal Touch Cruise Consultants, 113 W. Sunrise Hwy., Freeport, NY 11520; tel. 800/477-4441.

The Travel Company, El Camino Real, Suite 250, Dept. CT, Atherton, CA 94027; tel. 800/367-6090 or 415/367-6000.

Trips 'n Travel, 9592 Harding Avenue, Surfside, FL 33154; tel. 800/331-2745, in Florida 305/864-2222.

Vacations at Sea, 4919 Canal St., New Orleans, LA 70119; tel. 800/274-1572, in Louisiana 504/482-1572.

Worldwide Discount Travel Club ($50 annual membership), 1674 Meridian Ave., Miami Beach, FL 33139; tel. 305/534-2082.

Payment

Deposit Most cruises must be reserved with a refundable deposit of $200–$500 per person, depending upon how expensive the cruise is; the balance is to be paid one to two months before you sail. Don't let a travel agent pressure you into paying a larger deposit or paying the balance earlier. If the cruise is less than a month away, however, it may be legitimate for the agency to require you to pay the entire amount immediately.

If possible, pay your deposit and balance via credit card. This gives you some recourse if you need to cancel, and you can ask the credit card company to intercede on your behalf in case of problems. Don't forget to get a receipt.

Handling money over to your travel agent constitutes a contract, so before you pay your deposit, study the cruise brochure to find out the provisions of the cruise contract. What is the payment schedule and cancellation policy? Will there be any additional charges before you can board your ship, such as transfers, port fees, local taxes, or baggage charges? If your air connection requires you to spend an evening in a hotel near the port before or after the cruise, is there an extra cost?

Cancellation If you cancel your reservation 45–60 days prior to your scheduled cruise (the grace period varies from line to line), you may receive your entire deposit or payment back. You will forfeit some or even all of your deposit if you cancel any closer to cruise time. In rare cases, however, if your reason for canceling is unavoidable, the cruise line may decide, at its discretion, to waive some or all of the forfeiture. An average cancellation charge is $100 one month before sailing, $100 plus 50% of the ticket price 15–30 days before sailing, and $100 plus 75% of the ticket price between 14 days and 24 hours before sailing. If you fail to show up when the ship sails, you lose the entire amount. Many travel agents also assess a small cancellation fee.

Insurance Cruise lines sell cancellation insurance for about $50 per ticket (the amount varies according to the line, the number of days in the cruise, and the price you paid for the ticket).

Before You Go

Tickets, Vouchers, and Other Travel Documents

Some cruise companies will give you your cruise ticket and transfer vouchers (which will get you from the airport to the ship and vice versa) at the time you make the final payment to your travel agent. Depending upon the airline, and whether or not you have purchased a fly/cruise package, you may receive your plane tickets or charter flight vouchers at the same time; you may also receive vouchers for any shore excursions, although most cruise lines prefer to hand those over when you board your ship. There are some cruise companies that mail tickets, either to you or your travel agent, only after they have received payment in full. Should your travel documents not arrive when promised, contact your travel agent or call the cruise line directly on its toll-free line. Occasionally tickets are delivered directly to the ship for those who book late.

Once you board your ship you may be asked to turn over your passport for group immigration clearance (*see* Passports, below, and Embarkation in Arriving and Departing, below) or to turn over your return plane ticket so the ship's staff may reconfirm your flight home. Otherwise, be sure to keep all travel documents in a safe place, such as a shipboard safe-deposit box.

Cruise Ships

Crown Cruise Line

SS Crown Jewel
Specifications

Type of ship: Upscale Mainstream
Type of cruise: Traditional
Size: Small (20,000 tons)
Number of cabins: 410
Outside cabins: 69.5%

Passengers: 820
Crew: 300 (Filipino)
Officers: Northern European and Scandanavian
Year built: 1992

Overview

From mid-October to mid-November the *Crown Jewel* makes two trans-Panama canal voyages that call in Acapulco. One cruise sails from New York to San Diego, the other runs from Los Angeles back to Palm Beach, Florida.

With half the passenger capacity of many competitors, the *Crown Jewel* offers an intimate voyage replete with personal touches. Clever use of glass, however, creates an illusion of spaciousness. A skylight and three walls of windows brighten the dining room where the tiered seating allows unobstructed sea views, and one entire wall of the Crown Plaza, a five-deck atrium foyer, is glass—the views here are also spectacular. A grand staircase and glass elevator complete the space.

Cabins and Rates

	Beds	Phone	TV	Sitting Area	Fridge	Tub	Per Diem
Suites	D	●	●	●	●	○	$185–$200
Outside	T/D	●	●	◐	◐	○	$165–$185
Inside	T/D	●	●	○	○	○	$150–$165

Staterooms and suites are dressed in a subtle color scheme of mauves, pinks, blues, and greens set against beautiful wood trim. Every passenger is made to feel a bit spoiled: Complimentary fruit, champagne, and other amenities await your arrival; at night there's turn-down service.

Access for the Disabled

Four cabins (two inside, two outside) have handicapped access.

Crystal Cruises

Crystal Harmony
Specifications

Type of ship: Luxury mainstream
Type of cruise: Traditional
Size: Large (49,400 tons)
Number of cabins: 480
Outside cabins: 96%

Passengers: 960
Crew: 505 (European)
Officers: Norwegian and Japanese
Year built: 1990

Cruise Facilities

Ship	*Cruise Line*	*Size (in tons)*	*Type of Ship*	*Type of Cruise*	*Per Diem Rates ***	*Length of Cruise ***	*Number of Passengers*	*Passenger/Crew Ratio*
Crown Jewel	Crown Cruise Line	20,000	Upscale Mainstream	Traditional	$150-$200	21-day	820	
Crown Odyssey	Royal Cruises Line	34,250	Luxury Mainstream	Traditional/ Senior	$245-$645	12-day	1,052	
Crystal Harmony	Crystal Cruises	49,400	Luxury Mainstream	Traditional	$210-$1,150	10,17-day	960	
Dawn Princess	Princess Cruises	25,000	Upscale Mainstream	Traditional/ Senior	$128-$400	7,10-day	890	
Fair Princess	Princess Cruises	25,000	Upscale Mainstream	Traditional/ Senior	$128-$400	7,10-day	890	
Island Princess	Princess Cruises	20,000	Upscale Mainstream	Traditional	$156-$400	10,11-day	610	
Royal Viking Sun	Royal Viking Line	38,000	Luxury Mainstream	Traditional/ Senior	$335-$1,175	21-day	740	
Seabourn Spirit	Seabourn Cruise Line	10,000	Luxury Yacht-like	Traditional	$558-$885	12,14-day	212	
Westward	Norwegian Cruise Line	28,000	Mainstream	Traditional	$179-$442	7-day	829	

Sanitation Rating*	Disabled Access	Special Dietary Options	Gymnasium	Jogging Track	Swimming Pool	Whirlpool	Sauna/Massage	Deck Sports	Casino	Disco	Cinema/Theater	Library	Boutiques/Gift shops	Video Arcade	Child Care	Outlet Voltage
N/A	●	●	●	●	1	2	●	●	●	●	●	●	●	●	●	110AC
88	●	●	●	●	2	2	●	●	●	●	●	●	●	○	○	110AC 220AC
94	●	●	●	●	2	2	●	●	●	●	●	●	●	●	◐	110AC 220AC
86	◐	●	●	◐	3	0	●	●	●	●	●	●	●	●	●	110AC
87	◐	●	●	◐	3	0	●	●	●	●	●	●	●	●	●	110AC
87	●	●	●	●	2	0	●	●	●	●	●	●	●	●	◐	110AC
86	●	●	●	●	2	1	●	●	●	●	●	●	●	○	◐	110AC 220AC
91	●	●	●	●	1	3	●	●	●	○	○	●	●	○	◐	110AC 220AC
93	◐	●	●	●	2	0	●	●	●	●	●	●	●	○	●	110AC

*Sanitation ratings are provided by the Vessel Sanitation Program, Center for Environmental Health and Injury Control. Ships are rated on water, food preparation and holding, potential contamination of food, and general cleanliness, storage, and repair. A score of 86 or higher indicates an acceptable level of sanitation. According to the center, "a low score does not necessarily imply an imminent outbreak of gastrointestinal disease." Chart ratings come from the center's March 15, 1992 report. Not all ships are covered.

** Per Diem rates and length of cruise apply only to cruises that call in Acapulco or Ixtapa.

Overview From mid-October through late December, the *Crystal Harmony* makes six runs that call at Acapulco. The first four either originate or end here. These cruises all pass through the Panama Canal and last between 10 and 17 days.

The *Crystal Harmony* is a sleek and sophisticated ship that contradicts conventional wisdom. Not all new, state-of-the-art ships have to look like high-rise hotels floating on barges. Built and owned by a Japanese company, the ship is not only technologically advanced and superbly equipped, but tastefully decorated as well. Harmonious colors in trims and furnishings and a light-and-airy design give a sense of both luxury and simplicity. Neo-classical sculpture and plants are placed throughout the ship. At the center is a multilevel atrium, Crystal Plaza, a study in glass stairways and railings, brass fixtures, and dazzling white walls. The Vista Lounge is a beautiful wedding-white room with oversize observation windows. The Lido is covered by a retractable canopy. With one of the highest passenger/space ratios afloat, there's never a feeling of claustrophobia.

Cabins and Rates

	Beds	Phone	TV	Sitting Area	Fridge	Tub	Per Diem
Penthouses/ Suites	T/Q	●	●	●	●	●	$534–$1,162
Superior	T/Q	●	●	●	●	●	$413–$443
Deluxe/Deluxe Veranda	T/Q	●	●	●	●	●	$229–$409
Inside	T	●	●	●	●	●	$213–$229

Staterooms and cabins are large, beautifully decorated, and well equipped. All cabins have hair dryers and robes. The views from some cabins on the Horizon and Promenade decks are obstructed by lifeboats. Cabins on the Promenade Deck look out onto a public promenade rather than the sea.

Access for the Disabled Four cabins have been fitted for wheelchair access. Passengers must provide their own small, traveling wheelchairs.

Norwegian Cruise Line

MS Westward *Specifications*

Type of ship: Mainstream
Type of cruise: Traditional
Size: Medium (28,000 tons)
Number of cabins: 390
Outside cabins: 85%
Passengers: 829
Crew: 325 (international)
Officers: Norwegian
Year built: 1972

Overview In winter, seven-day cruises between Los Angeles and Acapulco leave on alternating Saturdays.

The ship was built in 1972, expanded in 1981, and refurbished when it became the *Westward* in 1991. Passengers tend to be middle-aged couples, the kind of folks you'd see strolling off the tennis courts or golf course. Like NCL's other ships, the *Westward* has extensive activities and interesting shore excursions.

A couple of NCL favorites are a mini-Olympics and the chance to meet a pro football player on every cruise.

Cabins and Rates

	Beds	Phone	TV	Sitting Area	Fridge	Tub	Per Diem
Penthouse Suite	T or D	●	●	●	●	●	$392–$442
Suite	T	●	●	●	●	●	$320–$385
Deluxe Outside	T	●	●	●	●	●	$300–$320
Outside	T	●	●	○	○	●	$225–$302
Inside	T	●	●	○	○	●	$179–$218

The *Westward* has spacious cabins decorated in warm sunset colors; most have bathtubs. Nine penthouse suites have large, open sitting areas, separate bedrooms, floor-to-ceiling windows, and a private balcony. The smaller suites also feature a separate bedroom, and concierge service is available to some.

Access for the Disabled The *Westward* has no wheelchair-accessible cabins. The ship does, however, have ramps into the public areas and accessible elevators, and the staff goes out of its way to accommodate requests.

Princess Cruises

TSS Dawn Princess and TSS Fair Princess
Specifications

Type of ship: Upscale mainstream
Type of cruise: Traditional/senior
Size: Medium (25,000 tons)
Cabins: 446
Outside Cabins: 51.2%
Passengers: 890
Crew: 500 (European)
Officers: Italian
Year built: 1957 (*Dawn Princess*), 1956 (*Fair Princess*)

Overview In winter both ships offer seven-day loops from Los Angeles for Cabo San Lucas, Mazatlán, and Puerto Vallarta, with three days at sea. They also have 10-day loops from Los Angeles to Puerto Vallarta, Zihuatanejo/Ixtapa, Acapulco, Mazatlán, and Cabo San Lucas, with four days at sea.

Both the *Dawn Princess* and *Fair Princess* are former Sitmar ships, and they're virtually identical. Built in 1956–57 as ocean liners and last refurbished in 1989, the ships have retained much of their original look, with teakwood decks, glass-paneled library bookshelves, muted pastel interiors, and wood paneling. As is often the case on converted ocean liners, however, passengers enjoy limited public spaces.

Cabins and Rates

	Beds	Phone	TV	Sitting Area	Fridge	Tub	Per Diem*
Suite	D	●	●	●	●	●	$327–$400

Mini-suite	T	●	●	●	●	○	$256–$350
Outside	T or U/L	●	○	○	○	○	$171–$260
Inside	T or U/L	●	○	○	○	○	$128–$210

Cabins are large and include oversize closets, full-length mirrors, and wood trim. Outside views of the cabins on the Aloha Deck are obstructed by lifeboats; cabins on the Baja Deck look out onto a public promenade, not the open sea.

Access for the Disabled Ramps exist throughout the ships; however, some areas remain inaccessible. Most of the elevators are accessible. There are ten wheelchair-accessible cabins onboard.

MV Island Princess *Specifications*

Type of ship: Upscale mainstream
Type of cruise: Traditional
Size: Medium (20,000 tons)
Cabins: 305
Outside cabins: 77.5%
Passengers: 610
Crew: 350 (international)
Officers: British
Year built: 1972 (*Island Princess*), 1971 (*Pacific Princess*)

Overview In winter the *Island Princess* makes 10- or 11-day transcanal sailings between Acapulco and San Juan. The eastbound Panama Canal itinerary calls at Costa Rica, Aruba, St. Croix, and St. Thomas, with four days at sea. The westbound itinerary stops at St. Thomas, Martinique, and Curaçao, with four days at sea. The *Island* also has a couple of seven-day one-way Mexican Riviera cruises between Los Angeles and Acapulco.

One of the smallest ships in the fleet, *Island Princess* may not sport many public rooms, but the vessel is spacious and attractive; it carries large crews, which results in superior service—from fresh flowers everywhere to white-gloved stewards.

Most outdoor activities are centered around the cloverleaf-shaped swimming pool, protected by a retractable canopy. The interior is modern and impressive—particularly the two-story lobby with its spectacular staircase, floor-to-ceiling mirrors, and glass paneling. The dining room is well-lit and roomy.

Cabins and Rates

	Beds	Phone	TV	Sitting Area	Fridge	Tub	Per Diem*
Suites	D or T	○	○	●	●	●	$292–$400
Outside Deluxe	T	○	○	●	●	○	$264–$285
Inside Deluxe	T	○	○	●	●	○	$249–$235
Outside	T	○	○	○	○	○	$211–$225
Inside	T	○	○	○	○	○	$156–$190

Some of the cabins on the Promenade Deck look out onto a public area rather than the open sea.

Access for the Disabled All public lavatories and some of the cabins are equipped to accommodate handicapped passengers. All four elevators are accessible to passengers confined to wheelchairs.

Royal Cruise Line

MS Crown Odyssey
Specifications

Type of ship: Luxury mainstream
Type of cruise: Traditional/senior
Size: Medium (34,250 tons)
Number of cabins: 526
Outside cabins: 78%
Passengers: 1,052
Crew: 470 (Greek)
Officers: Greek
Year built: 1988

Overview In winter, the *Crown Odyssey's* Panama Canal cruises sail between Acapulco or Los Angeles and San Juan, and include Caldera (Costa Rica) and some Caribbean ports.

The *Crown Odyssey* is ultramodern, more like a floating town than a classic cruise ship—and the *Odyssey's* crew makes you feel like its mayor. Passengers can wander around 12 decks. The interior is a mosaic of different textures and materials, including marble, wood, glass, stainless steel, and brass.

Much emphasis is placed on physical fitness. The Health Center, styled after a Roman bath, boasts tile walls with inlaid mosaics and Italian white rattan furniture.

Dining in the Seven Continents restaurant is an experience difficult to top. Royal Doulton china, European linen, and silver set the tone for meals that are superbly prepared and deftly served.

Cabins and Rates

	Beds	Phone	TV	Sitting Area	Fridge	Tub	Per Diem
Superior Deluxe Apartment	T/D	●	●	●	●	●	\$605–\$645
Suites	T/D	●	○	●	○	●	\$442–\$602
Superior Deluxe Outside	T	●	○	○	○	●	\$470–\$520
Deluxe Outside	T	●	○	○	○	◐	\$290–\$340
Deluxe Inside	T	●	○	○	○	◐	\$245–\$305

The suites on board the *Crown Odyssey* are spacious and comfortable. Wood paneling and trim are used extensively in both the cabins and the suites, which also provide fully mirrored closets, phones for worldwide communications, and 24-hour room service. The 16 Penthouse Deck suites are all decorated thematically and have private balconies, marble bathrooms, and butler service. The Superior Deluxe Suites and the Junior Suites on the Riviera Deck feature bay windows. The views from most cabins on the Lido Deck, however, are obstructed or partially obstructed by lifeboats.

Access for the Disabled Four cabins are equipped with wheelchair-accessible bathrooms.

Royal Viking Line

MS Royal Viking Sun *Specifications*

Type of ship: Luxury mainstream
Type of cruise: Traditional/senior
Size: Large (38,000 tons)
Number of cabins: 370
Outside cabins: 94.8%
Passengers: 740
Crew: 460 (European)
Officers: Norwegian
Year built: 1988

A winter Panama Canal cruise sails between Fort Lauderdale and San Francisco, visiting St. Thomas, Tortola, St. Barts, Bonaire, Aruba, Acapulco, and Cabo San Lucas.

Overview The *Sun*, Royal Viking's flagship, is relatively new (1988), and no expense was spared in outfitting it. The interior is luxurious and spacious, designed for maximum comfort even on very long voyages. A feeling of light and space is created by the use of floor-to-ceiling windows. Despite all the glass, the ship does have its share of small, private lounges, including the Oak Room with its wood-burning fireplace, leather upholstery, and wood paneling. The Grill Room, an à la carte (extra charge) restaurant, offers an alternative to the main dining room, with special menus prepared by a three-star chef. The *Sun*'s passenger-to-crew ratio is just about the lowest among cruise ships.

Cabins and Rates

	Beds	Phone	TV	Sitting Area	Fridge	Tub	Per Diem
Penthouse	T/K	●	●	●	●	●	$1,030–$1,175
Deluxe Bedroom	T/K	●	●	●	●	◐	$836–$936
Outside Double	T/K	●	●	●	●	◐	$390–$551
Inside Double	T	●	●	○	●	◐	$336–$400

Cabins on the *Sun* are oversized, beautifully furnished, and have all amenities. Cabins on the Promenade Deck look out onto a public area rather than the open sea.

Access for the Disabled Four handicapped-equipped staterooms have L-shaped bed configurations to give passengers in wheelchairs greater maneuverability. Anyone confined to a wheelchair must travel with a companion and provide one's own 22″ wheelchair.

Seabourn Cruise Line

Seabourn Spirit *Specifications*

Type of ship: Luxury, yachtlike
Type of cruise: Traditional
Size: Small (10,000 tons)
Number of cabins: 106
Outside cabins: 100%
Passengers: 212
Crew: 140 (international)
Officers: Norwegian
Year built: 1989 *(Spirit)*

Overview The *Spirit* offers Panama Canal transits in January and February, between Acapulco and Barbados (12 days) or Acapulco and Fort Lauderdale (14 days). The 12-day transit stops in Huatulco Bay (Mexico), Costa Rica, Curaçao, and St. Lucia. The 14-day transit starts in Acapulco and ends in Fort Lauderdale, with calls at Costa Rica, Curaçao, and the Dominican Republic.

Aesthetically, the *Seabourn Spirit* may be the finest cruise ship afloat. With its sleek lines and twin funnels that resemble airfoils, the *Seabourn Spirit's* profile makes other cruise vessels look cluttered and ungainly. The plentiful use of glass, brass, and marble gives the interior a similarly clean look, heightened by the ship's spaciousness. Peaches, blues, and soft beiges dominate, with additional splashes of color provided by paintings on the walls. The most popular room inside is the Club/Casino with its bar and piano, backed by sloping picture windows that form the stern wall. Spotlighting, potted plants, and glass partitions make this an attractive room for preprandial cocktails and after-dinner dancing.

Cabins and Rates

	Beds	Phone	TV	Sitting Area	Fridge	Tub	Per Diem
Regal Suite *Type C*	Q or T	●	●	●	●	●	$885
Regal Suite *Type B*	Q or T	●	●	●	●	●	$724
Seabourn Suite *Type A*	Q or T	●	●	●	●	●	$558

All cabins are equipped with safes. The Regal Suites in the front of the ship have curved bow windows that make you feel as though you are on your own private sailing yacht.

Access for the Disabled Three Seabourn Suites (type A) are organized for easier wheelchair access. All elevators, public areas, and public lavatories are accessible to passengers in wheelchairs. Disabled passengers are nevertheless required to travel with a nonhandicapped adult companion.

4 Exploring Acapulco

Acapulco is a city that is easily understood, easily explored. During the day the focus for most visitors is the beach and the myriad of activities that happen on and off it—sunbathing, swimming, waterskiing, parasailing, snorkeling, deep-sea fishing, and so on. At night, the attention shifts to the restaurants and discos. The Costera Miguel Alemán, the wide boulevard that hugs Acapulco Bay from the Scenic Highway to Caleta Beach (a little less than five miles), is central to both day and night diversions. All the major beaches, big hotels—minus the more-exclusive East Bay properties, such as Las Brisas, Pierre Marqués, and the Princess—and shopping malls are off the Costera. Hence most of the shopping, dining, and clubbing takes place within a few blocks of the Costera, and many an address is listed only as "Costera Miguel Alemán." Because street addresses are not often used and streets have no logical pattern, directions are usually given from a major landmark, such as CiCi or the Zócalo.

Old Acapulco, the colonial part of town, is where the Mexicans go to run their errands: mail letters at the post office, buy supplies at the Mercado Municipal, and have clothes made/repaired at the tailor. Here is where you'll find the Zócalo, the church, and Fort San Diego. Just up the hill from Old Acapulco is La Quebrada, where, five times a day, the cliff divers plunge into the surf 130 feet below.

The peninsula just south of Old Acapulco contains remnants of the first version of Acapulco. This primarily residential area has been prey to dilapidation and abandonment of late, and the efforts made to revitalize it—such as reopening the Caleta Hotel and opening the aquarium on Caleta Beach and the zoo on Roqueta Island—haven't met with much success. The Plaza de Toros, where bullfights are held sporadically, is in the center of the peninsula.

If you've arrived by plane, you've had a royal introduction to Acapulco Bay. Driving from the airport, via the Scenic Highway, the first thing you see on your left is the golf course for the Acapulco Princess. Just over the hill is your first glimpse of the entire bay, and it is truly gorgeous, day or night. Your tour continues after you've settled into your hotel.

Lovers of art and architecture and devotees of historic monuments should not expect a wealth of sites, and that's as it should be. Acapulco is perfect for those who enjoy relaxing at the beach and pool by day and gearing up for dining and dancing at night. And though there are sights worth seeing outside of Old Acapulco that can be reached easily on foot, that route is not recommended. Walking along the Costera with its traffic and congestion can be rather unpleasant, especially in the heat. If you do fancy an ambulatory tour, we suggest a stroll along the beach, stopping en route at one of the hotel bars for a frosty daiquiri or *cerveza* (beer).

Taxis are another inexpensive option. They cost about the equivalent of a bus ride in the United States (*see* Staying in Acapulco in Chapter 1 for detailed information on hiring a cab). Buses are dirt cheap, but slow and not air-conditioned. There are also tour operators eager to show you around. Consult the list of tour operators (*see* Staying in Acapulco in Chapter 1) or check the activities desk at the major hotels. A tour is also handy if you don't have a car and want to explore the lagoons east and west of Acapulco (*see* Chapter 10).

Numbers in the margin correspond to points of interest on the Roqueta Island, Old Acapulco, and the East Bay map.

1 **La Base,** the Mexican naval base next to Plaza Icacos, anchors the eastern terminus of the Costera. There are no tours.

2 The **Centro Cultural Guerrerense** is on the beach side of the Costera, just past the Hyatt Regency hotel. It contains a small archaeological museum and the Zochipala art gallery with changing exhibits. *Admission free. Open weekdays, 9–1 and 5–8.*

3 **CiCi** (short for Centro Internacional para Convivencia Infantil), on the Costera, is a water-oriented theme park for children. There are dolphin and seal shows, a freshwater pool with wave-making apparatus, water slide, mini-aquarium, and other attractions. *Admission: $7 adults; $5 children. Open daily 10–6.*

About a half mile past CiCi, on the right side of the Costera, is
4 **Centro Internacional** (the Convention Center), not really of interest unless you are attending a conference there. There is a **Mexican Fiesta** Tuesday, Thursday, and Saturday nights from 7 to 10:30 ($45 pays for the show, dinner and open bar; entrance to the show alone is $10).

Continue along the Costera, through the heart of The Strip,
5 until you reach **Papagayo Park,** one of the top municipal parks in the country for location, beauty, and variety. Named for the hotel that formerly occupied the grounds, Papagayo sits on 52 acres of prime real estate on the Costera, just after the underpass at the end of The Strip. Though aimed at children, there is plenty for all ages to enjoy. Youngsters enjoy the life-size model of a Spanish galleon like the ones that once sailed into Acapulco when it was Mexico's capital of trade with the Orient. There is an aviary, a roller-skating rink, a racetrack with mite-size Can Am cars, a replica of the space shuttle *Columbia,* bumper boats in a lagoon, and other rides. The aviary is Papagayo's best feature: Hundreds of species of birds flitter overhead as you amble down shaded paths. *Admission free, though rides cost $1–$3.50. Open daily 10–6.*

6 The sprawling **Mercado Municipal,** a few blocks from the Costera, is Acapulco at its most authentic. It is also the city's answer to the suburban shopping mall. Locals come to purchase their everyday needs, from fresh vegetables and candles to plastic buckets and love potions. (Many cab drivers get a 10% commission on whatever you buy at the nearby Mercado de Artesanías, so many will try to discourage you from going to the mercado. Their reasons are highly imaginative, such as "The mercado's souvenirs are covered with dangerous lead-based paint." This happens to be true, but it is true of most handcrafted pottery and ceramics in Mexico. Except for stoneware, which is safe, it is wise to use Mexican pottery only for decoration or for serving, never for cooking or storing. Often the lead content is in the glaze rather than in the clay. In any case, this shouldn't stop you from the experience of exploring the market, so just ignore the cab drivers.) Go between 10 AM and 1 PM and ask to be dropped off near the *flores* (flower stand) closest to the souvenir and craft section. If you've driven to the

mercado, locals may volunteer to watch your car; be sure to lock your trunk and tip about 35¢.

The stalls within the mercado are densely packed together but luckily are awning covered, so things stay quite cool despite the lack of air-conditioning. From the flower stall, as you face the ceramic stand, turn right and head into the market. There are hundreds of souvenirs to choose from: woven blankets, puppets, colorful wooden toys and plates, leather goods, baskets, hammocks, and handmade wooden furniture including child-size chairs. You can also find some kitschy gems: Acapulco ashtrays and boxes covered with tiny shells or enormous framed pictures of the Virgin of Guadalupe. Bargaining hard is the rule: Start at half the asking price. The exception is silver. Under no circumstance pay more than one-fourth the asking price for hallmarked jewelry. A bracelet will be offered for $50 but the price should drop to less than $20 within five minutes. The silver vendors speak English.

The mercado is patronized primarily by Mexicans and, like many markets, is divided into departments. One area sells locally made brushes and wooden spoons. In another, artisans put finishing touches on baskets and wooden furniture. Women sell rows of neatly arranged plastic buckets in a rainbow of colors. There are dozens of exotic blossoms—many arranged into FTD-like centerpieces—in the flower market. Prices are a fraction of what you'd pay at home. The beans, spices, and vegetable section has a number of unfamiliar tropical products. There is even a stand offering medicinal herbs from China along with good luck charms. The love potions have unusual packaging. "Take one home to dominate your mate or to effect a reconciliation" the label on one says. Allow at least an hour and a half to take it all in.

7 Built in the 18th century to protect the city from pirates, **El Fuerte de San Diego** is on the hill overlooking the harbor next to the army barracks in Old Acapulco. (The original fort, destroyed in an earthquake, was built in 1616.) The fort now houses the **Museo Historico de Acapulco,** under the auspices of Mexico City's prestigious Museum of Anthropology. The exhibits portray the city from prehistoric times through Mexico's independence from Spain in 1821. Especially noteworthy are the displays touching on the Christian missionaries sent from Mexico to the Far East and the cultural interchange that resulted. Exhibits are mounted in separate air-conditioned rooms of the old fort. In addition to the permanent collection, there are changing exhibits and a projection room. The museum sponsors lectures (in Spanish), meetings, and an occasional evening performance. The front desk has details. *Tel. 74/82–38–28. Admission: $3.50. Open Tues.–Sun. 10:30–4:30.*

Acapulco is still a lively commercial port and fishing center. If
8 you stroll along the **waterfront,** you'll see all these activities at the commercial docks. The cruise ships dock here, and at night Mexican parents bring their children to play on the small tree-lined promenade. Farther west, by the Zócalo, are the docks for the sightseeing yachts and smaller fishing boats. It's a good spot to join the Mexicans in people-watching.

9 The **Zócalo** is the center of Old Acapulco, a shaded plaza in front of **Nuestra Señora de la Soledad,** the town's modern but unusual—stark white exterior with bulb-shaped blue and yel-

Centro Internacional, **4**
Centro Cultural Guerrerense, **2**
CiCi, **3**
Fuerte de San Diego, **7**
La Base, **1**
La Quebrada, **10**
Mercado Municipal, **6**
Papagayo Park, **5**
Waterfront, **8**
Zócalo, **9**

Roqueta Island, Old Acapulco, and the East Bay

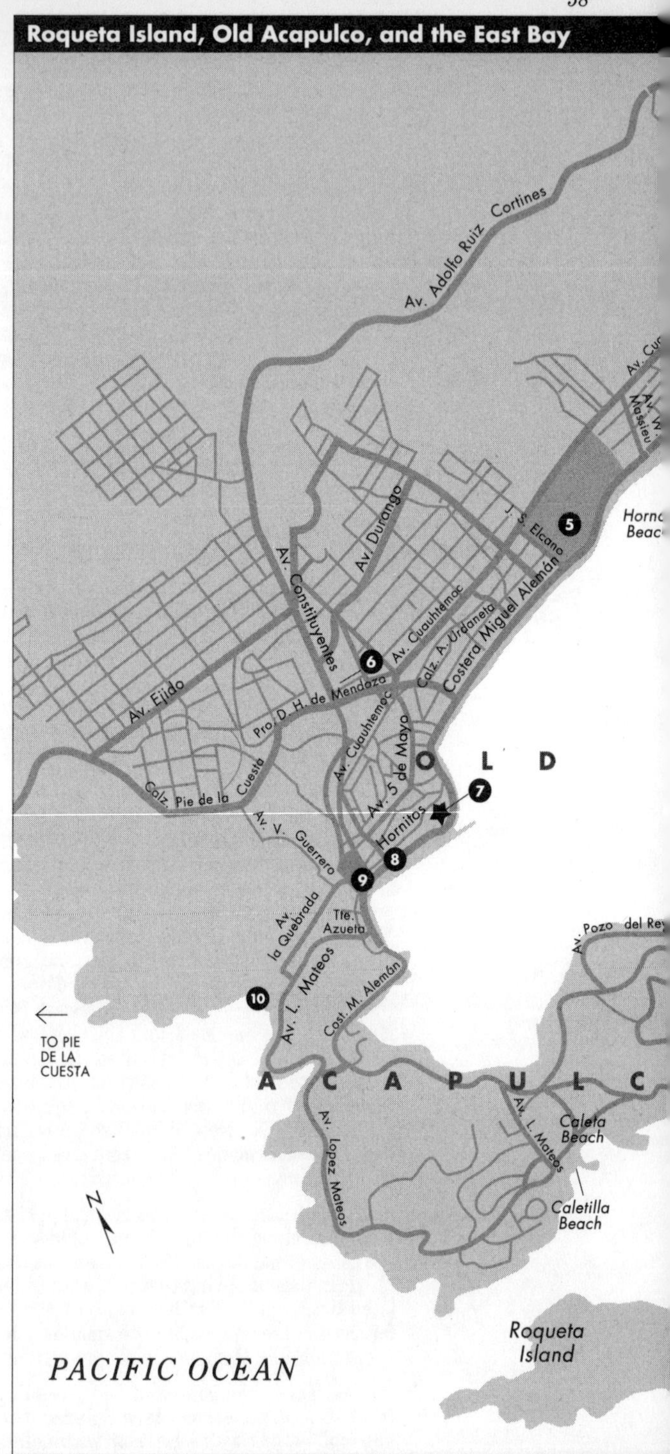

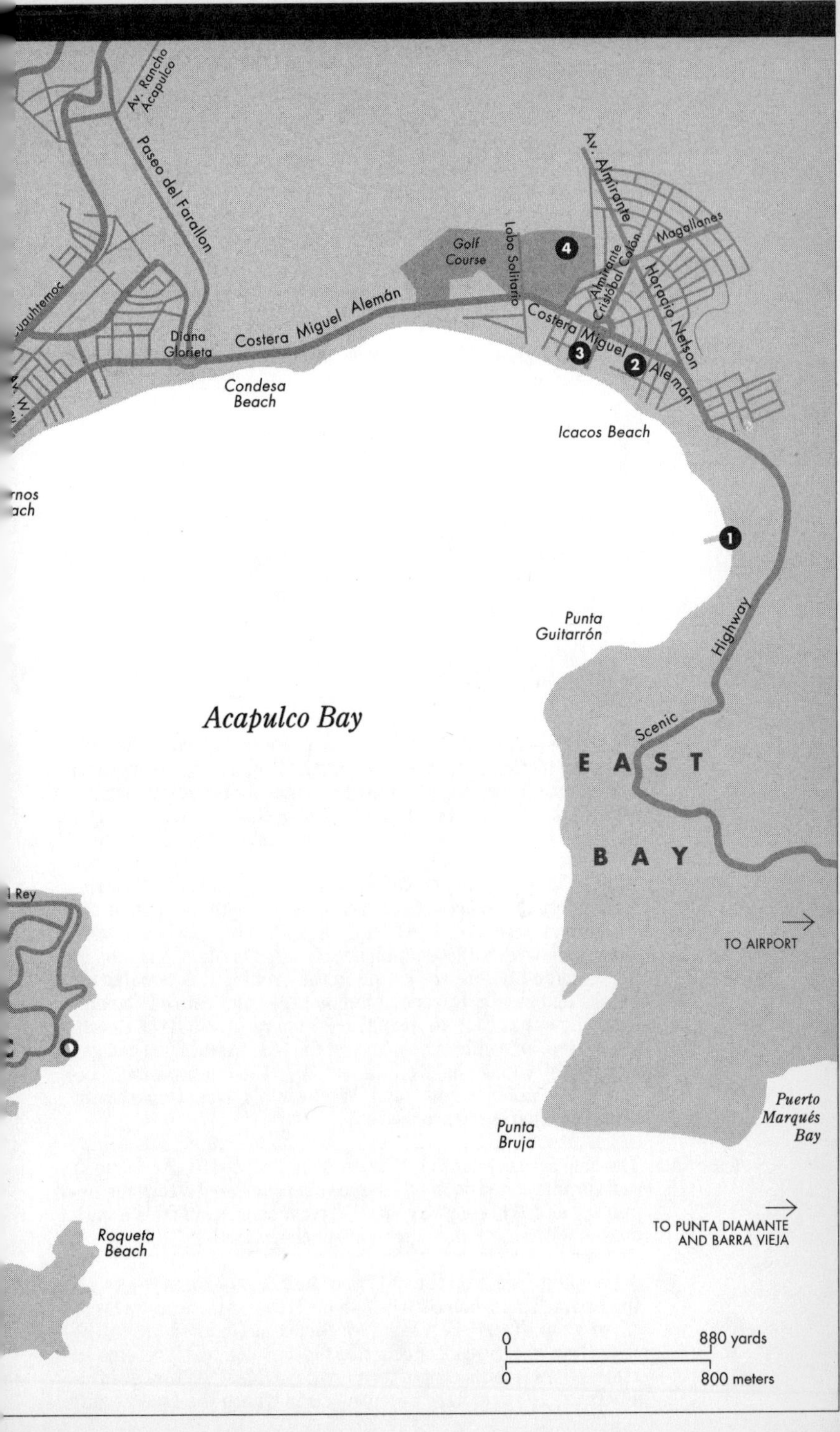
Av. Rancho Acapulco
Paseo del Farallon
Cuauhtemoc
Diana Glorieta
Costera Miguel Alemán
Condesa Beach
Golf Course
Lobo Solitario
Av. Almirante
Almirante Cristóbal Colón
Magallanes
Horacio Nelson
Costera Miguel Alemán
Icacos Beach
Punta Guitarrón
Acapulco Bay
Scenic Highway
EAST BAY
TO AIRPORT
Puerto Marqués Bay
Punta Bruja
TO PUNTA DIAMANTE AND BARRA VIEJA
Roqueta Beach
0 880 yards
0 800 meters

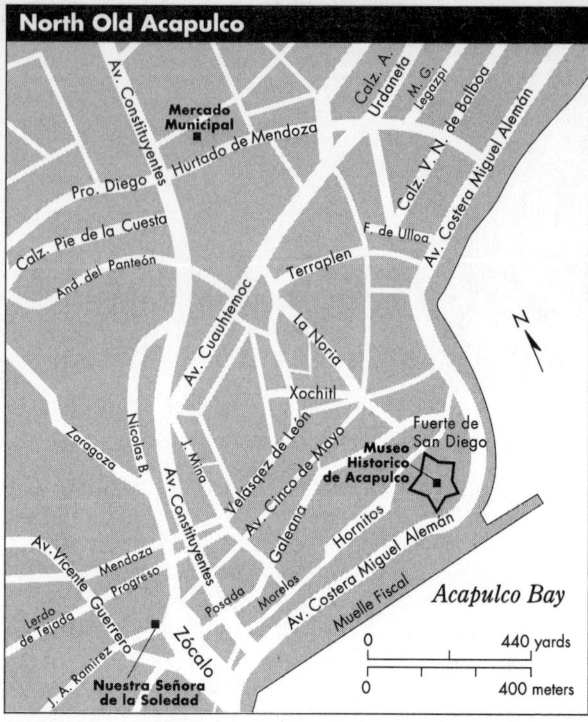

low spires—church. If there is any place in Acapulco that can be called picturesque or authentic, the Zócalo is it. Overgrown with dense trees, it is the hub of downtown, a spot for socializing. All day it's filled with vendors, shoeshine men, and people lining up to use the pay phones. After siesta, they drift here to meet and greet. On Sunday evenings there's music in the bandstand. There are several cafés and news agents selling the English-language *Mexico City News*, so tourists lodging in the area linger here, too. The Flor de Acapulco is a lovely old-fashioned café with a 1950s ambience. Groups of Mexicans stop in for breakfast before work, and in the evening it is popular for drinks and meals. European hippie types and retired Canadians hang out at Flor de Acapulco for hours. Around the Zócalo are several souvenir shops, and on the side streets you can get hefty, fruity milk shakes for about 50¢. The "flea market," inexpensive tailor shops, and Woolworth's (*see* Department Stores in Chapter 5) are nearby.

Time Out The café across from the Flor de Acapulco, below the German restaurant, at 455 de Mayo, serves *churros* every afternoon beginning at 4. This popular Spanish treat consists of fried dough dusted with sugar and dipped in hot chocolate.

10 A 10-minute walk up the hill from the Zócalo brings you to **La Quebrada.** This is home to the famous Mirador Hotel and a large silver shop, Taxco El Viejo (*see* Silver in Chapter 5). In the 1940s this was the center of action for tourists, and it retains an atmosphere reminiscent of its glory days. Most visitors eventually make the trip here because this is where the famous cliff

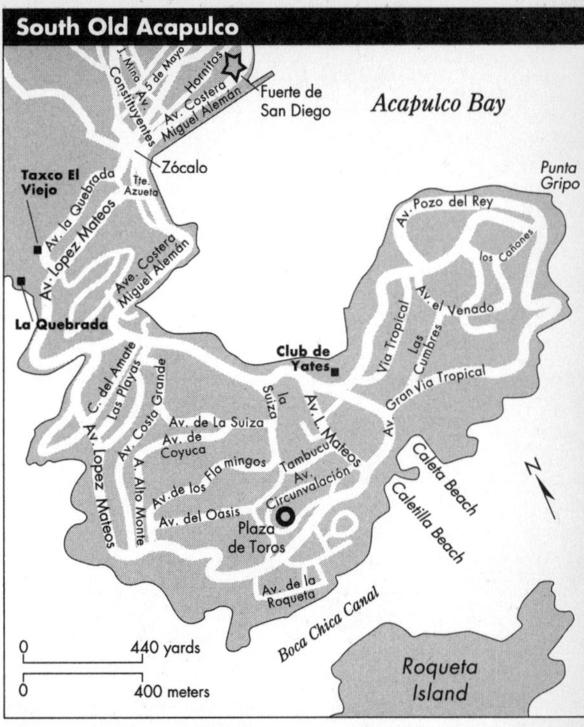

divers jump from a height of 130 feet every evening at 7:30, 8:30, 9:30, and 10:30. The dives are thrilling, so be sure to arrive early. Before they dive, the brave divers say a prayer at a small shrine near the jumping-off point. Sometimes they dive in pairs; often they carry torches.

What to See and Do with Children

CiCi and **Papagayo Park** (*see above*). They might also like the aquarium on Caleta beach, where there are pools, a toboggan, scuba diving, and (for rent) jet skis, inner tubes, and kayaks—not to mention clean rest rooms. From here you can take the launch to the small zoo on Roqueta Island, or a glass-bottom boat to La Quebrada and Puerto Marqués. *Aquarium admission: $5. Ferry service to Roqueta Island, including zoo admission: $3.50. Glass-bottom boat: $6.50.*

Palao's. This restaurant on Roqueta Island has a sandy cove for swimming, a pony, and a cage of monkeys. Children enjoy the motorboat ride out to the island (*see* Chapter 10).

Beto's. Another restaurant where children won't feel constrained, this is right on the beach at Barra Vieja (about 25 km east of Acapulco), with a child-size pool for swimming and a play tower for climbing.

Mimi's Chili Saloon and **Carlos 'n Charlies.** If your child misses familiar food (hamburgers, fries, etc.), these fun, festive eateries will fill the bill as well as young stomachs.

5 Shopping

There is quite a lot of shopping to do in Acapulco, and the abundance of air-conditioned shopping malls and boutiques makes picking up gifts and souvenirs all the more pleasurable. Except for the markets, most places shut for siesta. The typical hours of business are 10–1 and then 4–7, though these hours vary slightly. Most shops close on Sunday.

Though the fall of the peso has given most travelers to Acapulco a shopping edge, those who master the art of bargaining and understand how the Mexican sales tax (IVA) works will have their purchasing power increased even more.

Bargaining This is essential when dealing with street vendors, in small crafts shops, and in the mercado. Start at just below half the asking price and pay up to two-thirds. Vendors will usually drop the price by about one-third immediately. Then the tooth-pulling stage begins, when you haggle over one or two dollars. The best way to break a deadlock is to walk away and feign disinterest. They will soon come after you with a more reasonable offer.

IVA The standard sales tax in Mexico is known as an IVA, which is short for *impuesto valor agregado* (value added tax). It is 10%. Most purchases, including food, drink, and clothing, are taxed. But don't pay the IVA twice; it is often incorporated into the cost of an item. Look for signs in shop windows or alongside the price that say *IVA Incluido*, or ask the shopkeeper if IVA is part of the listed price.

Gift Ideas

Mexicans produce quantities of inexpensive collectibles and souvenirs such as colorful serapes, ceramics, glassware, silver, straw hats, leather, shell sculptures, wooden toys, carved walking canes, and, in season, Christmas ornaments. Most of these trinkets can be found everywhere. In fact, you may tire of the hawkers who traverse the beaches and approach passersby on the street. Crafts sold on the street include stone wind chimes, painted wooden birds (each about $3.50–$5), shell earrings for 50¢, shell sculptures, sets of wooden dishes, and rugs. Bargaining is essential in these situations (*see above*). Prices are often lower in the markets and on the street, so it makes sense to buy outside the shops or to visit the shops first, note the prices, and then venture to the markets to try and beat the store prices. Don't buy any article described as "silver" on the street. Street vendors sell a silver facsimile called alpaca. In the morning they buy bracelets from a wholesale supplier for 50¢ that they sell to unsuspecting tourists in the afternoon for $5. Buy silver in shops and look for the .925 hallmark, which means you are getting sterling. The large AFA (Artesanías Finas de Acapulco) crafts shop, though, has fixed prices and will ship, so this is the place to purchase onyx lamp stands and other larger items (*see* Food and Flea Markets, *below*). Clothes are another reasonably priced gift item. There are a couple of fashionable boutiques with designer clothes, but the majority of shops stock cotton sportswear and casual resort clothes. Made-to-order clothes are well made and especially reasonable. Otherwise, be careful, since quality is not high and many goods self-destruct a few months after you get back home.

Shopping

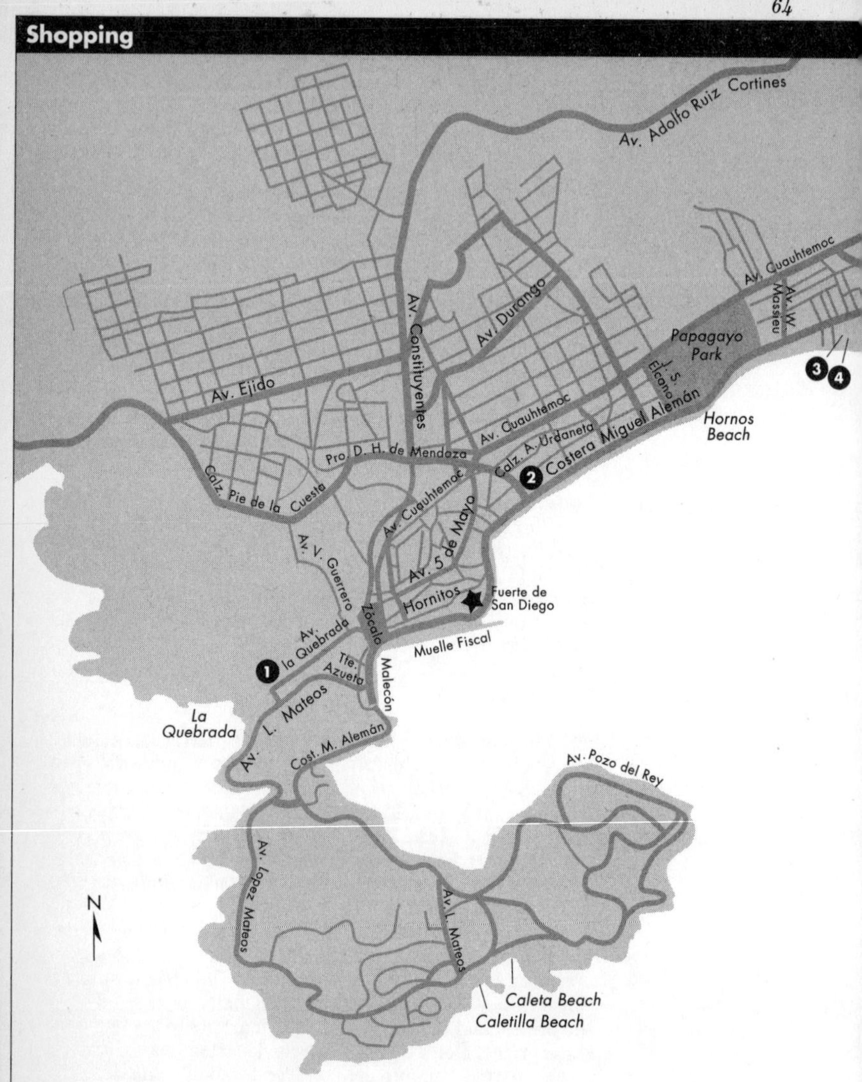

Aca Mall, **8**
Artesanías Finas de Acapulco, **10**
El Mercado de Artesanías, **2**
El Patio, **6**
Flamboyant Mall, **5**
Galería Plaza, **4**
Marbella Mall, **7**
Plaza Bahía, **3**
Plaza Condesa, **9**
Plaza Icacos, **11**
Princess Arcade, **12**
Taxco El Viejo, **1**

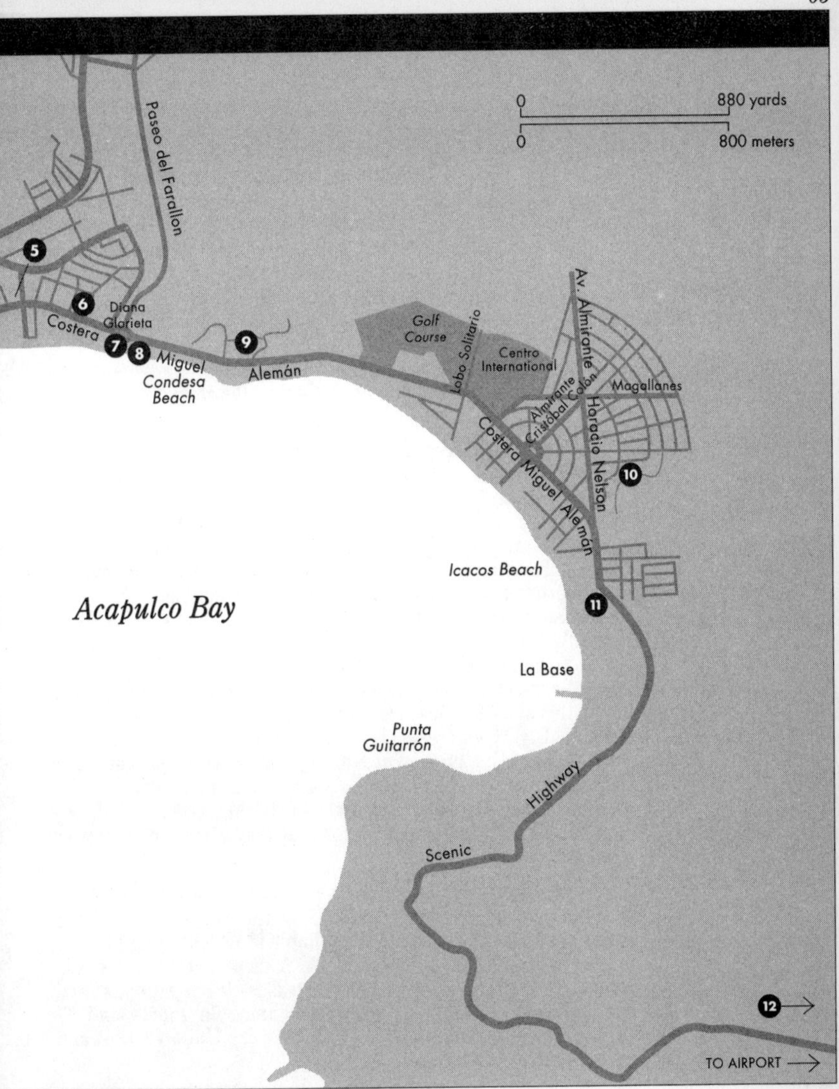
0
880 yards
0
800 meters
Paseo del Farallon
Diana
Glorieta
Costera
Miguel
Alemán
Condesa
Beach
Golf
Course
Lobo Solitario
Centro
International
Av. Almirante
Almirante
Cristóbal Colón
Magallanes
Horacio Nelson
Costera Miguel Alemán
Icacos Beach
Acapulco Bay
La Base
Punta
Guitarrón
Highway
Scenic
TO AIRPORT

Shopping Districts

The biggest shopping strip surrounds the Fiesta Americana Condesa Hotel and is where you can find Gucci, Acapulco Joe, Ocho Rios, Rubén Torres, Fiorucci, and others. Downtown (Old) Acapulco doesn't have many name shops, but this is where you'll find the inexpensive tailors patronized by the Mexicans, lots of little souvenir shops, and the flea market with crafts made for tourists. The tailors are all on Calle Benito Juárez, just west of the Zócalo. Also downtown are Woolworth's—which carries the same kinds of goods as in the United States—and a branch of Sanborns, a more upscale place.

Food and Flea Markets

The main market, **Mercado Municipal,** is described in detail in Chapter 4.

El Mercado de Artesanías is a twenty-minute walk from the Zócalo. Turn left as you leave Woolworth's and head straight until you reach the Multibanco Comermex. Turn right for one block and then turn left. When you reach the Banamex, the market is on your right. There are also "fleamarket" signs posted. The market itself is shamelessly inauthentic; everything here is made strictly for foreign consumption, so go just for the amusement. It is a conglomeration of every souvenir in town: fake tribal masks, the ever-present onyx chessboards, the $20 hand-embroidered dresses, imitation silver, hammocks, ceramics, even skin cream made from turtles. (Don't buy it because turtles are endangered and you won't get it through U.S. Customs.) *Open daily from 9 to 9.* If you don't want to make the trip downtown, try **Noa Noa** on the Costera at Calle Hurtado de Mendoza. It's a cleaner, more commercial version of the Mercado Municipal and also has T-shirts and jewelry, as well as the dozens of souvenirs available in the other markets.

Artesanías Finas de Acapulco (AFA) is one block north of the Costera behind the Baby O disco. All the souvenirs you have seen in town and lots more are available in 13,000 square feet of air-conditioned shopping space. AFA also carries household items, complete sets of dishes, suitcases, leather goods, and conservative clothing, as well as fashionable shorts and T-shirts. The staff is helpful. AFA ships to the United States and accepts major credit cards.

The **Crafts Shop,** in the same building as Taxco El Viejo in La Quebrada before you reach the Mirador Hotel, has not only all the usual crafts but also the best selection of glassware in Acapulco.

Two blocks west of the Zócalo is **Calle José M. Iglesia,** home to a row of little souvenir shops that have a smaller selection than the big markets, but many more T-shirts and more shell sculptures, shell ashtrays, and shell key chains than you ever imagined possible.

Art

Galerías Artesanales, at the Princess, carries the work of contemporary Mexican artists, including Felgueres, as well as handcrafts that almost border on art. *Open Mon.–Sat. 10–8.*

Galería Rudic, across from the Hyatt Continental, is one of the best galleries in town, with a good collection of top contemporary Mexican artists, including Armando Amaya, Leonardo Nierman, Norma Goldberg, Trinidad Osorio, José Clemente Orozco, and José David Alfaro Siqueiros. *Open weekdays 10–2 and 5–8.*

Galería Victor is the most noteworthy shop in the El Patio shopping center across from the Hyatt Continental. On display is the work of the late Victor Salmones. *Open 10–2 and 4–8. Closed Sun.*

The sculptor **Pal Kepenyes** continues to receive good press. His jewelry is available in the Hyatt Regency arcade. It's also on display in his house at Guitarrón 140. Good luck with his perennially busy phone number, tel. 74/84–47–38.

Sergio Bustamente's whimsical painted papier-mâché and giant ceramic sculptures can be seen at the Princess Hotel shopping arcade and at his own gallery (Costera Miguel Alemán 711-B, next to American Express). **El Dorado Gallery,** next door, carries works by his former partner, Mario Gonzáles.

Boutiques

The mall section (*see below*) lists clothing shops, but there are a few places, mainly near the Fiesta Americana Condesa Hotel, that are noteworthy. **Mad Max** has tasteful cotton separates in bold colors for children, and shirts sporting the shop's logo (all under $20). **Acapulco Joe, Rubén Torres, Polo Ralph Lauren, Benetton, Fiorucci,** and **OP** are scattered around the Costera, too. At No. 143 are three interconnected shops: Explora, Poco Loco, and Maria de Guadalajara. **Explora** and **Poco Loco** stock shirts imprinted with beer and alcohol logos, with casual separates and bathing suits, as well. The **Maria de Guadalajara** line of comfortable casual clothes for women is made from crinkly cotton in subdued and pastel colors. There are also a few high-fashion boutiques that will make clothes to order, and many can alter clothes to suit you, so it is always worth asking.

Sassafrass, in the Galería Plaza, is a boutique stocked with stylish bathing suits, shorts, and handpainted T-shirts for men and women.

Ocho Ríos, at the entrance to the Fiesta Americana Condesa and next door to the Galería Acapulco Plaza, has a line of smashing women's bathing suits for equally smashing bodies.

In Plaza Bahía, **Lassere** has a selection of very stylish casuals, designed in France and made in Mexico for men and women.

Marietta is located at the Acapulco Princess Hotel arcade and on the Costera at the Torre de Acapulco. It has a large collection that ranges from simple daywear to extravagantly sexy party dresses. This is a standby for expats in Acapulco. Though the clothes may seem expensive (cotton dresses from $70 to $150), they are quite a bit cheaper than they would be in the United States. It also has a good selection of men's shirts.

Pit, located in the Princess arcade, is another bonanza. It is one of the few places that carries sweaters and coats as well as bathing suits and light dresses.

Custom-made Clothes The most famous of the made-to-order boutiques is **Samy's** at Calle Hidalgo 7, two blocks west of the Zócalo, a little crammed shop next to a florist. It boasts a clientele of international celebrities and many of the important local families. Samy, the charming owner, takes all customers to heart and treats them like old, much-loved friends. He makes clothes for men and women, all in light cottons. The patterns are unusual and heavily influenced by Mexican designs, with embroidery and gauze playing a supporting role in the Samy look. The outfits are appropriate for trendy over-30s. Anything that doesn't fit can be altered, and Samy will even work with fabric that you bring in. Prices start at about $30. There is also a ready-to-wear line.

Esteban's, the most glamorous shop in Acapulco, is on the Costera near the Club de Golf. Like Samy, Esteban will make clothes to order and adapt anything you see in the shop. The similarity ends there. Esteban's clothes are far more formal and fashionable. His opulent evening dresses range from $200 to $1,000, though daytime dresses average $120. If you scour the racks, you can find something for $85. Esteban has a back room full of designer clothes.

Jewelry

Aha, on the Costera next to the Crazy Lobster, has the most unusual costume jewelry in Acapulco. Designed by owner Cecilia Rodriguez, this is really campy, colorful stuff that is bound to attract attention. Prices range from $12 to $300.

Emi Fors are tony jewelry shops owned by Mrs. Fors, a former Los Angelino. The stores stock gold, silver, and some semiprecious stones. There are two branches: Galería Plaza and the Continental Plaza.

Arles, at the Galería Acapulco Plaza, carries the beautiful Oro de Monte Alban collection of gold replicas of Oaxacan artifacts, as well as watches, handicrafts, and handpainted tin soldiers.

Leather

Leather goods are inexpensive in Mexico but generally not of the highest quality. So shop carefully and don't plan to pass on anything to your grandchildren. Best bets for quality are Gucci and Aries. **Gucci** sells shoes and accessories in Mexican versions of Italian designs that are much loved by fashionable Mexicans. It is a good place for men's shoes, and the prices are comparatively reasonable. Women's handbags range from $100 to $300. *Costera 102 near El Presidente, across from the Hyatt Continental, at El Patio, the Hyatt Regency, and the Galería Acapulco Plaza.*

Aries (Las Brisas Hotel), the other reputable leather-goods dealer in Acapulco, sells Mexican leather that has been sent to Spain to be cured, then returned to Mexico to be fashioned into luggage, handbags, and briefcases. Prices are a bit more than at Gucci but not substantially higher.

Silver

Many people come to Mexico to buy silver. Taxco, three hours away, is one of the silver capitals of the world (*see* Chapter 11). Prices in Acapulco are lower than in the United States but not dirt-cheap by any means. Bangles start at $8 and go up to $20; bracelets range from $20 to $60. Just look for the .925 sterling silver hallmark, or buy the more inexpensive silver plate that is dipped in several coats *(baños)* of silver. **Antonio Pineda** and **Los Castillo** are two of the more famous design names. Designs range from traditional bulky necklaces (often made with turquoise) to streamlined bangles and chunky earrings. Not much flatware can be found, although Emi Fors and Taxco El Viejo do carry some.

Taxco El Viejo (La Quebrada 830), in a large colonial building in Old Acapulco, has the largest silver selection in Acapulco. Pieces seen all over town crop up here as do more unusual designs. Also for sale are flatware and a large range of ornamental belt buckles. If you buy several pieces, you can request a discount. Beware of heavy-handed sales techniques such as offering to send a taxi to pick you up at your hotel, a tactic meant to make you feel obligated to buy something.

La Joya (Acapulco Plaza) stocks a good collection of inexpensive silver jewelry in modern designs and an extensive array of low-priced bangles (in the $6 range). Joya sells wholesale and will give a 30% discount on every item. *Open weekdays 9–6, Sat. 9–5.*

Dudu (Acapulco Princess shopping center) has the finest selection of silver jewelry and decorative pieces in town. There are signed pieces by Los Castillo (including brightly colored high-temperature ceramic dinnerware inlaid with silver), and enameled pieces by Miguel Pineda.

Malls

Malls are all the rage in Acapulco, and new ones are constantly being built. These range from the lavish air-conditioned shopping arcade at the Princess to rather gloomy collections of shops that sell cheap jewelry and embroidered dresses. Malls are listed below from east to west.

The **Princess's** cool arcade is one of Acapulco's classiest, most comfortable malls. Serious shopping takes place here. Best bets are quality jewelry, clothes, leather, accessories, and artwork. Even if you are staying on The Strip, it is worth the cab ride out here just to see the shops: Dudu offers beautiful silver jewelry and *objets d'art;* Pit carries women's clothes—jackets, coats and Mexican-accented dresses for $250 and casual daywear in the $150 range. Aca Joe and Fila have branches here, as does Bye Bye. Marietta has a large collection of men's and women's clothes. The handicrafts in ceramics, clay (including black clay pieces from Oaxaca), and papier-mâché at Galerías Artesanales straddle the line between crafts and art. Emil has a good choice of sportswear for men and women.

La Casita, which carries Mexican-inspired clothes for women, is the only shop left in **Plaza Icacos,** at the bottom of the hill, across from the Hyatt Regency. Across from the Fiesta Americana Condesa Hotel is the **Plaza Condesa,** which offers a cold-drink stand, an Italian restaurant, a weight-training center, and a greater concentration of silver shops than anywhere in Acapulco. Next door to Plaza Condesa is a high-tech, two-story building with a gym, OP for trendy sportswear, Rubén Torres, and Acapulco Joe. Two branches of Mad Max carrying children's inexpensive unisex clothes in basic colored cotton are here, too. The multilevel **Marbella Mall,** at the Diana Glorieta, has Peletier Paris jewelers and Bing's Ice Cream, as well as several restaurants and a Century 21 office. **Aca Mall,** which is on the other side of the Diana Glorieta, is all white and marble. Here you'll find Polo Ralph Lauren, Esprit, Perry Ellis, Amarras, Ellesse, and Marti (which carries a huge variety of sports equipment). **El Patio,** across from the Hyatt Continental, has two recommendable art galleries, Gucci, and a fairly generic collection of clothing and silver shops.

Plaza Bahía, next to the Acapulco Plaza, is a huge, completely enclosed and air-conditioned mall, where you can easily spend an entire day. Here you'll find Calvin Klein; Benetton; Aspasia, which carries a line of locally designed glitzy evening dresses and chunky diamanté jewelry; Bally; Armando's Girasol, with its distinctive line of women's clothing; restaurants and snack bars; Marti, which has every piece of sports equipment you could ever need; a video-games arcade; and silver and handicraft shops. The list goes on and on.

Galería Plaza is a new two-story structure of lusciously air-conditioned shops built around a courtyard. Except for the silver, you could find many similar items at home. But this is a good place to pick up some cotton sportswear or a pretty dress to wear to a disco. For fancier duds, Arles, upstairs, has hand-painted lead soldiers and the "Oro de Monte Alban" collection of gold replicas of pre-Hispanic jewelry found in Oaxaca. Guess! is one block west as you leave the plaza. Across from the Galería Plaza is the **Flamboyant Mall,** similar in style to El Patio.

Department Stores

Sanborns is the most un-Mexican of the big shops. It sells English-language newspapers, magazines, and books, as well as a line of high-priced souvenirs, but its Mexican glassware and ceramics cannot be found anywhere else in town. This is a useful place to come for postcards, cosmetics, and medicines. Sanborns's restaurants are recommended for glorified coffee-shop food. *The branch adjacent to the Condesa, Costera Miguel Alemán 209, is open until 1 AM; the downtown branch, Costera Miguel Alemán 1206, closes at 10:30 PM.*

Two branches of **Super Super** and **Gigante,** all on the Costera, and one Super Super downtown sell everything from light bulbs and newspapers to bottles of tequila and postcards. If you are missing anything at all, you should be able to pick it up at either of these stores or at the **Commercial Mexicana,** a store a little closer to The Strip. *Open until 9 PM; Super Super on La Costera until 11 PM, downtown until 8 PM.*

Woolworth's, at the corner of Escudero and Matamoros streets in Old Acapulco, is much like the five-and-dime stores found all over the United States, but with a Mexican feel. You can purchase American brands of shampoo for less than they cost at home, as well as paper goods, cheap clothes, handmade children's toys, and the ubiquitous Acapulco shell ashtrays. There are also several mini-Woolworths along the Costera. *Open until 9 PM.*

6 Sports and Fitness

Participant Sports and Fitness

Acapulco has lots for sports lovers to enjoy. Most hotels have pools, and there are several tennis courts on The Strip. The weight-training craze is beginning to catch on and gyms are opening. You'll find one at Plaza Condesa across from the Fiesta Americana Condesa Hotel.

Fishing Sailfish, marlin, shark, and mahimahi are the usual catches. Head down to the docks near the Zócalo and see just how many people offer to take you out for $35 a day. It is safer to stick with one of the reliable companies whose boats and equipment are in good condition.

Fishing trips can be arranged through your hotel, downtown at the Pesca Deportiva near the *muelle* (dock) across from the Zócalo, or through travel agents. Boats accommodating four to ten people cost $200–$500 a day, $60 by the chair. Excursions usually leave about 7 AM and return at 2 PM. You are required to get a license ($7) from the Secretaría de Pesca above the central post office downtown, but most fishing outfits take care of it. Don't show up during siesta, between 2 and 4 in the afternoon. For deep-sea fishing, **Arnold Brothers** (Costera Miguel Alemán 205, tel. 74/82–18–77) has well-maintained boats for five passengers (two lines). Small boats for freshwater fishing can be rented at **Cadena's** and **Tres Marías** at Coyuca lagoon.

Fitness and Swimming **Acapulco Princess Hotel** (Carretera Escénica, Km 17, tel. 74/84–31–00) offers the best fitness facilities, with five pools, 11 tennis courts—including two that are indoors *and* air-conditioned—and a gym with stationary bikes, Universal machines, and free weights. The Princess and its sister hotel, the Pierre Marqués, share two beautifully maintained 18-hole golf courses. Golf clubs are available to rent. Because the Princess is about nine miles from the city center, you can even swim in the ocean here, avoiding the pollution of Acapulco Bay. Beware: The waves are rough and the undertow is strong.

Villa Vera Spa and Fitness Center (Lomas del Mar 35, tel. 74/84–03–33) has three illuminated clay courts and a new spa and fitness center. Masseuses and cosmetologists give facials and massages inside or by the pool, as you wish. The fitness center is equipped with exercise machines (including step machines), free weights, and benches. You can purchase natural fruit juices at the bar and low-calorie meals in the dining room. Both the beauty center and gym are open to non-guests.

Westin Las Brisas (Carretera Escénica 5255, tel. 74/84–15–80) is the place to stay if you like to swim but don't like company or competition. Individual *casitas* come with private, or semiprivate, pools; the beach club has two saltwater pools, a Home Fitness System, and workout machines.

Most of the major hotels in town along the Costera Miguel Alemán also have pools, which is where you should do your swimming. In spite of the city's recent efforts to clean up Acapulco Bay, the sea opposite the city center is still to be avoided.

Golf There are two 18-hole championship golf courses shared by the Princess and Pierre Marqués hotels. Reservations should be made in advance (tel. 74/84–31–00). Greens fees are $50 for guests, and $60 for nonguests. There is also a public golf course at the Club de Golf (tel. 74/84–07–81) on The Strip across from the Acapulco Malibú hotel. Greens fees are $30 for nine holes.

Jogging As in Mexico City, jogging has caught on here among all classes of people. The only real venue for running in the downtown area, however, is along the sidewalk next to the seafront Costera Miguel Alemán. Early morning is the best time, since traffic is heavy along this thoroughfare during most of the day and the exhaust fumes can make running unpleasant. The sidewalk measures close to five miles, although your hotel will probably lie somewhere in the middle of the route. The beach is another option. Away from the city center, the best area for running is out at the Acapulco Princess Hotel, on the airport road. A 2-kilometer (1.2 mi) loop is laid out along a lightly traveled road and, in the early morning, you can also run along the asphalt trails on the golf course.

Scuba Diving **Divers de México,** owned by a helpful and efficient American woman, provides English-speaking captains and comfortable American-built yachts. A four- to five-hour scuba-diving excursion, including equipment, lessons in a pool for beginners, and drinks, costs about $55 per person. If you are a certified diver, the excursion is $45; if you bring your own equipment, it is $30. Divers de México also rents chairs on fishing boats for about $30 per person and runs three-hour sunset champagne cruises to watch the cliff divers (tel. 74/82–13–98 or 74/83–60–20).

Arnold Brothers (*see* Fishing, *above*) also runs daily scuba excursions ($30) and snorkeling trips.

Tennis Court fees range from about $7 to $20 an hour during the day, and are $2–$3 more in the evening. Non-hotel guests pay about $5 more per hour. Lessons, with English-speaking instructors, are about $25 an hour; ball boys get a $2 tip.

Acapulco Plaza, 4 clay courts, 3 lighted (tel. 74/84–80–50).
Acapulco Princess, 2 indoor courts, 9 outdoor (tel. 74/84–31–00).
Club de Tennis and Golf, across from Hotel Malibu, Costera Miguel Alemán (tel. 74/84–48–24).
Hyatt Regency, 5 lighted courts (tel. 74/84–12–25).
Pierre Marqués, 5 courts (tel. 74/84–20–00).
Tiffany's Racquet Club, Avenue Villa Vera 120, 5 courts (tel. 74/84–79–49).
Villa Vera Hotel, 3 lighted clay courts (tel. 74/84–02–24).

Water Sports Waterskiing, broncos (one-person motor boats), and parasailing can all be arranged for on the beach. Parasailing is an Acapulco highlight and looks terrifying until you actually try it. Most people who do it love the view and go back again and again. An eight-minute trip costs $10–$15 (tel. 74/82–20–56). Waterskiing is about $20 an hour; broncos cost $15 an hour. Windsurfing can be arranged at Caleta and most of the beaches along the Costera, but is especially good at Puerto Marqués. At Coyuca Lagoon, you can try your hand (or feet) at barefoot waterskiing. The main surfing beach is Revolcadero.

Spectator Sports

Bullfights The season runs from Christmas to Easter, and *corridas* are held—sporadically—on Sundays at 5:30. Tickets are available through your hotel or at the Plaza de Toros ticket window (open Mon.–Sat. 10–2 and Sun. 10:30–3; tel. 74/82–11–81). Tickets cost from $20 to $25, and a $25 seat in the first four rows—in the shade (*sombra*)—is worth the extra cost.

Beaches

The lure of sun and sand in Acapulco is legendary. Once you hit the beach, you may never want to leave, and you may never need to, except to enjoy Acapulco's other draw, its nightlife. Every sport is available and you can shop from roving souvenir vendors, eat in a beach restaurant, dance, and sleep in a *hamaca* (hammock) without leaving the water's edge. If you want to avoid the crowds, there are also plenty of quiet and even isolated beaches within reach. However, at some of these, such as Revolcadero and Pie de la Cuesta, there are a very strong undertow and strong surf, so swimming is not advised.

Though water sports are available on most beaches, consider the following before you bathc: Despite an enticing appearance and claims that officials are cleaning up the bay, it remains polluted. If this bothers you, we suggest you follow the lead of the Mexican cognoscenti and take the waters at your hotel pool.

Beaches in Mexico are public, even those that seem to belong to a big hotel. The list below moves from east to west.

Barra Vieja About 16 miles east of Acapulco, between Laguna de Tres Palos and the Pacific, this magnificent beach is even more inviting than Pie de la Cuesta because you're not bothered by itinerant peddlers and beggars (*see* Chapter 10).

Revolcadero A wide, sprawling beach next to the Pierre Marqués and Princess hotels, its water is shallow and waves fairly rough. People come here to surf and ride horses.

Puerto Marqués Tucked below the airport highway, this strand is popular with Mexican tourists, so it tends to get crowded on weekends.

Icacos Stretching from the naval base to El Presidente, this beach is less populated than others on The Strip. The morning waves are especially calm.

Condesa Facing the middle of Acapulco Bay, this stretch of sand has more than its share of tourists, especially singles. The beachside restaurants are convenient for bites between parasailing flights.

Hornos and Hornitos Running from the Paraiso Radisson to Las Hamacas hotels, these beaches are packed shoulder to shoulder with Mexican tourists. These tourists know a good thing: Graceful palms shade the sand and there are scads of casual eateries within walking distance.

Caleta and Caletilla On the peninsula in Old Acapulco, these two attract families. Motorboats to Roqueta leave from here.

Roqueta Island A ferry costs about $3.50 round-trip, including entrance to the zoo; the trip takes 10 minutes each way. Acapulqueños consider Roqueta Island their day-trip spot (*see* Chapter 10).

Pie de la Cuesta You'll need a car or cab to reach this relatively unpopulated spot, about 15 minutes west of town (*see* Chapter 10).

7 Dining

Introduction

Dining in Acapulco is more than just eating out—it is the most popular leisure activity in town. Every night the restaurants fill up, and every night the adventurous diner can sample a different cuisine: Italian, German, Japanese, American, Tex-Mex, and, of course, plain old Mex. The variety of styles matches the range of cuisines: from greasy spoons that serve regional specialties to rooftop gourmet restaurants with gorgeous views of Acapulco Bay. Most restaurants fall somewhere in the middle, and on The Strip there are dozens of palapa (palm frond)–roofed beachside restaurants, as well as wildly decorated rib and hamburger joints popular with visitors under 30.

One plus for Acapulco dining is that the food is garden fresh. Each morning the Mercado Municipal is abuzz with restaurant managers and locals buying up the vegetables that will appear on plates that evening. Although some top-quality beef is now being produced in the states of Sonora and Chihuahua, many of the more expensive restaurants claim that they import their beef from the States. Whether or not they're telling the truth, the beef is excellent in most places.

The following dishes are Mexican menu staples:

Caldo Rojo. A spicy red chicken broth filled with rice, chickpeas, carrots, zucchini, chicken, avocado, and cilantro (coriander). This hearty dish is found only in authentic Mexican restaurants.
Camarones. These jumbo shrimp, not caught in Acapulco, are tender if cooked right.
Ceviche. Don't pass up this popular appetizer said to have originated in Acapulco. It consists of raw shellfish or white fish fillets marinated in lime juice and makes a light starter to any meal.
Guacamole. The Mexican version of this avocado dip often includes onions, cilantro, tomatoes, and varying amounts of those hot little devils known as *chiles serranos*. It's a good idea to take a small taste before you dig in.
Huachinango. This locally caught red snapper is served whole or filleted. It is a mild fish and very filling, whether grilled or prepared in a light garlic sauce.
Langosta. This lobster is also fresh though not caught in the bay. It is more expensive and less meaty than its Atlantic relations.
Pozole. This thick hominy soup with nuggets of pork is found only in Mexican establishments.
Tortillas. A staple of the Mexican diet, these thin rounds of corn kernels that have been soaked in lime and then ground to a paste and made into a dough form the basis of enchiladas, tacos, and tostadas. In many restaurants, tortillas are served on the side instead of bread.

Establishments that cater to tourists purify their drinking water and use it to cook vegetables. In smaller restaurants, ask for bottled water with or without bubbles (*con* or *sin gas*); the brand often served is Tehuacán, or just ask for *agua mineral* to receive a bottle of club soda. The usual rules apply at the local restaurants: eat only cooked vegetables, and no matter where you are, it is sensible to peel all fruit. The small stands on the street serve inexpensive, filling food—a plate of tacos usually costs about $1. But before you eat, look around to note the fly count. Contrary to popular belief, most Mexican dishes are spicy but not necessarily *picante* (hot). Chili sauces are served in bowls on the side so you can adjust the spiciness to your taste; the green chili sauce adds a mild tang, but the red is very strong and should be approached with care. Most hotels have breakfast buffets; in restaurants you'll have a choice of sweet rolls and coffee, fruit salad, pancakes, or *huevos rancheros* (fried eggs on a tortilla, with spicy tomato sauce). Manzanilla, an herbal tea, is served. Mexicans eat breakfast at any time in the morning. Lunch, the main meal of the day, is served from 2 to 4 PM. Dinner is late by American standards, and many restaurants don't get crowded until about 9, leaving less time to kill if you are planning to hit the discos later.

Service is usually good but often slow. Most waiters and managers have been in the business for a long time and take pride in what they do. One advantage to slow service is that restaurants don't close until the last customer has left, so it is easy to enjoy a meal at leisure. Tipping 10% to 15% is expected.

Some decent wines are now being produced in Mexico. Imported wines are readily available, too, though they tend to be far more expensive than the domestic varieties. But cocktails are an Acapulco specialty, and some restaurants serve as many different drinks as they have dishes. (For a complete discussion of imbibing in Mexico, *see* Discos in Chapter 9.)

Health food has finally hit. The Villa Vera bar serves fresh-fruit and vegetable drinks, and the restaurant has diet lunch platters; there are also numerous cafés that have fruit shakes and fruit salad platters. In the Tex/Mex and American restaurants, you can often find a big salad bar loaded with fresh vegetables, but, as always, digestive discretion is advised.

The top restaurants in Acapulco can be fun for a splurge and provide very good value. Even at the best places in town, dinner rarely exceeds $35 per person, and the atmosphere and views are fantastic. Ties and jackets are out of place, but so are shorts or jeans. You may have to taxi back to your hotel to change. Gourmets and epicures be warned: Haute cuisine is not to be found. Although the food is fresh and carefully prepared, it does not compare with what is available in Europe or in large North American cities. Ordering something that is not produced locally is asking for trouble. Asparagus, for example, is often canned, artichokes are usually not up to scratch, and many chefs have not mastered the art of preparing a truly subtle sauce. Reservations are advised for all restaurants in the very expensive and expensive categories. Unless stated, all are open daily from 6:30 or 7 PM until the last diner leaves.

Highly recommended restaurants are indicated by a star ★.

Category	**Cost***
Very Expensive	over $45
Expensive	$25–$45
Moderate	$15–$25
Inexpensive	under $15

**per person excluding drinks, service, and sales tax (10%)*

Very Expensive

French **Le Gourmet.** Although its food is wildly inconsistent, this restaurant, in the Acapulco Princess hotel, is thought by many to be one of Acapulco's premier establishments. Many people staying down on the Costera brave the 15-minute taxi ride to partake of a tranquil meal in a plush setting. The French menu has all the classics: vichyssoise, steak au poivre sautéed in cognac, and such Acapulco favorites as lobster and red snapper fillets. The atmosphere is luxurious and genteel, with roomy, comfortable chairs, silent waiters, and air-conditioning. *Acapulco Princess Hotel, tel. 74/84–31–00. Reservations advised. AE, DC, MC, V.*

Gourmet ★ **Coyuca 22.** This is possibly the most expensive restaurant in Acapulco; it is certainly one of the most beautiful. Entering Coyuca is like walking onto a film set. Diners eat on terraces that overlook the bay from the west, on a hilltop in Old Acapulco. The understated decor consists of Doric pillars, sculptures, and large onyx flower stands near the entrance. Diners gaze down on an enormous illuminated obelisk and a small pool. The effect is like eating in a partially restored Greek ruin sans dust. The tiny menu centers on seafood, with lobster the house specialty. Prime ribs are also available. *Avenida Coyuca 22 (a 10-minute taxi ride from the Zócalo), tel. 74/82–34–68 or 83–50–30. Reservations required. AE, DC, MC, V. Closed Apr. 30–Nov. 1.*

Expensive

Continental **Maximilian's.** An exception to the rule that says hotels don't serve top-quality food is this Acapulco Plaza restaurant. A haven for American expatriates who like to dress up and come for a treat, it is one of few beachside restaurants with air-conditioning. Lobster bisque, duck, and seafood cooked with classic ingredients are the specialties, and steak is available, too. *Acapulco Plaza, tel. 74/85–80–50. Reservations advised. AE, DC, MC, V.*

Italian ★ **Casa Nova.** This restaurant in the exclusive Las Brisas area has fantastic sunset views of all Acapulco. It specializes in southern Italian cuisine, and the pastas are homemade. You might try the Fettuccine Scampi, prepared with shrimp, mushrooms, and scallops; the grilled veal chops; or the grilled fresh Norwegian salmon. The piano bar is open until midnight. *Scenic Hwy. 5256, tel. 74/84–68–19 or 84–68–16. Reservations a must on weekends. Dress: casual, but no shorts or T-shirts. AE, DC, MC, V.*

Seafood ★ **Blackbeard's.** A dark, glorified coffee shop with a pirate ship motif, Blackbeard's—owned by the proprietors of Mimi's Chili Saloon—has maps covering the tables in the cozy booths, and the walls are adorned with wooden figureheads. At the entrance there's an unfortunate lion, which the owner feels adds to the atmosphere. Every movie star, from Bing Crosby to Liz Taylor, who ever set foot here has his or her photo posted in the lounge. A luscious salad bar and jumbo portions of shrimp, steak, and lobster keep customers satisfied. A new disco on the premises starts throbbing at 10:30 PM. *Costera Miguel Alemán, tel. 74/84–25–49. Reservations advised. AE, DC, MC, V.*

Fodor's
Hawaii

It's easy to recognize a good place when you see one.

American Express Cardmembers have been doing it for years.

The secret? Instead of just relying on what they see in the window, they look at the door. If there's an American Express Blue Box on it, they know they've found an establishment that cares about high standards.

Whether it's a place to eat, to sleep, to shop, or simply meet, they know they will be warmly welcomed.

So much so, they're rarely taken in by anything else.

Always a good sign.

Moderate

American

★ **Carlos 'n Charlies.** This is without a doubt the most popular restaurant in town; a line forms well before the 6:30 PM opening. Part of the Anderson group (with restaurants in the United States and Spain as well as Mexico), Carlos 'n Charlies cultivates an atmosphere of controlled craziness. Prankster waiters, a jokester menu, and eclectic decor—everything from antique bullfight photos to a tool chest of painted gadgets hanging from the ceiling—add to the chaos. The crowd is mostly young and relaxed, which is what you need to be to put up with the rush-hour traffic noise that filters up to the covered balcony where people dine. The menu straddles the border, with ribs, stuffed shrimp, and oysters among the best offerings. *Costera Miguel Alemán 999, tel. 74/84–12–85 or 84–00–39. No reservations. AE, DC, MC, V.*

D'Joint. Locals as well as tourists love D'Joint—a claustrophobic restaurant with a funky, publike atmosphere and a popular sports bar—so, in season, prepare for a wait. In addition to the usual steaks, salads, and nachos, prime ribs are the house specialty. The four types of roast beef sandwiches are another hit. After your meal, try "sexy coffee"—cappuccino with liqueur. *Costera Miguel Alemán 79, next door to the Hotel Acapulco Malibú, tel. 74/84–19–13. No reservations. AE, DC, MC, V. Closed one week in summer.*

Embarcadero. A nautical motif pervades Embarcadero, which is well-loved by both Acapulco regulars and resident Americans. It is designed to look like a wharf with the bar as the loading office. Wooden bridges lead past a fountain to the thatched eating area, piled high with wooden packing crates and maps. The food is American with a Polynesian touch. You can have deep-fried shrimps with garlic sauce, tempura, chicken, or steak. The "salad barge" is enormous. *Costera Miguel Alemán, west of CiCi Park, tel. 74/84–87–87. Open 6 PM–midnight. No reservations. AE, DC, MC, V. Closed Mon. out of season.*

★ **Hard Rock Café.** A bar, restaurant, and dance hall filled with rock memorabilia, this is one of the most popular spots in Acapulco, and with good reason. The southern-style food—fried chicken, ribs, chili con carne—is very well prepared and the portions are more than ample. The taped rock music begins at noon, and a live group starts playing at 11 PM. There's always a line at the small boutique on the premises where you can buy sports clothes and accessories bearing the Hard Rock label. *Costera Miguel Alemán 37, tel. 74/84–66–80. AE, MC, V.*

Sanborns. Both branches of this all-purpose store have dining rooms. The food is basic coffee-shop fare, with an extensive all-day breakfast menu offering steak, shrimp, and an enormous array of baked goods. Sanborns on the Costera has the best American coffee around and a terrace with a view of the bay. In the mornings, sit under the canopy or on the left side of the patio to avoid the sun. *Costera Miguel Alemán 1226, next to Condesa del Mar hotel, tel. 74/84–44–65, open till 1 AM; Costera Miguel Alemán 209, next to the post office in Old Acapulco, tel. 74/82–61–67, open till 11 PM. No reservations. AE, MC, V.*

Continental

★ **Madeiras.** It vies with its neighbor Miramar for most chichi place in Acapulco, and there are fierce arguments as to which has the best food. Madeiras is very difficult to get into; many people make reservations by letter before their arrival. At the very least, call the minute you get to Acapulco. Children under 8 are not welcome, however. All the tables at Madeiras have a

Dining

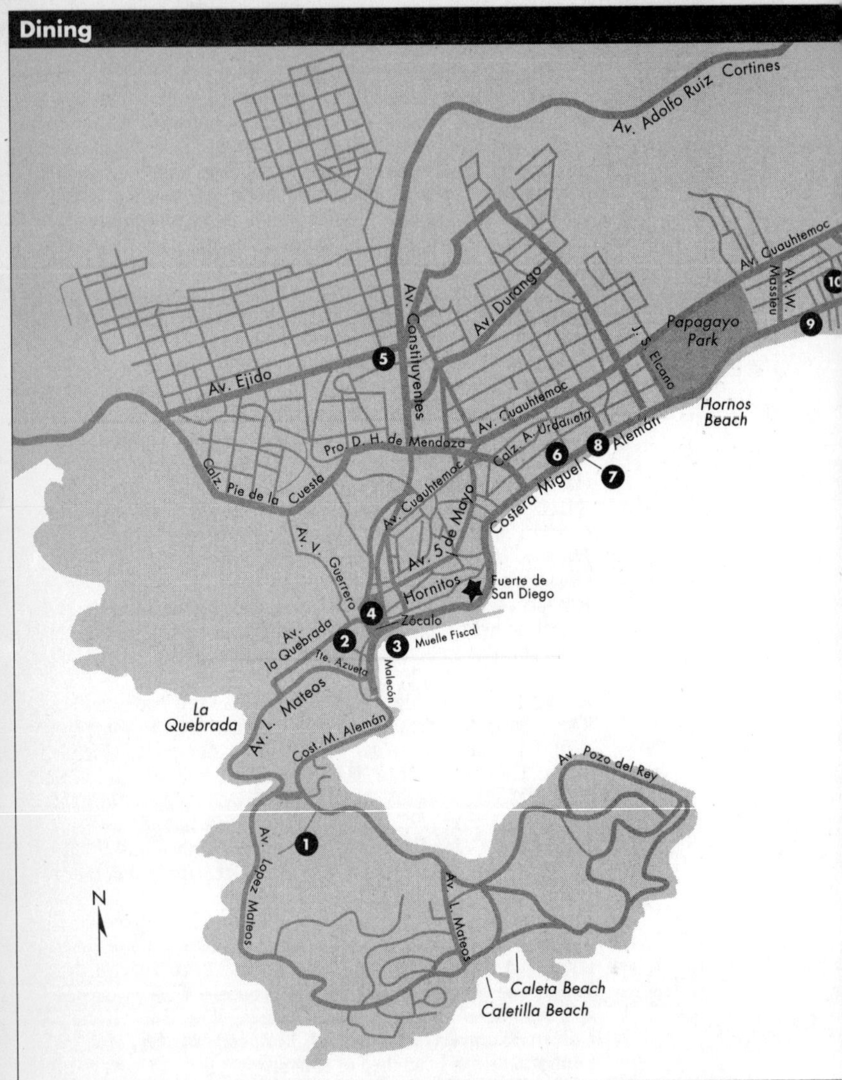

Acapulco Fat Farm, **2**
Barbarroja, **14**
Bella Italia, **8**
Beto's, **18**
Beto's Barra Vieja, **32**
Beto's Safari, **19**
Blackbeard's, **17**
Carlos 'n Charlies, **20**
Casa Nova, **31**
Coyuca 22, **1**
Crazy Lobster, **13**
D'Joint, **23**
El Cabrito, **25**
El Fuerte del Virrey, **21**
Embarcadero, **26**
Hard Rock Café, **24**
Hard Times, **22**
Le Gourmet, **33**
Los Rancheros, **28**
Madeiras, **30**
Maximilian's, **11**
Mimi's Chili Saloon, **16**
Miramar, **29**
Normandie, **6**
100% Natural, **10**
Pancho's, **12**
Paradise, **15**
Sanborns, **3, 27**
Sirocco, **7**
Tlaquepaque, **5**
Woolworth's, **4**
Zorrito's, **9**

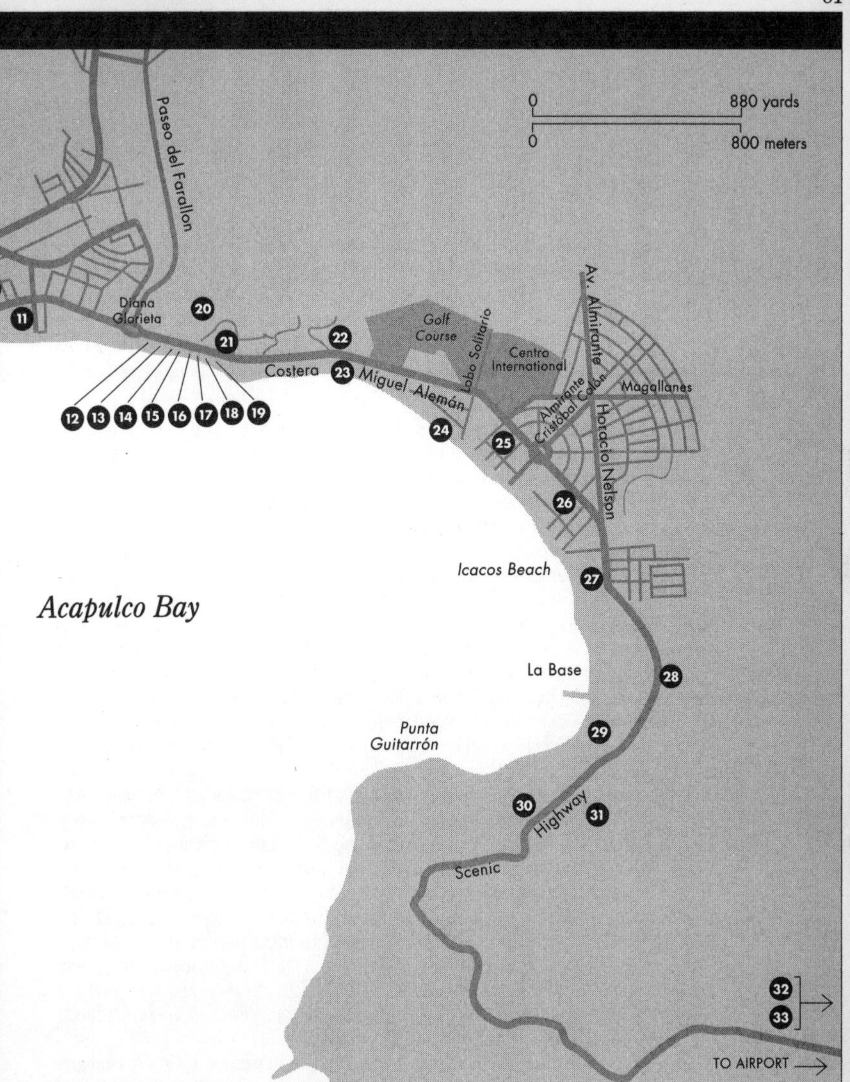
0
880 yards
0
800 meters
Paseo del Farallon
Diana Glorieta
Golf Course
Lobo Solitario
Centro International
Av. Almirante
Almirante Cristóbal Colón
Magallanes
Horacio Nelson
Costera
Miguel Alemán
Acapulco Bay
Icacos Beach
La Base
Punta Guitarrón
Highway
Scenic
TO AIRPORT
11
12
13
14
15
16
17
18
19
20
21
22
23
24
25
26
27
28
29
30
31
32
33

view of glittering Acapulco by night. The furniture is certainly unusual: the bar/reception area has art nouveau-style carved chairs, plump sofas, and startling coffee tables made of glass resting on large wooden animals. All the dishes and silverware were created by silversmiths in the nearby town of Taxco. Dinner is served from a four-course, prix fixe menu and costs about $25 without wine. Entrées include the delicious Spanish dish of red snapper in sea salt, tasty chilled soups, stuffed red snapper, and a choice of steaks and other seafood, as well as the *crepas de huitlacoche* (huitlacoche, or cuitlacoche, is a corn fungus that was a delicacy to the Aztecs). Desserts are competently prepared but have no special flair. There are two seatings, at 6:30 and 9. Unfortunately, diners coming at the later time may find selections limited. *Scenic Highway just past La Vista shopping center, tel. 74/84-73-16. Reservations required. AE, DC, MC, V.*

French **El Fuerte del Virrey.** El Real at El Fuerte del Virrey has already set up house as one of Acapulco's best. The setting is unlike any in Acapulco: an antiques-filled dining room and bar and a military museum—all in a building designed to look like an 18th-century fort. Lavish floral arrangements decorate the entrance to the dining area, and high wooden booths ensure intimate meals. Several private rooms are also available for small groups, as is the lusciously cool wine cellar. Chef Leonardo Anzures produces some of the best food in Acapulco by melding the cuisines of Mexico and France. Octopus stew in cognac and oysters and red snapper baked in pastry are some of the specialties, but beef lovers also will find a healthy selection. *El Fuerte del Virrey, Roca Sola 17, Club Deportivo (behind Carlos 'n Charlies), tel. 74/84-33-21. Reservations not required. AE, DC, MC, V.*

★ **Miramar.** Light wood furniture and a fountain provide the decoration for this understated place, but the real glamour comes from the view of the bay and the flickering lights of Acapulco. Traditional dishes, like pâté and lobster thermidor, are served alongside classics with a new twist: ceviche with a hint of coconut and red snapper papillote. Shrimp mousse and duck are both specialties. Miramar is not as intimate as its neighbor, Madeiras, and many large groups from the Princess book long tables, so the noise level is rather high. *Scenic Highway at La Vista shopping center, tel. 74/84-78-74. Reservations advised. AE, D, MC, V. Closed Sept.-Oct.*

Normandie. Recognized as the only authentic French restaurant in town, this small place is run by the charming Nicole Lepine. The Normandie has pastel blue walls and a little fountain reminiscent of a Parisian tearoom, and the platters of cakes near the door add to this impression. The menu touches all bases, including beef bourguignon and seafood gratinée. *On the Costera near the Super-Super, tel. 74/85-19-16. AE, MC, V. Closed Apr. 1-Dec. 1.*

Italian **Bella Italia.** For more than 20 years, Bella Italia has been run by an Italian family. Although old-time Acapulqueños claim the food is not what it once was, it is still very good, and there's always a crowd partaking of the many pasta dishes served with baskets of crispy hot rolls in a cool palapa-roof hut overlooking the ocean. The clam sauce is superb. *Costera Miguel Alemán, opposite Hotel El Cid (a five-minute taxi ride from The Strip), tel. 74/85-17-57. No reservations or credit cards.*

Mexican

Los Rancheros. With a view of the water in the posh East Bay, here's Mexican food at about half what you'd pay at Madeiras or Miramar. The decor is colorful, folksy Mexican with paper streamers, checked tablecloths, and lopsided mannequins in local dress. Specials include *carne tampiqueña* (fillet of beef broiled with lemon juice), chicken enchiladas, and *queso fundido* (melted cheese served as a side dish to chips). Live music noon to midnight, daily. *Scenic Highway just before Extasis disco (on the left as you head toward the airport), tel. 74/84-19-08. MC, V.*

Pancho's. The only source for Mexican food right on the beach, Pancho's is open for lunch and dinner. During the day you get a free drink with your meal. Though the food is good, the selection is rather generic. *Costera Miguel Alemán, behind the El Pescador restaurant in the Continental Plaza, tel. 74/84-30-08. No reservations. AE, MC, V.*

Mixed Menu

★ **Hard Times.** With an unusually large menu for Acapulco, Hard Times features the usual Tex-Mex dishes as well as plenty of barbecue, fresh fish, and the largest salad bar in town. The dining area is an attractive open terrace, with a partial view of the bay. Although right in the center of The Strip, Hard Times is a tranquil haven—decorated with palms and incandescent lights—in which to enjoy generous portions of American food and, sometimes, jazz. Arrive early; there is often a wait in high season. *Costera Miguel Alemán, across from the Calinda Quality Hotel (look for the red neon lights), tel. 74/84-00-64. Reservations advised during high season. AE, DC, MC, V. Closed Sun. during summer.*

Seafood

Barbarroja. Eating at this outdoor restaurant is very much like sitting on the deck of a ship. A large mast does virtually nothing to block the view of the street, so don't bother coming here if you want privacy. This is a good place for seafood: Lobster tail with filet mignon is the house specialty, but there are also chicken-and-seafood combos and a four-course tourist special for $20. A courtesy half-bottle of wine or after-dinner liqueur comes with the à la carte dinner. Steer clear of the ice-cold, but tasteless, strawberry daiquiris. *Costera Miguel Alemán, next to Paradise, tel. 74/84-59-32. AE, DC, MC, V. Open for dinner only.*

Crazy Lobster. Sharing owners with Beto's, Crazy Lobster also shares appearance: a palapa roof outside but hanging plants and a big tank of tropical fish within. Every Friday, Saturday, and Sunday night, a live trio provides a soft background to the quick and friendly service. Broiled lobster and shrimp are the specialties. *Costera Miguel Alemán, next to Paradise, tel. 74/84-59-74. Reservations not required. AE, MC, V. Open 10 AM to midnight.*

Paradise. This is the leading beach-party restaurant. T-shirted waiters drop leis over your head as you arrive and hand roses to the ladies. The menu (primarily seafood) has the same number of dishes as drinks, a pretty good indicator of what this place is like. Paradise has one of the biggest dance floors in Acapulco and live music day and night. Chaos reigns at lunchtime (from 2 to 5), and the mood picks up again from 8:30 to 10:30. Expect a young crowd. *Costera Miguel Alemán 107, next to Mimi's Chili Saloon, tel. 74/84-59-88. No reservations. AE, DC, MC, V.*

Sirocco. This beachside eatery is numero uno for those who crave Spanish food in Acapulco. The tile floors and heavy wooden furniture give it a Mediterranean feel. Specialties include *pulpo en su tinta* (octopus in its own ink) and 10 varieties of fresh fish. Order paella when you arrive at the beach—it takes a half hour to prepare. *Costera Miguel Alemán, across from Super-Super, tel. 74/85-23-86 and 74/85-94-90. Reservations not required. AE, MC, V. Open for lunch and dinner, 2-10 PM.*

Inexpensive

American **Woolworth's.** The Old Acapulco branch has an air-conditioned coffee shop with a large menu of Mexican and American food. If you get a sudden urge for a BLT or hot fudge sundae, come here. *J.R. Escudero 250, next to Sanborns downtown, tel. 74/82-56-83.*

Health Food ★ **100% Natural.** Six family-operated restaurants specialize in light, healthful food—yogurt shakes, fruit salads, and sandwiches made with whole-wheat bread. The service is quick and the food is a refreshing alternative to tacos, particularly on a hot day. Look for the green signs with white lettering. *Costera Miguel Alemán 204, near the Acapulco Plaza, no phone. Another branch is near the Acapulco Princess Hotel, tel. 74/85-39-82. No credit cards.*

★ **Zorrito's.** The old Zorrito's, a rather dingy but popular café that filled up with partygoers snacking between discos, is no longer, but a new, very clean restaurant of the same name is now attracting tourists. The menu features a host of steak and beef dishes, and the special, *filete tampiqueña*, comes with tacos, enchiladas, guacamole, and frijoles. *Costera Miguel Alemán and Anton de Alaminos, next to Banamex, tel. 74/85-37-35. No reservations. AE, MC, V.*

Mexican **El Cabrito.** This is another local favorite for true Mexican cuisine and ambience. The name of the restaurant—"the goat"—is also its specialty. In addition you can choose among mole; forged cheese; jerky with egg, fish, and seafood; and other Mexican dishes. *Costera Miguel Alemán, between Mariscos Pipo and Ninas, tel. 74/84-77-11. No reservations. MC, V.*

★ **Mimi's Chili Saloon.** Right next door to Paradise is this two-level wooden restaurant decorated with everything from Marilyn Monroe posters to cages of tropical birds and a collection of ridiculous signs. It's frequented by those under (and frequently over) 30 who gorge on Tex-Mex, onion rings, and excellent burgers and wash them down with peach and mango daiquiris. Or the waiters will bring you anything on the menu next door at Blackbeard's. Be prepared for a wait in the evenings. *Costera Miguel Alemán, tel. 74/84-25-49, at Blackbeard's. No reservations. AE, MC, V. Closed Mon. and Labor Day (May 1).*

★ **Tlaquepaque.** As hard to find as it is to pronounce, this is one of the best restaurants in Acapulco. It's well worth the 15-minute cab ride into the northwestern residential section of Acapulco (tell your driver it is around the corner from where the Oficina de Tránsito used to be). Owner/chef José Arreola was a chef at the Pierre Marqués for 15 years and he takes his job very seriously. Don't insult him by asking if the water is purified or if the vegetables are safe. The menu is 100% Mexican, excellent and authentic. If your party numbers four or more, Señor Arreola likes nothing better than to select a family-style meal, which can include quail liver tostadas, deep fried tortillas, and *chiles rellenos*. The alfresco dining area sits on a stone terrace bordered by pink flowering bushes and an abandoned well. The outside tables have a perfect view of the kitchen filled with locally made pots. Thursday is *pozole* day, when a thick soup of hominy and pork is served. *Calle Uno, Lote 7, Colonia Vista Alegre, tel. 74/85-70-55. Reservations advised Thurs. only (pozole day). Closed Mon. Cash only.*

Mixed Menu **Acapulco Fat Farm.** High-school and college students at the Acapulco Children's Home run this cozy place in the center of town. The specialties include ice cream made with all natural ingredients, U.S.-style cakes and pies, sandwiches, hamburgers, and good Mexican food as well. The background music is classical, which is unusual for Acapulco, and there's an exhibition of paintings and masks, as well as a book exchange. *Juárez 10, tel. 74/83-53-39. No reservations. No credit cards.*

Seafood ★ **Beto's.** By day, you can eat right on the beach and enjoy live music; by night, this palapa-roofed restaurant is transformed into a dim and romantic dining area lighted by candles and paper lanterns. Whole red snapper, lobster, and ceviche are recommended. There is a second branch next door and a third—where the specialty is *pescado a la talla* (fish spread with chili and other spices and then grilled over hot coals)—at Barra Vieja beach. *Beto's, Costera Miguel Alemán, tel. 74/84-04-73. Beto's Safari, Costera Miguel Alemán, next to Beto's, tel. 84-47-62. Beto's Barra Vieja, Barra Vieja beach, no phone. Reservations unnecessary at all three branches. AE, MC, V.*

8 Lodging

Introduction

Accommodations in Acapulco run the gamut from sprawling, big-name complexes with nonstop amenities to small, family-run inns where hot water is a luxury. Wherever you stay, prices are reasonable compared with those in the United States, and service is generally good, since Acapulqueños have been catering to tourists for 40 years. Mexican hotels are rated by the Mexican government on the star system, from 1- to 5-star. (Fodor's recommended accommodations are noted with one star, which is *not* based on the government's star system.) Properties with three or more stars, for example, must fulfill certain requirements, such as a TV in every room and a central location. The criteria are a little confusing and sometimes irrelevant. A better gauge is price. Accommodations above $80 (double) are air-conditioned (but you can find air-conditioned hotels for less) and include a mini-bar, TV, and a view of the bay. There is usually a range of in-house restaurants and bars, as well as a pool. Exceptions exist, such as Las Brisas, which, in the name of peace and quiet, has banned TVs from all rooms. So if such extras are important to you, be sure to ask ahead. If you can't afford air-conditioning, don't panic. Even the cheapest hotels have cooling ceiling fans. Other points to keep in mind when making reservations:

- Ask for a room on one of the upper floors to avoid noise from the pool and bar areas, and on the bayside, for the view and to avoid street noise.
- Request a bath if necessary; many hotels have just showers in the majority of rooms.
- Low-season rates can mean a saving of 15%–40%.
- December 24–January 4 is the height of high season, closely followed by Semana Santa (the week before Easter). Book early to avoid disappointment.

Toll-free numbers are listed for hotels that use them. If you get stuck without a room, the Office of Tourism at Costera Miguel Alemán 187 (tel. 74/85–13–04) can make inquiries. Unless stated, all hotels are open 365 days a year.

Because Acapulco is a relatively new resort, it lacks the converted monasteries and old mansions found in Mexico City. But the Costera is chockablock with new luxury high rises and local franchises of such major U.S. hotel chains as Hyatt and Sheraton. Since these hotels tend to be characterless, your choice will depend on location and what facilities are available. Villa Vera, Acapulco Plaza, Las Brisas, and both Hyatts have tennis courts as well as swimming pools. The Princess and Pierre Marqués share two 18-hole golf courses, and the Malibú is across from the Club de Tennis and Golf. All major hotels can make water-sports arrangements.

In Acapulco geography is price, so where you stay determines what you pay. The most exclusive area is the Acapulco Diamante, home to some of the most expensive hotels in Mexico. Travelers come here for a relaxing, self-contained holiday; the Acapulco Diamante hotels are so lush and well equipped that most guests don't budge from the minute they arrive. The minuses: Revolcadero Beach is too rough for swimming (though great for surfing), and the East Bay is a 15-minute (expensive) taxi ride from the heart of Acapulco. There is also very little to do in this area except dine at three of Acapulco's better restaurants (Madeiras, Casa Nova, and Miramar), and dance at the glamorous Extravaganzza and Fantasy discos.

Highly recommended hotels are indicated by a star ★.

Category	Cost*
Very Expensive	$185–$285
Expensive	$100–$185
Moderate	$55–$100
Inexpensive	under $55

**All prices are for a standard double room, excluding 10% sales (called IVA) tax.*

Acapulco Diamante

Very Expensive ★ **Acapulco Princess.** This is the first hotel you come to from the airport. Three pyramid-shaped buildings, the Princess has the largest capacity of any hotel in Acapulco. The hotel's fact sheet makes fascinating reading: 50 chocolate cakes are consumed daily and 2,500 staff meals are served. The Princess is one of those mega-hotels always holding at least three conventions with an ever-present horde in the lobby checking in and greeting their fellow dentists or club members. But more rooms equals more facilities. The Princess has eight restaurants, five bars, a disco, tennis, golf, and great shopping in a cool arcade. The pool near the reception desk is sensational—fantastic tropical ponds with little waterfalls and a slatted bridge leading into a swimming/sunning area. It forms a jungle backdrop to the lobby, which is always fresh and cool from the ocean breezes. Rooms are light and airy, with cane furniture and crisp yellow and green rugs and curtains. Guests can also use the facilities of the hotel's smaller sibling, the Pierre Marqués; a free shuttle bus provides transport. Accommodations include breakfast and dinner (mandatory in high season). *Box 1351 Playa Revolcadero, tel. 74/84–31–00 or 800/223–1818. 1,019 balconied rooms, with bath. Facilities: two 18-hole golf courses, 11 tennis courts (2 indoor), 4 freshwater pools, 1 saltwater pool, 8 restaurants, 5 bars, disco, banquet rooms. AE, DC, MC, V.*

Camino Real Acapulco Diamante. Acapulco's newest hotel was still under construction as we went to press but should be open by the time you read this. It's set on a secluded beach surrounded by tropical gardens and will have "modern Mexican" decor. *Playa Pichilingue, tel. (Westin in U.S.) 800/228–3000. 160 rooms with ocean view, 2 terraced pools, tennis courts, fitness center, shopping arcade, restaurants, bars. CC. TK.*

★ **Las Brisas.** This Westin hotel claims the dubious distinction of "most expensive hotel in Mexico"; some say it's overpriced, but at least you get a lot for your money. Privacy is a major advantage (especially in rooms with a private pool) in this spread-out yet self-contained luxury complex; most of the facilities are open only to guests, though outsiders with a reservation may dine at the El Mexicano restaurant any day but Wednesday or Saturday, and La Concha Beach Club is open to nonguests on Wednesday for shrimp and fillet night. There are almost three employees per guest during the winter season. Transportation is by white and pink jeep. You can rent one for $60 to $70 a day, including tax, gas, and insurance; or, if you don't mind a wait, the staff will do the driving. And transport is necessary—it is a good 15-minute walk to the beach restaurant, and all the facilities are far from the rooms. Everything at Las Brisas is splashed with pink, from the bedspreads and staff uniforms to the stripes in the middle of the road. Attention to detail is Las Brisas's claim to fame: Rooms are stocked with cigarettes, liquor, and snacks. Flowers are scattered daily on the private pools and beds; a complimentary bowl of fresh fruit arrives each afternoon. Hotel registration takes place in a comfortable lounge to avoid lines, and Las Brisas arranges for guests to receive only crisp new bills. There is a small "disco" (actually a video bar), and a nouvelle Mexican restaurant (the food quality is inconsistent) overlooks the tennis courts. Lunch is taken at the often-deserted La Concha, an exclusive beach club that has two saltwater pools. There is also an art gallery and a few other stores. On Thursday a jeep caravan winds through plantations to a lagoon where pink and white canoes carry guests to jungle picnic grounds for lunch, mariachis, and canoe and burro races. Friday night is Mexican Fiesta, with a rooftop buffet, razorless cockfights, and fireworks. A little Mexican village is set up, and locals selling crafts are bused in so that guests will have a chance to bargain. This, more than anything, reveals how isolated Las Brisas is, since bargaining in Mexico starts practically the moment you step off the plane. Tipping is not allowed, but a service charge of $20 a day is added to the bill. The rate includes Continental breakfast. *Box 281, Carretera Escénica 5255, tel. 74/84–15–80 or 800/228–3000, fax 74/84–22–69. 309 rooms with bath. Facilities: beach club, fitness machines, 2 saltwater pools, 1 freshwater pool, Jacuzzi and sauna, 4 lighted tennis courts, water sports, 4 restaurants, 1 bar, 2 conference rooms. AE, DC, MC, V.*

★ **Pierre Marqués.** This hotel is doubly blessed: It is closer to the beach than any of the other East Bay hotels, and guests have access to all the Princess's facilities without the crowds. In addition, it has three pools and five tennis courts illuminated for nighttime play. Rooms are furnished identically to those at the Princess, but duplex villas and bungalows with private patios are available. Many people stay here to relax, then hit the Princess's restaurants and discos at night—the shuttle bus runs about every ten minutes. Accommodations include mandatory breakfast and dinner in high season. *Box 474, Playa Revolcadero, tel. 74/84–20–00 or 800/223–1818. 344 rooms with bath. Facilities: two 18-hole golf courses, 5 tennis courts, 3 pools, valet service, bar, 3 restaurants, shops. Open only during the winter season. AE, DC, MC, V.*

Expensive

Sheraton Acapulco. Perfect for those who want to enjoy the sun and the sand but don't have to be in the center of everything, this Sheraton is isolated from all the hubbub of the Costera and is rather small in comparison with the chain's other properties in Mexico. The rooms and suites are distributed among 17 villas that are set on a hillside on secluded Guitarrón beach 6 miles (10 km) east of Acapulco proper. Rooms for the handicapped and nonsmokers are available, and all units have private balconies and a sweeping view of the entire bay. *Costera Guitarrón 110, tel. 74/84–37–37 or 800/325–3535. 226 rooms and 8 suites with bath. Facilities: 2 pools, 2 restaurants, 2 bars, water sports. AE, DC, MC, V.*

Lodging

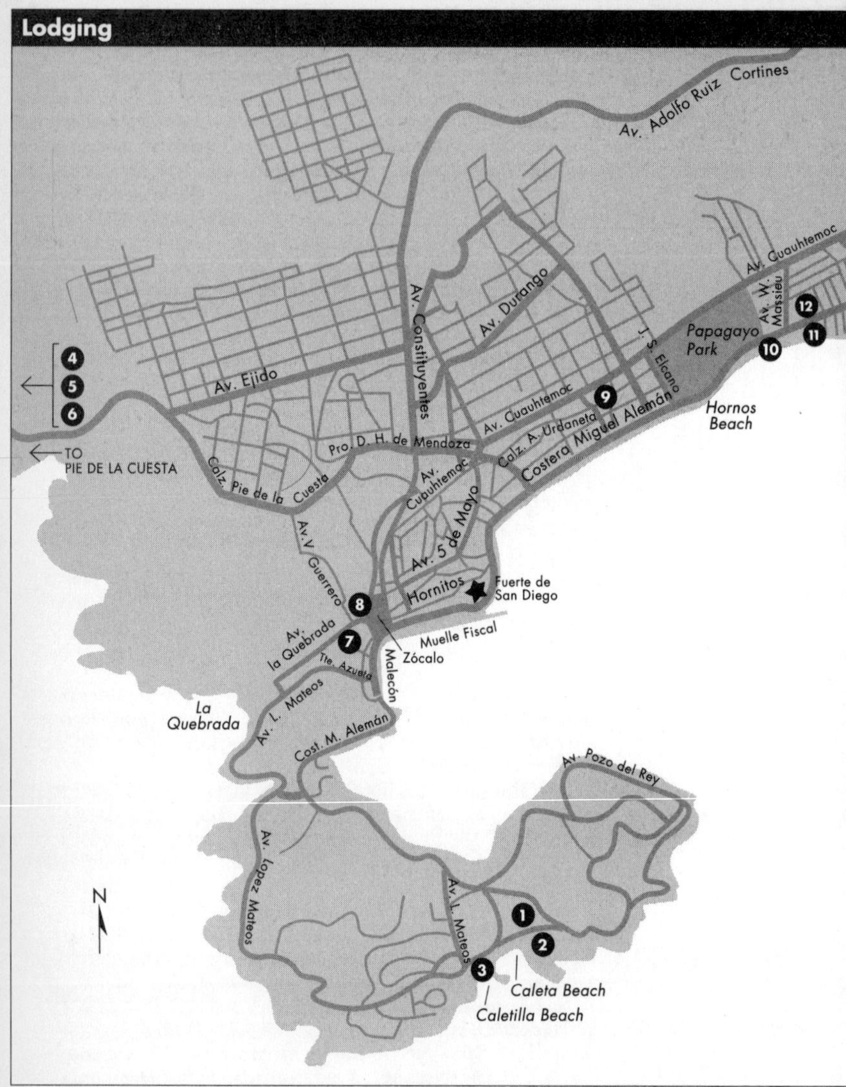

Av. Adolfo Ruiz Cortines
Av. Durango
Av. Constituyentes
Av. Ejido
Av. Cuauhtemoc
Av. W. Massieu
Papagayo Park
J. S. Elcano
Calz. A. Urdaneta
Costera Miguel Alemán
Hornos Beach
Pro. D. H. de Mendoza
TO PIE DE LA CUESTA
Calz. Pie de la Cuesta
Av. Cuauhtemoc
Av. 5 de Mayo
Av. V. Guerrero
Hornitos
Fuerte de San Diego
Muelle Fiscal
Zócalo
Malecón
Av. la Quebrada
Tte. Azueta
Av. L. Mateos
La Quebrada
Cost. M. Alemán
Av. Pozo del Rey
Av. Lopez Mateos
Av. L. Mateos
N
Caleta Beach
Caletilla Beach

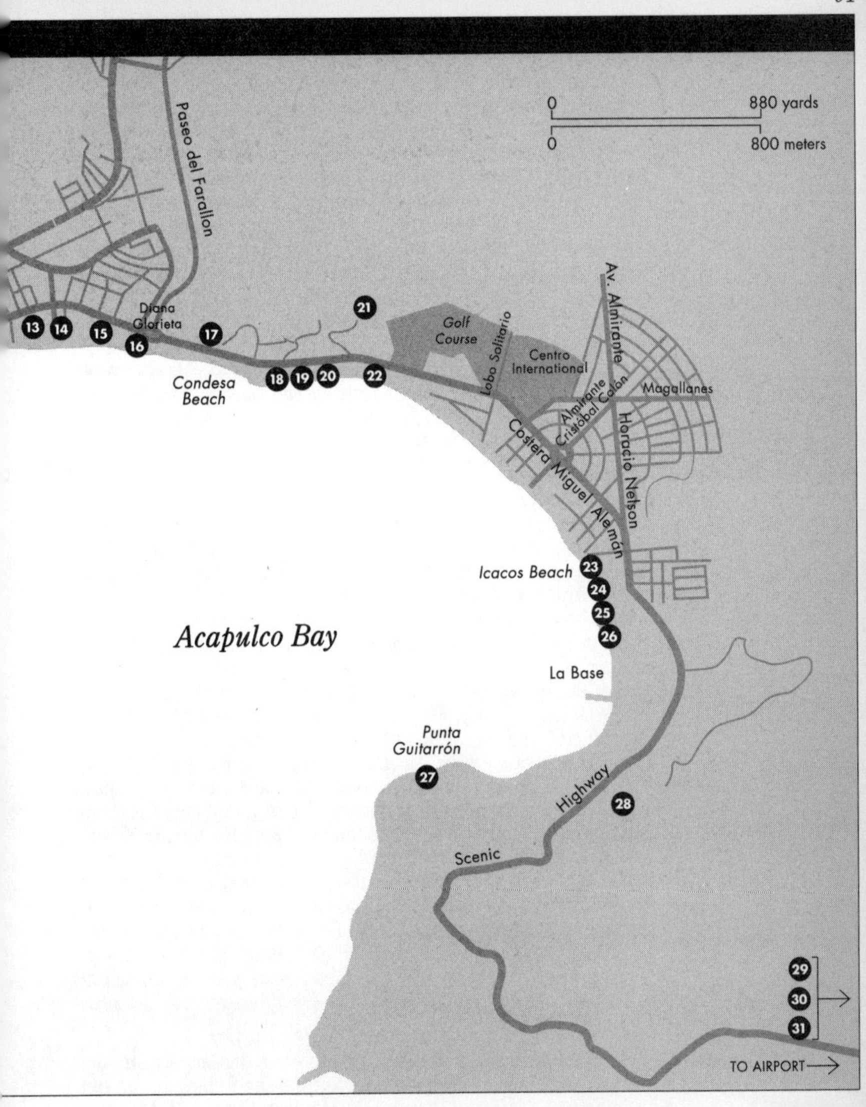
0
880 yards
0
800 meters
Paseo del Farallon
Diana
Glorieta
Condesa
Beach
Golf
Course
Lobo Solitario
Centro
International
Av. Almirante
Almirante
Cristóbal Colón
Magallanes
Horacio Nelson
Costera Miguel Alemán
Icacos Beach
Acapulco Bay
La Base
Punta
Guitarrón
Highway
Scenic
TO AIRPORT
13
14
15
16
17
18
19
20
21
22
23
24
25
26
27
28
29
30
31

The Strip

"Costera" is what locals call the Costera Miguel Alemán, the wide shoreline highway that leads from the bottom of the Scenic Highway, around the bay, then past Old Acapulco. The Paraíso Radisson Acapulco Hotel anchors the end of The Strip. This area is where you'll find discos, American-style restaurants, airline offices, and the majority of the large hotels. It is also home base for Americans—lounging on the beaches, shopping in the boutiques, and generally getting into the vacation spirit. Acapulco's best beaches are here, too. The waves are gentle and water sports are plentiful. Hotels on the Costera take full advantage of their location. All have freshwater pools and sun decks, and most have restaurants/bars overlooking the beach, if not on the sand itself. Hotels across the street are almost always cheaper than those on the beach. And because there are no private beaches in Acapulco, all you have to do to reach the water is cross the road.

Very Expensive ★

Villa Vera. A five-minute drive north of the Costera leads to one of Acapulco's most exclusive hotels. Guests are primarily affluent American business travelers, actors, and politicians. This luxury estate, officially the Villa Vera Hotel and Racquet Club, is unequaled in the variety of its accommodations. Some of the villas, which were once private homes, have their own pools. Casa Lisa, the swankiest, costs $1,300 a day. Standard rooms, in fashionable pastels and white, are not especially large. No matter. No one spends much time in the rooms. The main pool, with its swim-up bar, is the hotel's hub. During the day, guests lounge, lunch, snack, and swim here (a diet menu is available for calorie-conscious guests). By night, they dine at the terraced restaurant, with its stunning view of the bay. Though Villa Vera's guests rarely leave the premises, taxis and tours are available. There's a new exercise facility, and three championship tennis courts host the annual competition for the Miguel Alemán and Teddy Stauffer cups. For those guests who don't have their own cars, transportation is by hotel jeep. Book well in advance; guests have been known to make reservations for the following year as they leave. *Box 560, Lomas del Mar 35, tel. 74/84-03-33 or 800/223-6510. 80 rooms with bath. Facilities: pool with swim-up bar, 3 lighted tennis courts, sauna and massage, water sports, beauty salon, restaurant, banquet room. AE, DC, MC, V.*

Expensive

Acapulco Plaza. This Holiday Inn resort is the largest and one of the newest hotels on the Costera. Like the Princess, the Plaza has more facilities than many Mexican towns: 12 bars and restaurants, four tennis courts, Jacuzzis, steam baths, and two pools. The Plaza Bahía next to the hotel is the largest shopping mall in town. As if that weren't enough, another shopping center, the Galería Acapulco Plaza, is right in front of the hotel. Maximilian's (*see* Chapter 7) serves quality Continental fare. The lobby bar is most extraordinary—a wooden hut, suspended by a cable from the roof, reached by a gangplank from the second floor of the lobby. About 35 people can fit inside the bar, which overlooks a garden full of flamingos and other exotic birds. Guest rooms tell the same old story: pastels and blond wood replacing passé dark greens and browns. People rave about the rooms and facilities, but we have heard several reports of inferior service and unfriendly treatment at the front desk. *Costera Miguel Alemán 123, tel. 74/85-80-50 or 800/*

HOLIDAY. 1,008 rooms with bath. Booked solid Dec. 20–Jan. 3. Facilities: health club, sauna, freshwater pools, 4 lighted tennis courts, water sports, 5 restaurants, 7 bars, conference rooms. AE, DC, MC, V.

Calinda. Part of the Choice Hotels chain, this hotel is big, popular, and well-established, with a largely American following. Rooms are spacious and bright and have recently been spruced up with brown rugs and the ubiquitous pink-and-blue-pastel bedspreads and curtains. In case it isn't hot enough, the Calinda is one of the few hotels in Acapulco that has a sauna. At happy hour everyone gathers in the small lobby to enjoy the live music. There's a very popular Mexican Fiesta on Wednesday. *Costera Miguel Alemán 1260, tel. 74/84–04–10 or 800/228–5151. 356 rooms with bath. Facilities: 2 pools, water sports, 3 restaurants, bar, lounge, nightclub open during the high season, conference rooms. AE, DC, MC, V.*

Continental Plaza Acapulco. No one spends time in the air-conditioned lobby here simply because the pool area is so inviting. Lush tropical foliage surrounds the town's largest pool, a little wooden bridge leads to Fantasy Island, and the beach is just steps away from the sun deck. A cafeteria overlooks the whole scene, as do bayside accommodations. All rooms in this 14-story property are furnished in "generic Acapulco"—cane headboards and adequate writing desks. The Regency Club (10th floor) is a private level of suites, almost like a little hotel of its own. Complimentary breakfast and cocktails are served, and no children are allowed. *Box 214, Costera Miguel Alemán, tel. 74/84–09–09; 800/228–9000 (individuals); 800/492–8639 (groups). 435 rooms with bath. Facilities: gym, pool, sauna and steam room, water sports, golf, access to the tennis courts at the Hyatt Regency, 3 restaurants, night club, 2 bars, conference rooms. AE, DC, MC, V.*

El Presidente. Because the El Presidente, with its great pool area and large rooms, has been around for so long, it has practically become an Acapulco landmark. It has had its ups and downs, but it's been taken over by Colony Resorts and Hotels and is once again looking good. Rooms in the west tower have been redecorated in peach and white, with pinkish-gray carpeting. The somewhat less expensive ones in the east tower have tile floors, "antiqued" furniture, and wrought-iron chairs. The spacious marble-floored lobby catches a delightful breeze and is one of the coolest places in Acapulco. *Costera Miguel Alemán 89, tel. 74/84–17–00 or 800/777–1700. 384 rooms and 18 suites with bath. Facilities: pool, gym, 3 restaurants, 2 bars.*

★ **Fiesta Americana Condesa Acapulco.** Right in the thick of the main shopping/restaurant district, the Condesa, as everyone calls it, is ever popular with tour operators. The rooms are furnished with wall-to-wall pastel plushness. This is the best hotel on the Costera. *Costera Miguel Alemán 1220, tel. 74/84–26–03 or 800/FIESTA–1. 500 rooms with bath. Facilities: 2 pools, water sports, 4 restaurants, bar, conference rooms. AE, DC, MC, V.*

Hyatt Regency Acapulco. Another mega-hotel that you never have to leave, this property is popular with business travelers and conventioneers. (Ex-President López Portillo used to stay in—what else?—the Presidential Suite.) All the rooms were recently redecorated in soft pastels. Four tennis courts, four restaurants (including a beachside seafood place and a Mexican dining room), four bars, and a lavish shopping area provide the action. The Hyatt is a little out of the way, a plus for those who seek quiet. Rooms on the west side of the hotel are preferable for those who want to avoid the noise of the maneuvers at the neighboring naval base. *Costera Miguel Alemán 1, tel. 74/84–28–88 or 800/223–1234. 690 rooms with bath. Facilities: 4 tennis courts, pool, sauna and massage, shops, 4 restaurants, 3 bars, 6 conference rooms, parking. AE, DC, MC, V.*

★ **Paraíso Radisson.** The last of the big Strip hotels is a favorite of tour groups, so the lobby is forever busy. The rooms look brighter and roomier since the management replaced the heavy Spanish-style furniture with light woods and pastels. Guests lounge by the pool or at the beachside restaurant by day. The rooftop Gaviotas restaurant provides a sensational view of the bay at night. The pool area is rather small and the beach can get crowded, but the restaurants are exceptionally good and the staff couldn't be nicer. Book early—the hotel is often full in high season with tour groups. *Costera Miguel Alemán 163, tel. 74/85–55–96 or 800/228–9822. 422 rooms with bath. Facilities: pool, sauna, 2 restaurants, coffee shop, bar, water sports, shops, 5 conference rooms. AE, DC, MC, V.*

★ **Ritz.** From its brightly painted exterior, it's clear that the Ritz is serious about vacations. The lobby also is seriously colorful. Parties are a hotel specialty; outdoor fiestas are held weekly, and every night is Italian night in the lobby restaurant. The pink and rattan rooms add to the 1950s beach-party flavor. *Box 259, Costera Miguel Alemán and Magallanes, tel. 74/85–75–44 or 800/527–5919. 252 rooms with bath. Facilities: pool, wading pool, sauna, water sports, beach clubs, 3 restaurants, 3 bars (including a beach bar), disco, conference rooms. AE, DC, V.*

Moderate

Acapulco Days Inn. Returning visitors will remember this as the former Romano's Le Club, a comfortable, old-fashioned kind of hotel, located at the east end of the Costera, close to but not quite in the center of things. It's just a block from the beach and has a pool and sundeck, restaurants, and bars. *Costera Miguel Alemán 2310, tel. 74/84–53–32 or 404/728–4315. 334 rooms with bath. Facilities: pool, 3 restaurants, 3 bars. AE, DC, MC, V.*

Acapulco Malibú. This place consists of a five- and a six-story building of time-shared apartments that are rented out when vacant. It is very popular with families who appreciate the children's pool and shaded garden. The rooms are small and, although recently renovated, not especially glamorous. Wooden shutters help the air-conditioning keep the rooms cool. There is now TV, and water sports and other activities can be arranged. *Costera Miguel Alemán 20, tel. 74/84–10–70, fax 74/84–09–94. 80 rooms, showers only. Facilities: pool, restaurant. AE, DC, MC, V.*

Copacabana. Here's a good buy if you yearn for a modern hotel in the center of things. The staff is efficient and helpful, the ambience relaxed and festive. The lobby and pool (with a swim-up bar) are always crowded with people enjoying themselves. The psychedelic pseudo-Mexican lemon-and-lime hues pervade the halls and bedrooms. *Tabichines 2, tel. 74/84–32–60 or 800/221–6509. 422 rooms, showers only. Facilities: pool, 2 restaurants, 2 bars, shops, conference rooms. AE, DC, MC, V.*

Gran Motel Acapulco. This is a find for its reasonable price and central location. Bare walls and floors and blond-wood furniture give the newly decorated rooms a monastic appeal. The small pool has a bar, but there is no restaurant. Ask to stay in the old section, where the rooms are larger and quieter and have a beach view. *Costera Miguel Alemán 127, tel. 74/85-59-92. 88 rooms with bath. Facilities: pool, 3 lighted tennis courts, bar, parking. MC, V.*

Hotel Acapulco Tortuga. A helpful staff and prime location make the "Turtle Hotel" an appealing choice. It is also one of the few non-beach hotels to have a garden (handkerchief-size) and a pool where most of the guests hang out. At night, the activity shifts to the lobby bar, with the crowd often spilling out onto the street. The downside of this merriment is the noise factor: The lower rooms open onto balconies above the lobby, while the rooms facing east enjoy regular broadcasts from the neighboring building's generator. Avoid the lower rooms on the west side of the building, which have a charming view of a brick wall. The best bet is a room facing west on an upper floor. All rooms have blue-green pile rugs and small tables. Breakfast is served in the lobby café; lunch and dinner can be taken in the more formal restaurant. *Costera Miguel Alemán 132, tel. 74/84-88-89 or 800/832-7491. 252 rooms with bath. Facilities: pool, swim-up bar, lobby bar, 2 restaurants, snack bar, conference rooms. AE, DC, MC, V.*

La Palapa. All the rooms at this hotel are roomy suites, but the light and dark beige that seems to cover everything (there's even a piece of framed tweed decorating the walls) is dreary. Round tables and a bar (you supply the booze) do provide a homey feeling, and all rooms face the ocean. The beachside pool has a swim-up bar and the new health club has a weight room, sauna, massage, exercise classes, and a juice bar. The clientele includes Mexicans, Canadians, and Americans, all here for long stays. *Fragata Yucatán 210, tel. 74/84-53-63. 333 rooms with bath. Facilities: pool, 3 restaurants, 2 bars, water sports, coffee shop, conference rooms. AE, DC, MC, V.*

★ **Maralisa Hotel and Beach Club.** The Villa Vera's sister hotel sits on the beach side of the Costera. The sun deck surrounding two small pools—palm trees and ceramic tiles—is unusual and picturesque. The rooms are light, decorated in whites and pastels. This is a small, friendly place; all rooms have TVs and balconies, and the price is right, especially since guests have access to all Villa Vera's facilities. *Box 721, Enrique el Esclavo, tel. 74/85-66-77 or 800/448-8355. 90 rooms with bath. Facilities: 2 pools, private beach club, water sports, restaurant, bar. AE, DC, MC, V.*

Inexpensive

Autotel Ritz. This former relative of the Ritz is a good buy for its location. Thus it attracts bargain-hunters and senior citizens. The uncarpeted rooms are simply decorated, but the furniture is chipped and smudged with paint. Facilities include a restaurant, a decent-size pool with a bar, and room service until 9 PM. Rooms not on the Costera are quite quiet. The Autotel Ritz is recommended for those who want a fairly central location without paying top dollar. A useful note for nonguests: The long-distance surcharge is half what it is at many other hotels. *Avenue Wilfrido Massieu, Box 257, tel. 74/85-82-84 or 800/448-8355. 102 rooms with bath. Facilities: pool, restaurant, bar. AE, DC, MC, V.*

Old Acapulco

Moving off The Strip and west along the Costera leads you to downtown Acapulco, where the fishing and tour boats depart, and the locals go about their business. The central post office,

Woolworth's, and the Mercado Municipal are here, along with countless restaurants where a complete meal can cost as little as $5. The beaches here are popular with Mexican vacationers, and the dozens of little hotels attract Canadian and European bargain-hunters.

Moderate

★ **Boca Chica.** This small hotel is in a secluded area on a small peninsula, and its terraced rooms overlook the bay and Roqueta Island. It's a low-key place that's a favorite of Mexico City residents in the know. There's a private beach club with a natural saltwater pool for guests, and a seafood, sushi, and oyster bar. Accommodations include mandatory breakfast and dinner in high season. *Caletilla Beach, tel. 74/83-66-01 or 800/346-3942. 40 rooms. Facilities: 2 pools. AE, DC, MC, V.*

Caleta. Seasoned visitors to Acapulco will recognize the familiar white exterior and navy-blue awnings of the Caleta, which has been around since the early '50s. One of Acapulco's first luxury hotels, it has had something of a roller-coaster existence during the last 10 years, but it seems to be making a comeback as an all-inclusive resort. Accommodations cost less than average ($116 a night for two), yet include all meals (buffet style) and domestic drinks. Half the rooms have been redecorated and now sport new rugs, drapes, and bedspreads, marble baths, and TVs with satellite reception. The hotel stands on a cliff, with Caleta beach and Roqueta Island on one side and a small, almost private cove on the other. *Cerro San Martín 325, tel. 74/83-99-40. 261 rooms with bath. Facilities: 2 pools (one salt-water), 2 restaurants, bar, disco. AE, DC, MC, V.*

Hotel Misión. Two minutes from the Zócalo, this attractive budget hotel is the only colonial hotel in Acapulco. The English-speaking family that runs the Misión lives in a traditional house built in the 19th century. A newer structure housing the guest rooms was added in the 1950s. It surrounds a greenery-rich courtyard with an outdoor dining area. The rooms are small and by no means fancy, with bare cement floors and painted brick walls. But every room has a shower, and sometimes there is even hot water. The Misión appears in several European guidebooks, so expect a Continental clientele. The best rooms are on the second and third floors; the top-floor room is large but hot in the daytime. *Calle Felipe Valle 12, tel. 74/82-36-43. 27 rooms, showers only. No credit cards.*

★ **Playa Hermosa.** Right behind the El Cid Hotel and steps away from Playa Hornos and the Normandie restaurant is this tiny hotel. Owner Edward Mackissack's guests return every year, so in high season rooms are hard to come by. Staying here is a good way to make friends. The mostly above-40 guests meet on the patio/dining room for drinks every night, although every spring brings a contingent of students from the University of Texas. Built in 1936, Playa Hermosa was originally Ed Mackissack's private home, and it still feels like it. Each room is unique, with a Japanese print in one, a low coffee table in the next. Even the hallways are decorated with prints and furnished with chairs. There are shelves of English books, a garden, and a pool. With its Old Acapulco ambience, this is one of the more charming hotels around. All rooms have hot water, breakfast is included, and lunch can be provided if ordered the day before. *Vasco Núñez de Balboa, tel. 74/85-14-91. 20 rooms, showers only. Facilities: pool, restaurant, bar. No credit cards.*

Plaza las Glorias El Mirador. The old El Mirador has been taken over by the Plaza las Glorias chain, which is part of the Sidek conglomerate responsible for marina and golf developments all over Mexico. Very Mexican in style—white with red tiles—the Plaza las Glorias is set high on a hill with a spectacular view of Acapulco and of the cliff divers performing at La Quebrada. *Quebrada 74, tel. 74/83-11-55. 143 rooms with bath. Facilities: 3 pools, 2 restaurants (including La Perla restaurant-nightclub). AE, DC, MC, V.*

Inexpensive **Belmar.** With its white exterior and green awnings, this stately resort hotel—typical of the 1950s—looks like a ship landlocked in the middle of a huge garden. It's situated on a hill a few blocks from Caleta beach and is a favorite with budget travelers. The rooms are spacious, simple, clean, and comfortable, with large terraces. The walls are white, but almost everything else is some shade of green. This is one of the few Acapulco hotels with a rooftop restaurant; it has a great view of the bay. *Av. de los Cumbres and Gran Vía Tropical, tel. 74/82-15-26. 70 rooms with bath (50 with air-conditioning, 20 with fans). Facilities: pool, wading pool, miniature golf, bar. AE, MC, V.*

Condos and Apartment Rentals

Numerous real estate agents, rental agents, and time-share companies have offices in Acapulco. Your travel agent can provide details, and the following addresses can be helpful. Prices for a three-bedroom apartment range from $150 to $250 a day and often include a pool and view of the bay. Beware of pushy salespeople. An invitation to a free breakfast is a common ploy, and when you arrive you will be set upon by avid real estate agents who will suggest that you put the first installment on your credit card. Unfortunately, the management of Bella Italia (*see* Chapter 7) has been known to let condo publicists operate from its dining room, not a welcome interruption to your dinner. Ron Lavender can arrange for villa rentals (tel. 74/84-04-05). For time-share condos, the Secretariat of Tourism recommends Napoli S.A. at Hernán Cortés 43, tel. 74/85-81-80, and Torre Playa Sol, Costera Miguel Alemán 1252, tel. 74/84-62-38 or 74/84-80-50. The family that owns Hotel Fiesta and Hotel Isabel also rents efficiencies. Contact Amueblados Etel, Pinzona 92 in Old Acapulco, tel. 74/82-22-41.

9 The Arts and Nightlife

Acapulco has always been famous for its nightlife, and justifiably so. For many visitors the discos and restaurants are just as important as the sun and sand. The minute the sun slips over the horizon, The Strip comes alive with people milling around window-shopping, deciding where to dine, and generally biding their time till the disco hour. Obviously, you aren't going to find great culture here; theater efforts are few and far between and there is no classical music. But disco-hopping is high art in Acapulco. And for those who care to watch, there are live shows and folk dance performances. The tour companies listed in Chapter 1 can organize evening jaunts to most of the dance and music places listed below.

Entertainment

Lienzo Charro, near the Princess, has shows that feature Mexican horseback riders and folkloric dances. Performances are given Tuesday, Wednesday, and Saturday, from 7 to 10 PM. The cost, including dinner, open bar, contests, gifts, and free transportation, is about $32. Acuario Tours opposite the Plaza also organizes visits here.

The **Acapulco International Center** (also known as the convention center) has two shows nightly featuring mariachi bands, singers, and the "Flying Indians" from Papantla. The show with dinner and drinks costs about $42; entrance to the show alone is $10. Performances begin at 7:30 and 10. For $30, there's a Mexican fiesta at the **Marbella Shopping Center** on Monday, Wednesday, and Friday nights during the winter season, and on Wednesday and Friday, off-season, at 8 PM. Javier de Leon's folkloric ballet performs at the **Calinda Hotel.** On Friday, at El Mexicano restaurant in **Las Brisas** hotel, the fiesta starts off with a *tianguis* (marketplace) of handicrafts and ends with a spectacular display of fireworks.

The famous **cliff divers** at La Quebrada (*see* Chapter 4) perform every night at 7:30, 8:30, 9:30, and 10:30. **Divers de México** organizes sunset champagne cruises that provide a fantastic view of the spectacle from the water. For reservations, call 74/82–13–98, or stop by the office downtown near the *Fiesta* and *Bonanza* yachts. The *Fiesta, Bonanaza* (tel. 74/83–18–03 or 83–25–31 for both), and *Aca Tiki* (tel. 74/84–61–40) all run nightly cruises of the bay that include dinner, drinks, and a show. All boats leave from downtown near the Zócalo. Many hotels and shops sell tickets, as do the ticketsellers on the waterfront. At the Colonial, on the Costera next door to Extasis, there's a professional **ski show** Tuesday through Sunday at 9 PM (tel. 74/83–91–07).

Don't forget the nightly entertainment at most hotels. The big resorts have live music to accompany the early-evening happy hour, and some feature big-name bands from the United States for less than you would pay at home. Many hotels sponsor theme parties—Italian Night, Beach Party Night, and similar festivities.

Dance

Nina's is a dance hall specializing in salsa music. *On The Strip near CiCi, tel. 74/84–24–00.*

Flamenco performances take place at **La Flor de Acapulco Condesa.** A $30 tab includes dinner with wine and the show; $13 includes the show, two drinks, and tips. *Costera Miguel Alemán 112, near Carlos 'n Charlies, tel. 74/84–40–00. Nightly at 10:15.*

Film

If there is a hit movie you missed last year, chances are good that it will turn up—in English with Spanish subtitles—at one of the cinemas in town. The theaters are quite modern and comfortable; admission is about $1.50. Check the local papers for hours.

Discos

The legendary Acapulco discos are open 365 days a year from about 10:30 PM until they empty out, often not until 4 or 5 AM. Reservations are advisable for a big group, and late afternoon or after 9 PM are the best times to call. New Year's Eve requires advance planning.

The discos are very civilized, in that everyone gets a table and runs up a tab to be paid at the end of the night. Most clubs charge a cover (between $10 and $18), which is paid as you enter or put on your bill. The cover sometimes includes drinks, and these average $3 to $5 for local beverages and $6 for imported brands. After-dinner liqueurs run about $6, and imported champagne is the most expensive of all—$125–$150 per bottle. Many discos distribute free passes or have $10 all-you-can-drink nights, so watch for people handing them out on the street. In some places you can buy membership only for the time you are in town.

Tip just about everybody. The waiter should receive 15% of your tab or at least $4 if drinks are included in the cover charge. The headwaiter who seats you should get at least $2 or $3 before seating you, and the doorman merits $1. Leave change (about 50¢) for bathroom attendants. Tipping is a good practice if you plan to come back. Even if you don't plan to come back, remember that Mexican wages are low and that tips are salary.

Many of the discos attempt to maintain a glamorous veneer by posting outside a superior- and sullen-looking doorman who decides who may enter. Don't be intimidated; this is for appearance's sake only. You can wait outside for 10 minutes and find the place almost empty when you get in and everyone inside casually dressed. Some discos, such as Fantasy, don't like to have too many single men and keep them waiting until there are an equal number of single women inside. Women never have a problem, but if you want to meet people, the best place to sit is at the bar. Things don't really start moving till 11:30, and until people are warmed up, it can take a while to be asked to dance. Those without much stamina start to leave around 2 AM, but most stick it out till 3 or 4, at least.

The best tables are those on the edge of the dance floor, and "Siberia," the worst seats, is the upper reaches away from the music. But where to sit is a subjective judgment. If you want to actually hold a conversation, Siberia might be more to your liking. Tables near the dance floor are often cramped and the noise level is high.

Don't worry about what to wear—no one dresses to kill in Acapulco. Fantasy is the only nightclub where people dress up, and even there it seems that only women make a major effort. In general, disco garb is pretty and elegant, but by no means on the cutting-edge of fashion. Men are accepted anywhere in slacks and shirts. Women can wear just about anything, even shorts if they look good. The most common outfits are pastel cotton dresses or separates worn with fancy jewelry. It is hot inside, even though the air-conditioning works, so a jacket is not necessary. Some women do get dolled up and the effect is always appreciated, so if you do have a slinky dress or low-cut something that you have been saving for a special occasion, wear it in Acapulco or, better yet, at Fantasy, where clubbers cultivate a sophisticated air.

Wherever you go, you will face the question of what to drink, and because Acapulco is cocktail crazy, you have your work cut out for you. The most popular drinks are daiquiris and other drinks based on rum or tequila. The local rum, when mixed with Coke, becomes the smooth and syrupy Cuba libre. Tequila and mescal are both made from the fermented juices of the maguey plant, with tequila being the smoother of the two. Tequila is the heart of a margarita or it can be mixed with 7-Up to become a popper, a local specialty. When this blend is served in a coconut shell, it is aptly named *coco loco*. Mexicans usually drink their tequila straight with salt and lemon or sometimes follow it with a beer chaser. Take note: Tequila can be very strong. Conmemorativo, the top-of-the-line tequila, is a bit smoother. Gusano, a brand of mescal, comes with a worm at the bottom of the bottle, and it makes an, ahem, unusual gift for the unlucky stay-at-homes.

Mexicans love beer, and in some working-class joints it can cost as little as 50¢. Corona is currently fashionable in the United States, but Superior, Victoria, and Bohemia are the Buds and Millers of Mexico. Negra Modelo and Dos Equis are dark. Soft drinks are served everywhere, but not diet colas. Bottled mineral water and juices are widely available. Avoid ice if you are having stomach trouble or want to keep from having stomach trouble.

Except for Tiffany, Fantasy, and Extravaganzza, all the discos are on The Strip and, except for Le Dome, are in three different clusters. They are listed here roughly from east to west:

Tiffany, the posh disco at the Princess Hotel, is a bit more sedate than other places in town. It's great for people who enjoy conversation as well as dancing because the sound system directs the music toward the dance floor. *Princess Hotel, tel. 74/84-33-95.*

Extravaganzza. Acapulco's newest and most splendiferous disco was inaugurated in late 1989. Word has it that it cost over $3 million to build—absolutely everything was imported—and it has the ultimate in light and sound. It accommodates 700 at a central bar and in comfortable booths, and a glass wall provides an unbelievably breathtaking view of Acapulco Bay. No food is served, but Los Rancheros is just a few steps away. The music (which is for all ages) starts at 10:30. *On the Scenic Highway to Las Brisas, tel. 74/84-71-64.*

Fantasy is without a doubt one of the most exclusive of all the discos in Acapulco. If there are any celebrities in town, they'll be here, rubbing elbows with or bumping into local fashion designers and artists—since Fantasy is quite, shall we say, snug. As we've said already, this is one of the only discos where people really dress up, the men in well-cut pants and shirts, and the women in racy outfits and cocktail dresses. The crowd is 25–

50 and mainly in couples. Singles gravitate to the two bars in the back. A line sometimes forms, so people come here earlier than to other places. By midnight the dance floor is so packed that people dance on the wide windowsills that look out over the bay. At 2 AM there is a fireworks display. Capacity is 300, so although seating is cramped, all seats have a view of the floor. "Siberia" consists of an upstairs balcony. Around the floor are long plastic tubes filled with illuminated bubbles, and there is a good light show. In spite of everyone's proximity to the sound system, it is just possible to have a conversation—although not about anything complicated. A glassed-in elevator provides an interesting overview of the scene and leads upstairs to a little shop that stocks T-shirts and lingerie. *On the Scenic Highway, next to Las Brisas, tel. 74/84-67-27.*

Magic is all black inside and has a fabulous light show each night after midnight. This is a good-size place with tables on tiers looking down at the floor. This is one of the few discos where on weekdays you can find a fair number of Mexicans. Any day of the week, this is a good bet to catch up on the Top 10 from Mexico City, as well as the American dance hits. The atmosphere is friendly and laid-back. *Across the Costera from Baby O, tel. 74/84-88-15.*

Baby O and Le Dome (*see below*) are both old favorites. Even mid-week, Baby O is packed. The dance floor is a New York City subway at rush hour, the bar is Grand Central Terminal. Coming here is not a comfortable experience, nor is it quiet or peaceful; it is total chaos. Baby O bucks the trend of most discos in Acapulco. Instead of the usual mirrors and glitz, Baby O resembles a cave in a tropical jungle, with simple plants and walls made of a strange stonelike substance. The crowd is 18–30 and mostly tourists, although many Mexicans come here, too. In fact, this is one of Acapulco's legendary pick-up spots, so feel free to ask someone to dance. When the pandemonium gets to you, retreat to the little hamburger restaurant. Watch your step at all times, however, to avoid falling on the tables and waiters. The architect clearly thought he was designing for acrobats. *Costera Miguel Alemán 22, tel. 74/84-74-74.*

Hard Rock Café, filled with rock memorabilia, is part bar, part restaurant, part dance hall, and part boutique. It's one of the most popular spots in town. The food is southern style—ribs, fried chicken, hamburgers—and the portions are enormous. When the live music starts at 11 PM, waiters and customers alike get into the act. *Costera Miguel Alemán 37, next to CiCi, tel. 74/84-66-80.*

Le Dome, an Acapulco standby, is still one of the hot spots. Even before the music starts at 11:30, there is already a small crowd at the door, and in spite of the capacity of 800, this club is always full. Le Dome doesn't look very different from other clubs on The Strip—it has the usual black wall and mirror mix, although it does have a larger video screen than most. Le Dome is the only club in Acapulco, if not in the world, where you can play basketball, yes, basketball, every Wednesday. Winners get a bottle of tequila. *Costera Miguel Alemán 402, next door to Fiorucci, tel. 74/84-11-90.*

Discobeach is Acapulco's only alfresco disco and its most informal one. The under-30 crowd sometimes even turns up in shorts. The waiters are young and friendly, and every night they dress to a different theme. One night they're all in togas carrying bunches of grapes, the next they're in pajamas. Other nights feature a Hawaiian luau or a mock bullfight. Every Wednesday, ladies' night, all the women receive flowers. The coco loco is the house special. *On The Strip, one minute east of Eve's, tel. 74/84-70-64.*

News is billed as a "disco and concert hall." Disco it is—and it's enormous, with seating for 1,200 people in love seats and booths, but "concert hall" is just a figure of speech. There are different theme parties and competitions nightly—bikini contests on Tuesday, and Carnival Night (with lambada and limbo contests and a Brazilian-style show) on Thursday. Winners walk off with a bottle of champagne or dinner for two; occasionally the prize has been a trip to Hawaii. From 10:30 (opening time) to 11:30, the music is slow and romantic; then the disco music and the light show begin, and they go on till dawn. *Costera Miguel Alemán, across from the Hyatt Regency, tel. 74/84-59-02.*

Delirio used to operate under the name Jackie O, but now one can only sigh nostalgically for the days when the bathrooms were preciously dubbed "Jackie O" and "Aristotle." Comfortable is the operative word here; big booths and wrap-around sofas all have a view of the dance floor. Lasers and lights penetrate the seating area without irritating, and there are numerous relatively quiet spaces. *Opposite the Hyatt Continental, tel. 74/84-08-43.*

Planet is very sophisticated. The seats are comfortable armchairs and sofas with a good view for people-watching. The managers wear suits, and the disco is an art gallery—the walls are covered with tasteful renditions of the beach and other typical Mexican scenes. In addition to the usual videos and disco music, there is a show every night during the winter season (Friday and Saturday night during the rest of the year), complete with mariachis. This club is less crowded than most. There is always room to dance. The crowd is mostly Mexican. *Calle Vicente Yañez Pinzón 12, just behind Delirio, tel. 74/84-82-95.*

Antillanos has replaced the old Cats, which is, sadly, no more. Now it's all palm "trees" and lanterns, the crowd is mostly local, and the music is strictly salsa and tropical. The live groups start playing at 10:30, and at midnight there's a drag show. The $15 cover charge includes local-brand drinks. *Juan de la Cosa 32, tel. 74/82-72-35. Open Tues.–Sun.*

Cheers, a video bar, opens only for the big football and baseball games, championship boxing matches, etc. *Ritz Hotel, Costera Miguel Alemán and Magallanes, tel. 74/85-73-36, ext. 1314.*

X-rated Shows

There is a strip club called the **Afrocasino** in La Huerta, Acapulco's sleazy, depressing red-light district. All the taxi drivers know where it is. If you decide to go, have the waiter call you a cab when you are ready to leave. **Rebecca's** is another infamous nightspot-cum-bordello where two women and one man do what's billed as a live "sex" act involving weird activities with toilet paper. Basically, these are cheesy night spots—good places to avoid.

10 Short Excursions from Acapulco

Roqueta Island

A respite from the crowds on the main beaches, Roqueta Island is visited chiefly by Mexicans. Ask your taxi driver to take you to the *embarcadero* (wharf) near Caleta and Caletilla beaches. From there you can see the island—a mere 10 minutes away by motorboat. Tickets are available from specially designated offices and from boys with their own ticket books. Contrary to what is printed on the ticket, the price should be about $2 round-trip. When you buy your ticket, ask which boat it is for because each company's boat is marked with a different color. Retain the stub; it is for your return trip. For about $6.50 you can buy a ticket for the glass-bottom boat, which takes 45 minutes and detours for a look at the marine life as well as the sunken statue of the Virgin of Guadalupe. The last boat from Roqueta back to the mainland leaves at 5 PM. *Also see below.*

Once on Roqueta you'll find several simple restaurants frequented by Mexicans. The energetic may want to make the half-hour climb up to the *faro* (lighthouse). It is an overgrown route and fairly strenuous, but the view at the top makes up for it—from there you have a bird's-eye view of the entire bay. Just take the walkway to the right of the landing and proceed upward.

If you bear right and walk for about five minutes along a rather narrow, broken-down walkway (damaged in a fire and not for the fainthearted), you will eventually reach **Palao's,** a palapa-roof restaurant that serves lobster and fish caught in the bay in front of the restaurant. A two-course lunch will cost about $12. Palao's is decorated with all sorts of tribal paintings and motifs, and the effect is that of being inside a tropical hut. It is popular with tour operators, so if you arrive when there is a group here, you may catch the performance of Indian dances. This tour is not recommended, though, since the buffet served to groups is of very poor quality and includes a locally caught shellfish that most fishermen usually toss back. Come alone and choose what you eat. Palao's has its own little cove—alas, sometimes very polluted—and offers snorkeling and scuba diving equipment for rent. Local fishermen, displaying homemade shell sculptures, stand in the water with their boats and will take you for a paddle around the bay. Children love Palao's because there is a cage of monkeys and a friendly little horse they can pet. If you want to come only to Palao's and not to the rest of Roqueta, don't pay for a boat ticket. Palao's has its own motorboat, *La Coneja* (The Rabbit), which leaves from Caleta and Caletilla. Palao's also has an excursion boat that takes off from its dock at Costera Miguel Alemán 100, next to the *Fiesta* pier. The trip includes buffet lunch, as well as a performance of the Indian dances, and there's an open bar on board. It costs $25. *Open daily for lunch. Groups need reservations, tel. 74/82–43–13. No credit cards.*

Pie de la Cuesta

Pie de la Cuesta is a 25-minute drive through one of the least scenic parts of Acapulco, so it's a place most visitors want to stay put in, or else visit only once. This long stretch of pretty and fairly deserted beach is famous for sensational sunsets and for the entrancing Coyuca Lagoon behind it. The water on the

Pacific side is rough, and a terrific undertow makes swimming treacherous. The lagoon is a luscious blue and is surrounded with dense vegetation and birds. The thick plant life makes swimming in it uncomfortable, but you can hire a boat to take you around the lagoon and to the bird sanctuary at Preciado Island, and then to Montosa Island to the Estevez family's restaurant for a lunch of fish and mescal. There are also several restaurants on both the lagoon and the beach, so it's easy to spend the day. This is also the place for freshwater fishing.

To get to Pie de la Cuesta, turn off the Costera at the Artisans' Market onto Calle Mendoza, head west (following the signs to Pie de la Cuesta or Ixtapa/Zihuatanejo) until you see the ocean, then take the Pie de la Cuesta turnoff. Or hire a taxi—and try not to pay more than $15. If you want to spend the night, there are two hotels (*see below*).

Tres Marías and **Club El Zapito,** on the lagoon, are small clubs where you can rent a boat for waterskiing or for trips on the lagoon. The price is about $30 an hour. You can also rent a two-person hang glider at the rate of $30 for 15 minutes. If either place is crowded, order lunch when you arrive for whatever time you prefer.

Next door to Tres Marías is **Cadena's Club Náutico.** Besides ski and excursion boats for $30 an hour, you may also choose from backgammon and ping-pong. Some people cross back over to the beach during the day for sunbathing and beachside drinks. Or rent a hammock to lounge in for $1.50, or as little as 30¢ at Hotel Casablanca. Whenever you come, though, be sure and stay for the sunset. The sight is dramatic, and many applaud when it is over.

Lodging There are three little hotels at Pie de la Cuesta. **Casablanca** is a very simple family-run operation with rooms for $15 a day and a restaurant that serves all meals. *Book in advance by writing Bungalows y Restaurante Casablanca, Playa Pie de la Cuesta 3270, Acapulco, Guerrero, Mexico.*

The more upscale **Ukae Kim** is a delight. It's a collection of small buildings surrounded by shaded gardens, with 20 rooms on Pie de la Cuesta beach and nine rooms on the lagoon side. Guests can spend time at the two pools or at the bars, all of which are open to nonguests for $5. The rooms, which are priced from $40 to $55, are rustic, spacious, and charmingly furnished, with mosquito netting over the beds; several of them have Jacuzzis. *Pie de la Cuesta 356, Acapulco, Gro. There is no local phone. Reservation requests should be directed to a Mexico City address: Ukae Kim Hotel, Av. 515, No. 40, Unidad Aragón, 07979 México, tel. 5/760–7955.*

Costa Club Acapulco is the newest hotel in the area, just beyond the military base. The 150 tile-roof bungalow-style rooms are quite ample; each has its own terrace. They are grouped in modules of two strewn over a sprawling property that is bisected by the highway (a bridge over the road joins the two sections), so that some are on the ocean side and others on the lagoon side. Golf carts transport guests back and forth. Meals, most recreational activities, and entertainment are included in the rate. *Av. Pie de la Cuesta S/N, Acapulco, Gro. tel. 74/83–76–74 or (in Mexico City) 5/520–6457. 150 rooms with bath. Facilities: 2 tennis courts, 2 pools, amphitheater, 2 bars, 2 restaurants. AE, DC, MC, V.*

Off the Beaten Track

Popular though Pie de la Cuesta is, tourists rarely venture beyond to the western part of Coyuca and the isolated, flower-filled lagoon. Once you get to Pie de la Cuesta, follow the road down; turn right just before you get to the army base. Drive for half an hour until you can't go any farther and you will come upon a remarkable place: a whole village of fishermen who continue their lives practically untouched by the tourist explosion in Acapulco. The community has its own little church and cluster of houses, and the people are friendly and will take you for boat rides on the lagoon. The price varies, however, so ask at your hotel or at one of the restaurants, and be prepared to bargain. There are several small seafood restaurants, and most managers will be happy to lend you a hammock if you want to spend the night.

Nothing remains untouched in Acapulco for long, and now that the western end of the lagoon has been "discovered" other developers will surely follow. On the road leading to the fishing village, 12.5 kilometers (8 miles) after the army base, is **Maebba Beach Club** (downtown office tel. 74/85–84–64), at Playa Mogote. Here you'll find a pool, water toboggan, volleyball court, a buffet lunch served daily at 2, and a tennis court. $32 includes transportation, a visit to a tropical plantation, a cruise on the Coyuca Lagoon, lunch, and a few hours at the club.

In the other direction, 16 miles east of town, is **Barra Vieja,** the barrier beach that separates Laguna de Tres Palos from the ocean. It is well worth an excursion, and is even more unpopulated than Pie de la Cuesta. Here you can fish and swim in the lagoon and hire small boats to venture into the jungle, and there are several fish restaurants (including **Beto's,** the nicest, which is no more expensive than the others) that serve *pescado a la talla* (broiled whole fish on a skewer) for around $10 a kilo (2.2 pounds).

11 Taxco, the Silver City

Introduction

It's a picture-postcard look—Mexico in its Sunday best: White stucco buildings nuzzling cobblestoned streets, red-tile roofs and geranium-filled window boxes bright in the sun. Taxco (pronounced **tahss**-co), a colonial treasure that the Mexican government declared a national monument in 1928, tumbles onto the hills of the Sierra Madre in the state of Guerrero. Its silver mines have drawn people here for centuries. Now its charm, mild temperatures, sunshine, and flowers make Taxco a popular tourist destination.

Hernán Cortés discovered Taxco's mines in 1522. The silver rush lasted until the next century, when excitement tapered off. Then, in the 1700s a Frenchman, who Mexicanized his name to José de la Borda, discovered a rich lode that revitalized the town's silver industry and made him exceedingly wealthy. After Borda, however, Taxco's importance faded, until the 1930s and the arrival of William G. Spratling, a writer/architect from New Orleans. Enchanted by Taxco and convinced of its potential as a silver center, Spratling set up an apprentice shop, where his artistic talent and his fascination with pre-Columbian design combined to produce silver jewelry and other artifacts that soon earned Taxco its worldwide reputation as the Silver City. Spratling's inspiration lives on in his students and their descendants, many of whom are the city's current silversmiths.

Essential Information

Important Addresses and Numbers

The area code for Taxco is 762.

Tourist Information Both the **Federal Tourist Office** (tel. 762/2–15–25) and the **State Tourist Office** (tel. 762/2–22–79) are located in the Convention Center on Calle Florida (open weekdays 10–2 and 4–7), and there are tourist information booths on both the northern and southern entrances to town along Highway 95.

Emergencies Best handled through hotels.

Pharmacies Local pharmacies rotate staying open all night.

Getting There

There are several ways to travel to Taxco from Acapulco, and all involve ground transport.

By Car It takes about 2½ hours to make the drive from Acapulco to Taxco, now that the new road connecting the town to Highway 95 eliminates most of the tortuous hairpin turns of the previous route. A new superhighway connecting Acapulco to Cuernavaca, which should be finished by winter 1993 (much of it is already open), promises to cut down on driving time even more. It is also common practice to hire a chauffeured car or a taxi. Check with your hotel for references and prices.

If you are traveling from Ixtapa/Zihuatanejo, it is wiser to go through Acapulco and pick up the highway to Cuernavaca than to take Highway 124, which looks shorter on paper but is solitary and full of treacherous curves.

By Bus First-class **Estrella de Oro** buses leave Acapulco several times a day from the Terminal Central de Autobuses de Primera Clase (Av. Cuauhtemoc 1490, tel. 74/85–87–05). The cost for the approximately four-hour ride is about $7 one way. The Taxco terminal is at Avenida John F. Kennedy 126 (tel. 762/2–06–48). First-class **Flecha Roja** buses depart Acapulco several times a day from the Terminal de Autobuses (Av. Cuauhtemoc 97, tel. 74/82–03–51). The one-way ticket is about $6.50. The Taxco terminal for this line is at Avenida John F. Kennedy 104 (tel. 762/2–01–31). To get to Taxco from Ixtapa/Zihuatanejo, you must change buses in Acapulco.

Escorted Tours Many Mexico City–Acapulco tour packages include a one-night stay in Taxco. There are no organized tours from Ixtapa/Zihuatanejo, but private tours can be arranged through most travel agencies: You fly to Mexico City, are driven by a guide to Taxco (where you remain one or more nights), and then fly back from Mexico City.

Getting Around

Unless you're used to byways, alleys, and tiny streets, maneuvering anything bigger than your two feet through Taxco will be difficult. Fortunately, almost everything of interest is within walking distance of the Zócalo. Minibuses travel along preset routes and charge only a few cents, and Volkswagen bugs provide inexpensive (average $2) taxi transportation. Remember that Taxco's altitude is 5,800 feet. If you have come from sea level, wear sensible shoes for negotiating the hilly streets, and take it easy on your first day.

Exploring

Numbers in the margin correspond to points of interest on the Taxco Exploring map.

1 Begin at the **Zócalo,** properly called **Plaza Borda,** heading first
2 into the **Church of San Sebastián and Santa Prisca,** which dominates the main square. Usually just called Santa Prisca, it was built by French silver magnate José de la Borda in thanks to the Almighty for his having literally stumbled upon a rich silver vein. The style of the church—sort of Spanish baroque meets rococo—is known as churrigueresque, and its pink exterior is a stunning surprise.

Just a block from the Zócalo, behind Santa Prisca, is the
3 **Spratling Museum,** formerly the home of William G. Spratling (*see* Introduction, *above*). This wonderful little museum explains the working of colonial mines and displays Spratling's collection of pre-Columbian artifacts. *Porfirio Delgado and El Arco. Small entrance fee. Open daily 10–5.*

4 **Casa Humboldt,** a few blocks away, was named for the German adventurer Alexander von Humboldt, who stayed here in 1803. The Moorish-style 18th-century house has a finely detailed facade. At press time it was being remodeled to house a museum of colonial art. *Calle Juan Ruiz Alarcón 6.*

5 Down the hill from Santa Prisca is the **Municipal Market,** which is worth a visit, especially early on Saturday or Sunday morning.

Casa Humboldt, **4**
Municipal Market (Mercado), **5**
Plaza Borda (Zócalo), **1**
Santa Prisca, **2**
Spratling Museum, **3**

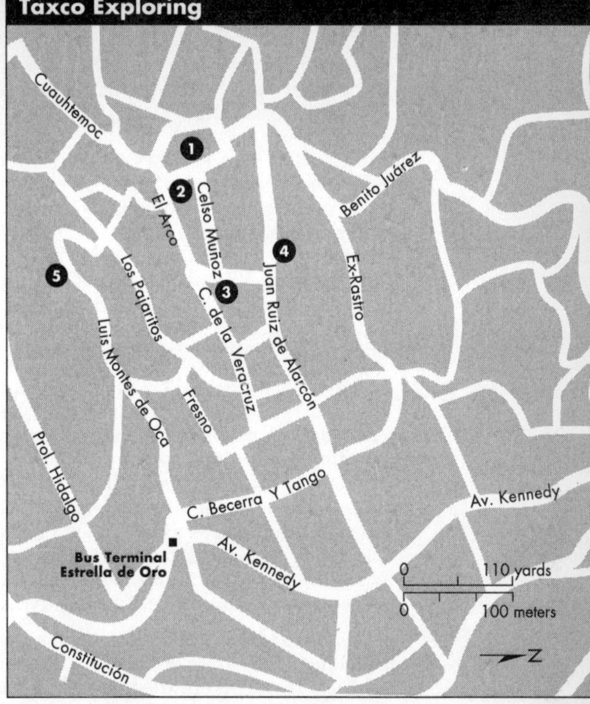

Time Out Around the plaza are several *neverías* where you can treat yourself to an ice cream in a delicious fruit flavor, or maybe even coconut.

Off the Beaten Track

About 15 minutes northeast of Taxco are the Caves of Cacahuamilpa (Grutas de Cacahuamilpa). The largest caverns in Mexico, these 15 large chambers comprise 12 kilometers (8 miles) of geological formation. Only some caves are illuminated. A guide can be hired at the entrance to the caves. Check with the tourist information office for specifics.

Shopping

Silver Most of the people who visit Taxco come with silver in mind. Three types are available: sterling, which is always stamped .925 (925 parts in 1,000) and is the most expensive; plated silver; and the inexpensive *alpaca*, which is also known as German silver or nickel silver. Sterling pieces are usually priced by weight according to world silver prices, and of course fine workmanship will add to the cost. Work is also done with semiprecious stones; you'll find garnets, topazes, amethysts, and opals. If you plan to buy, check prices before leaving home. When comparison shopping in the more than 200 silver shops in Taxco, you will see that many carry almost identical merchandise, although a few are noted for their creativity. Among them:

Galería de Arte Andrés (Av. John F. Kennedy 28) has unique designs created by the personable Andrés Mejía.
Pineda's Taxco (Plaza Borda) has fine designs and fine workmanship.
Los Castillo (Plazuela Bernal 10) is the most famous and decidedly one of the most exciting silver shops; it's known for innovative design and for combining silver with ceramics and such other metals as copper and brass. The artisans are disciples of Spratling.
The Spratling Workshop (south of town on Highway 95) turns out designs using the original Spratling molds.
Joyería Elena Ballesteros (Celso Muñoz 4) is a very elegant shop with work of outstanding design.

Local Wares Lacquered gourds and boxes from the town of Olinala, masks, bowls, straw baskets, bark paintings, and many other handcrafted items native to the state of Guerrero are available from strolling vendors and spread on the cobblestones at "sidewalk boutiques." **Acácia** (Convention Center, Calle Florida) has an interesting selection of Guerrero handicrafts. **Gracias a Dios** (Bernal 3) has women's clothing, with brightly colored ribbons and appliqués, designed by Tachi Castillo, as well as a less original selection of crafts. **La Calleja** (Calle Arco 5, 2nd floor) has a wide and well-chosen selection of native arts and handcrafts.

Sunday is market day, which means that artisans from surrounding villages descend on the town, as do visitors from Mexico City. It can get crowded, but if you find a seat on a bench in Plaza Borda, you're set to watch the show and peruse the merchandise that will inevitably be brought to you.

Sports and Fitness

You can play golf or tennis, swim and ride horses at various hotels around Taxco. Call to see if the facilities are open to nonguests. Bullfights are occasionally held in the small town of Acmixtla, 6 km (3.75 mi) from Taxco. Ask at your hotel about the schedule.

Dining

Gastronomes can find everything from tagliatelle to iguana in Taxco restaurants, and meals are much less expensive than in Acapulco.

Moderate ($20–$30)

Cielito Lindo. This charming restaurant features a Mexican-international menu. Give the Mexican specialties a try, for example, *pollo en pipian verde*, a chicken simmered in a mild, pumpkinseed-based sauce. *Plaza Borda, tel. 762/2-06-03. Open daily, breakfast–dinner. No reservations. Dress: casual. MC, V.*

★ **La Taberna.** This is the latest venture of the proprietors of Bora Bora, Taxco's popular pizza place. The menu is varied, with the likes of pastas, beef Stroganoff, and crepes to choose from.

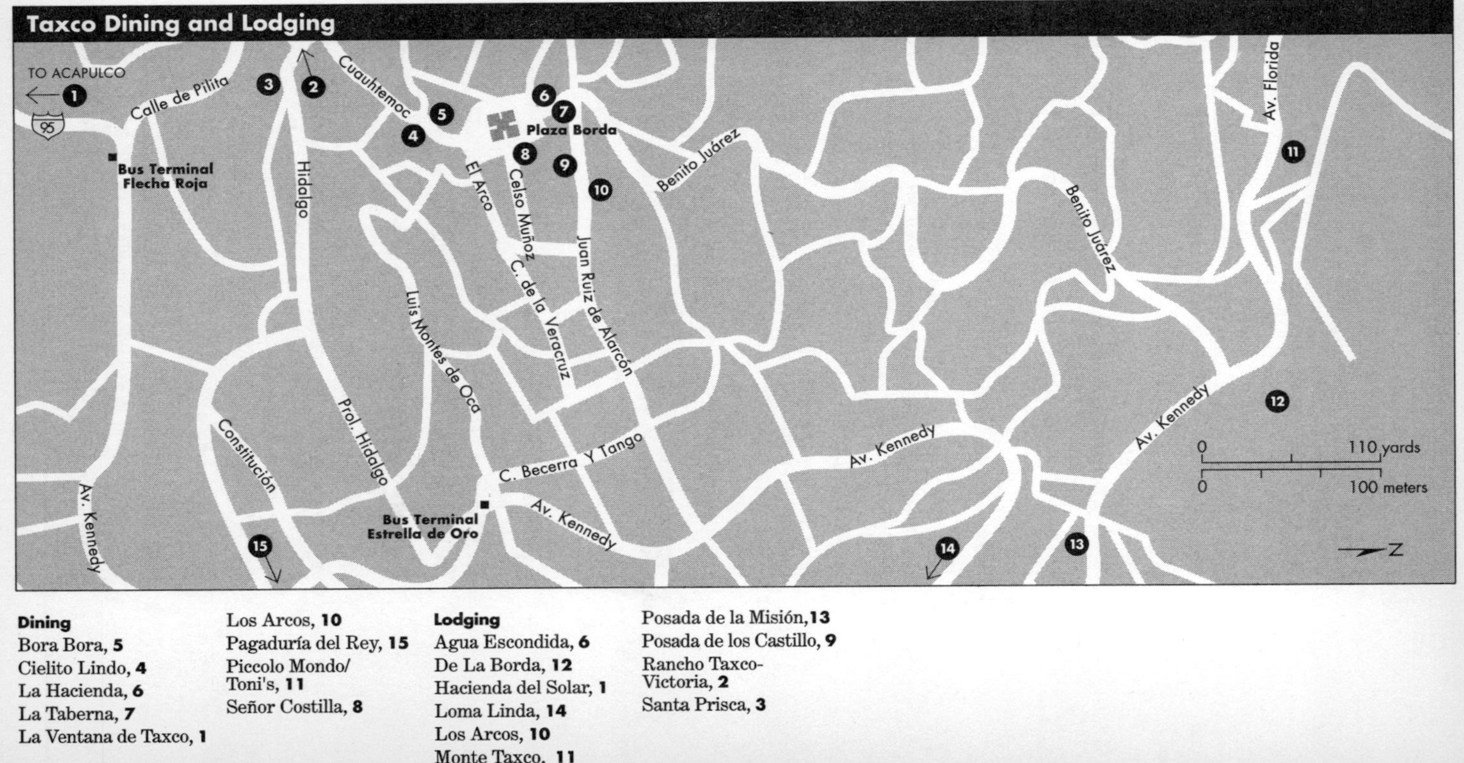

Dining
Bora Bora, **5**
Cielito Lindo, **4**
La Hacienda, **6**
La Taberna, **7**
La Ventana de Taxco, **1**
Los Arcos, **10**
Pagaduría del Rey, **15**
Piccolo Mondo/ Toni's, **11**
Señor Costilla, **8**

Lodging
Agua Escondida, **6**
De La Borda, **12**
Hacienda del Solar, **1**
Loma Linda, **14**
Los Arcos, **10**
Monte Taxco, **11**
Posada de la Misión, **13**
Posada de los Castillo, **9**
Rancho Taxco-Victoria, **2**
Santa Prisca, **3**

Benito Juárez 8, tel. 762/2–52–26. Reservations suggested. Dress: casual. MC, V.

★ **La Ventana de Taxco.** Mario Cavagna traveled from Como, Italy, to Taxco with many of his favorite recipes intact. That food, coupled with Mexican specialties and a fantastic view, make this the town's finest. *Hacienda del Solar Hotel, Hwy. 95, south of town, tel. 762/2–05–87. Reservations required on weekends. Dress: casual. AE, MC, V.*

Pagaduría del Rey. In the Posada Don Carlos, south of town via Avenida John F. Kennedy, this restaurant has a long-standing reputation for Continental fare served in comfortable surroundings. *Calle H. Colegio Militar (formerly Cerro de la Bermeja), tel. 762/2–34–67. Reservations not necessary. Dress: casual. Open daily breakfast–dinner. MC, V.*

Toni's. Prime rib and lobster are the specialties. There's also a great view and a romantic setting. *Monte Taxco Hotel, tel. 762/2–13–00. Reservations required. Dress: casual. AE, DC, MC, V.*

Inexpensive (under $15)

★ **Bora Bora.** Exceptionally good pizza is what's on the menu here. *Callejón de las Delícias, behind Paco's Bar, tel. 762/2–17–21. No reservations. Dress: casual. MC, V.*

La Hacienda. In the Hotel Agua Escondida, this charming restaurant serves Mexican and international specialties. The best buy: the daily fixed-price meal called a *comida corrida. Guillermo Spratling 4, tel. 762/2–06–63. Open daily, breakfast–dinner. No reservations. Dress: casual. MC, V.*

Los Arcos. This local favorite serves international cuisine in a delightful patio setting. *At the Hotel los Arcos, tel. 762/2–18–36. Reservations advised. Dress: casual. AE, MC, V.*

Piccolo Mondo. More casual than its neighbor Toni's, this place serves pizza baked in a wood-burning brick oven and meats and chicken charcoal broiled at your table. *Monte Taxco Hotel, tel. 762/2–13–00. Reservations advised. Dress: casual. AE, DC, MC, V. Closed Mon.–Thurs.*

Señor Costilla. That's right. This translates as Mr. Ribs, and the whimsical name says it all. The Taxco outpost of the zany Anderson chain serves ribs and chops in a restaurant with great balcony seating. *Plaza Borda, tel. 762/2–32–15. Reservations advised. Dress: casual. MC, V.*

Lodging

Whether your stay in Taxco is a one-night stopover or a few days' respite from the madness of Acapulco, there are several categories of hotel to choose from within Taxco's two types: the small inns nestled on the hills skirting the Zócalo and the larger, more modern hotels on the outskirts of town.

Moderate ($65–$100)

★ **Hacienda del Solar.** This intimate and elegant small resort (off Hwy. 95 south of town) has well-appointed rooms. Its restaurant is the top-notch La Ventana de Taxco (*see above*). *Box 96, 40200, tel. 762/2–03–23. 22 rooms with bath. Facilities: 1 tennis court, pool. MC, V.*

Monte Taxco. A colonial style predominates at this hotel, which has a knockout view and two restaurants, a disco, and nightly entertainment. *Box 84, Lomas de Taxco, 40200, tel. 762/2-13-00. 160 rooms with bath. Facilities: 3 tennis courts, 9-hole golf course, horseback riding. AE, DC, MC, V.*

Inexpensive ($40–$65)

De la Borda. Long a Taxco favorite, but getting very run-down now, the hotel's rooms overlook town from its hillside perch. There's a restaurant with occasional entertainment, and many bus tours en route from Mexico City to Acapulco stay overnight here. *Box 6, Cerro del Pedregal 2, 40200, tel. 762/2-00-25. 95 rooms with bath. Facilities: pool. MC, V.*

★ **Posada de la Misión.** Laid out like a village, this hotel is close to town and has dining room murals by the noted Mexican artist Juan O'Gorman. *Box 88, Cerro de la Misíon 84, 40230, tel. 762/2-00-63. 150 rooms with bath. Facilities: pool, tennis court. AE, DC, MC, V.*

Rancho Taxco-Victoria. This in-town hotel, in two buildings connected by a bridge over the road, is under the same management as the De la Borda, and suffers from the same neglect. It has its rooms done in classic Mexican decor. There's also the requisite splendid view. *Box 83, Carlos J. Nibbi 5, 40200, tel. 762/2-00-10. 100 rooms with bath. Facilities: 2 pools, restaurant, bar. AE, MC, V.*

Santa Prisca. The patio with fountains is a plus at this colonial-style hotel. *Cena Obscuras 1, 40200, tel. 762/2-00-80. 40 rooms. Facilities: restaurant, bar. AE, MC, V.*

Very Inexpensive (under $40)

Agua Escondida. A favorite with some regular visitors to Taxco, this small hotel has simple rooms decorated with Mexican-style furnishings. *Guillermo Spratling 4, 40200, tel. 762/2-07-26. 50 rooms with bath. Facilities: pool, La Hacienda restaurant. MC, V.*

Loma Linda. This is a basic motel on the highway just east of town. *Av. John F. Kennedy 52, 40200, tel. 762/2-02-06. 90 units. Facilities: pool, restaurant, bar. AE, MC, V.*

Los Arcos. An in-town inn, Los Arcos has a fine restaurant (*see* Dining, *above*). *Calle Juan Ruiz de Alarcón, 40200, tel. 762/2-18-36. 30 rooms with bath. Facilities: heated pool. MC, V.*

Posada de los Castillo. This inn in town is straightforward, clean, and good for the price. *Juan Ruiz de Alarcón 7, 40200, tel. 762/2-13-96. 15 rooms. Facilities: restaurant, bar. DC, MC, V.*

The Arts and Nightlife

The Arts

Festivals Taxco has no abundance of cultural events, but it's noted for its festivals, which are an integral part of the town's character. These fiestas provide an opportunity to honor almost every saint in heaven with music, dancing, marvelous fireworks, and lots of fun. The people of Taxco demonstrate their pyrotechnical skills with set pieces—wondrous "castles" made of bamboo. (Note: Expect high occupancy at local hotels and inns during fiestas.)

January 18, the feast of Santa Prisca and San Sebastián, the town's patron saints, is celebrated with music and fireworks.

Holy Week, from Palm Sunday to Easter Sunday, brings processions and events that blend Christian and Indian traditions, the dramas involving hundreds of participants, images of Christ, and, for one particular procession, black-hooded penitents. Most events are centered on Plaza Borda and the Santa Prisca Church.

September 29, Saint Michael's Day (Dia de San Miguel), is celebrated with regional dances and pilgrimages to the Chapel of Saint Michael the Archangel.

November 8, the Monday following the Day of the Dead celebrations on November 1 and 2, is the day the whole town takes off to a nearby hill for the Fiesta de los Jumiles. The *jumil* is a crawling insect that is said to taste strongly of iodine and is considered a great delicacy. Purists eat them alive, but others prefer them stewed, fried or combined with chili in a hot sauce.

In **late November or early December,** the National Silver Fair (Feria Nacional de la Plata) draws hundreds of artisans from around the world for a variety of displays, concerts, exhibitions, and contests held around the city.

Nightlife

Travelers should satisfy their appetite for fun after dark in Acapulco. Although Taxco has a disco or two, a couple of piano bars, and some entertainment, the range is limited.

Still, you might enjoy spending an evening perched on a chair on a balcony or in one of the cafés surrounding the Plaza Borda. Two traditional favorites are the **Bar Paco** and **Bertha's,** where a tequila, lime, and club-soda concoction called a "Bertha" is the house specialty.

Or immerse yourself in the thick of things, especially on Sunday evening, by settling in on a wrought-iron bench on the Zócalo to watch the children, lovers, and fellow people-watchers.

Most of Taxco's nighttime activity is at the Monte Taxco hotel, either at the **Windows** discotheque or at **Tony Reyes's,** where the price of the show includes a performance of the Papantla fliers, dancing, drinks, and transportation. On Saturday nights, there's a buffet, a terrific fireworks display (Taxco is Mexico's fireworks capital), and a show put on by the hotel's employees.

Some of the best restaurants, like La Ventana de Taxco, have music.

12 Ixtapa and Zihuatanejo

Introduction

In Ixtapa/Zihuatanejo, 3½ hours by car (250 kilometers/150 miles) up the coast from Acapulco, you can enjoy two distinct lifestyles for the price of one—double value for your money.

Ixtapa/Zihuatanejo is a complete change of pace from hectic Acapulco. The water is comfortably warm for swimming, and the waves are gentle. The temperature averages 78° year-round. During the mid-December–Easter high season, the weather is sunny and dry, and in the June–October rainy season, the short, heavy showers usually fall at night.

Ixtapa (pronounced ees-**tah**-pah), where most Americans stay—probably because they can't pronounce Zihuatanejo (see-wha-tah-**nay**-ho)—is big, modern, and scarcely 17 years old. Exclusively a vacation resort, it was invented and planned, as was Cancún, by Fonatur, Mexico's National Fund for Tourism Development. Large world-class hotels cluster in the Hotel Zone around Palmar Bay, where conditions are ideal for swimming and water sports, and just across the street are a couple of football fields' worth of shopping malls. The hotels are well spaced; there's always plenty of room on the beach, which is lighted for strolling at night; and the pace is leisurely.

Zihuatanejo, which means "land of women" in Purepecha, the language of the Tarascan Indians, lies 5 kilometers (3 miles) to the southeast. According to legend, Caltzontzin, a Tarascan king, chose this bay as his royal retreat and enclosed it with a long protective breakwater, which is known today as Las Gatas. After the Spanish conquest in the 16th century, the conquistadors sailed from here on the first voyage to the Philippines (which eventually became the center of Spanish trade with the Orient).

Zihuatanejo is an old fishing village that has managed to retain its charm; but it's also the area's commercial center, with banks and airline offices, and its *malecón* (waterfront) and cobblestoned streets are lined with hotels, restaurants, and boutiques.

In Ixtapa, Grupo Sidek, the conglomerate responsible for the marina complex in Puerto Vallarta, is developing a 173.5-hectare (429-acre) site on Palmar Bay. The Marina Ixtapa's plans call for a 500-slip marina, a yacht club, hotels, condominiums, condo-hotels, private homes, beach and tennis clubs, an 18-hole golf course, and a shopping center, all of which should be completed by the end of 1993.

The northern end of Zihuatanejo Bay is the site of another development, this one known as Puerto Mío. The project calls for a total of 500 units, including a hotel, a condo-hotel, and villas. A 35-suite hotel, restaurant, bar, and 60-slip marina are already operating.

Essential Information

Important Addresses and Numbers

Ixtapa/Zihuatanejo's area code is 753; its zip code is 40880.

Tourist Information The **tourist office** (tel. 753/4-30-71 or 753/4-22-07) is across the street from the Municipal Palace in Zihuatanejo; it's open daily 9-3 and 6-8.

Banks In Ixtapa, there is a **Bancomer** in the La Puerta Shopping Mall. Banks in Zihuatanejo include **Banamex** (Calle Cuauhtémoc 4), **Multibanco Comermex** (Calle Vicente Guerrero at Ramírez), and **Banca Serfín** (Calle Benito Juárez 22). Generally, banks exchange money only from 10 to 12:30.

Ixtapa's Casa de Cambio (private money exchange) is in the Los Patios Shopping Mall; the one in Zihuatanejo is on Calles Galeana and Nicolás Bravo (tel. 753/4-28-00). Hours are 9-2 and 4-6.

Emergencies Best handled through the hotels, most of which have a doctor on staff.

Post Office The post office is on Calle Catalina González in Zihuatanejo, four blocks from the beach.

Getting There

By Plane You can fly direct to Ixtapa on **Mexicana Airlines** from San Francisco and Los Angeles via Guadalajara, and from Chicago via Mexico City. **Delta** flies to Ixtapa nonstop from Los Angeles. Both **Mexicana** and **Aeromexico** have daily nonstop service from Mexico City and most other major cities in Mexico, but there is no direct air service from Acapulco.

By Car The trip from Acapulco is a 3½-hour drive over a good road that passes through small towns and coconut groves and has some quite spectacular ocean views for the last third of the way. At three inspection stops, soldiers checking for drugs and arms generally only look into the car and wave you on. Travelers from Mexico City may be tempted by Highway 134, which appears to be a more direct route; but it's solitary and full of curves, and most drivers prefer the longer route through Acapulco.

By Bus **Estrella de Oro** and **Flecha Roja** offer deluxe service (which means that the air-conditioning and toilets are likely to be functioning) between Acapulco and Zihuatanejo. The trip takes about five hours and costs $6. You must reserve and pick up your ticket one day in advance and get to the terminal at least a half hour before departure. Estrella de Oro buses leave from the Terminal Central de Autobuses de Primera Clase (Av. Cuauhtémoc 1490, tel. 74/85-87-05). The Flecha Roja buses leave from the Terminal de Autobuses (Av. Cuauhtémoc 97, tel. 74/82-03-51). Bus service from Mexico City is through Acapulco.

Escorted Tours

Most Acapulco-based travel agencies can set up one-day tours to Ixtapa/Zihuatanejo for about $50-$150, including guide, transportation (car, minibus, or bus), and lunch. If your hotel travel desk can't arrange it for you, contact **Turismo Caleta** (Calle Andrea Dória 2, tel. 74/84-61-72), **Fantasy Tours** (Costera Miguel Alemán 50, tel. 74/84-25-28), or **Excursiones Acapulco** (Costera Miguel Alemán 40, Suite 204, tel. 74/84-65-54).

Getting Around

Unless you plan to travel great distances or to visit remote beaches, taxis and buses are by far the best way to get around. Rental cars cost about $100 per day; jeeps about half that.

By Taxi Taxis are plentiful, and fares are reasonable. The average fare from the Ixtapa Hotel Zone to Zihuatanejo or to Playa La Ropa or Playa Quieta is about $4. There's no problem getting cabs, and there are taxi stands in front of most hotels.

By Bus The buses that operate between the hotels and from the Hotel Zone to downtown Zihuatanejo run approximately every 20 minutes and charge about 20¢.

By Motor Scooter Scooters can be rented at **Hola Renta Motos** (next door to the Villa Sakura restaurant in the El Portal shopping center; no phone) for $10–$15 an hour.

By Pedicab Pedicabs (*carcachas*) decorated with balloons can be rented in the shopping mall across the street from the Dorado Pacifico hotel for $10 per hour. Bikes cost $1 per hour. The rental tent is open daily 9–8.

By Car Rental-car offices in Zihuatanejo: **Dollar** at the Dorado Pacífico hotel (tel. 753/3–20–25) and at the Hotel Krystal (tel. 753/3–03–33, ext. 1110), and **Hertz** (Calle Nicolás Bravo 9, tel. 753/4–30–50 or 753/4–22–55). In Ixtapa: **Avis's** only office is in the airport (tel. 753/4–22–48), and the other companies have branches there. Jeeps can be rented at the airport from **Dollar** (tel. 753/4–23–14). A medium-size car runs about $100 per day, including insurance and mileage; jeeps are half that.

Exploring

No matter where you go in Ixtapa/Zihuatanejo, you get the fresh-air, great-outdoors feeling of a place in the making, with plenty of room to spare.

Zihuatanejo is a tropical charmer. The seaside promenade overlooks the town dock and cruise-ship pier; tiny bars and restaurants invite you to linger longer. From town, the road soars up a hill that has a handful of restaurants and hotels perched on breezy spots overlooking the bay. Another sprinkling of hotels surrounds pancake-flat **Madera Beach. La Ropa,** farther along, is Zihuatanejo's most popular beach and the location of one of Mexico's best small hotels, Villa del Sol. **Las Gatas** beach, beyond, lined with dive shops and tiny restaurants, is also popular, but is accessible only by water.

On the opposite end of the area, about five minutes beyond the Ixtapa Hotel Zone, is pretty **Playa Quieta,** a small beach used by Club Med. From here, you can take a boat ride to **Isla Ixtapa** for pennies and spend a wonderful day in the sun far from other people. Once the boat lands, take the path to the other side of the island for better sunning and swimming.

For another perspective, take a three-hour cruise for $25 on the 12-passenger catamaran *Tequila* (tel. 753/3–00–07). It cruises the bay with a stop for snorkeling at Isla Ixtapa. **Sailboats of the Sun** (tel. 753/3–07–82) sets sail weekdays at 10 AM from the Puerto Mío marina in Zihuatanejo for a seven-hour cruise that includes a stop for snorkeling and a fresh-fish lunch at Ixtapa Island. Both the *Tequila* and Sailboats of the Sun also have two-hour sunset cruises of Zihuatanejo Bay.

Shopping

At last count, there were seven shopping malls in Ixtapa. La Puerta, the first one built, is now flanked by terra-cotta-colored Ixpamar, colonial-style Los Patios, and bright white Las Fuentes. The ubiquitous **Aca Joe** and **Polo Ralph Lauren** are in Las Fuentes, as is **Africán,** which carries 100%-cotton safari-style clothing for men and women. **Ferrioni** is in La Puerta; **Chiquita Banana,** a good source of decorative items for your house, and **La Fuente,** which sells clothes with native-inspired designs, are in Los Patios. **El Amanecer,** selling some of the best folk art in the state, is in Ixpamar. Don't let the modern facades and sparkling decor fool you: Most prices are within everyone's range. A heavy wool sweater costs about $25; a giant T-shirt, less than $10; a hand-painted souvenir—a vase or animal of clay or lacquer, made with skills that have endured for centuries—might cost less than $5. There is sometimes free live entertainment on the patio at Ixpamar.

Downtown Zihuatanejo has a municipal minimarket and a host of tiny stores. You must go inside to discover bargains in souvenirs and decorations, T-shirts, and embroidered dresses. On Calle Vicente Guerrero is one of the best handicrafts shops in all of Mexico—**Coco Cabaña,** which is owned by the same people who run Coconuts restaurant. **Los Almendros,** at Calles Guerrero and Alvarez, has an especially good selection of handpainted ceramics from Oaxaca, and at **La Zapoteca,** on the waterfront, you'll find hand-loomed woolen rugs, wall hangings, and hammocks. On Calle Juan N. Alvarez, Indians sell baskets and other handmade wares that they bring from the surrounding areas.

Sports and Fitness

Although several hotels have tennis courts, and there are two beautiful championship golf courses in Ixtapa, most of the outdoor activities in Ixtapa/Zihuatanejo center on the water. At the **water-sports center** in front of Villa del Sol on La Ropa you can arrange for waterskiing, snorkeling, diving, and windsurfing.

Deep-sea Fishing Yellowfin tuna can run as large as 22 pounds, and mahimahi, known as *dorado* in Mexico, weigh in at 40 to 50 pounds. Boats with captain and crew can be hired at the **Cooperativa de Lanchas de Recreo and Pesca Deportiva** (Av. Ruíz Cortines 40 at the Zihuatanejo pier; tel. 753/4–20–56), or through **Turismo Caleta** (La Puerta shopping center in Ixtapa, tel. 753/3–04–44). The cost is $80 to $100 for a boat with two lines, and up to $250 for a boat with four to six lines. There's a sailfish tournament in December. You can have your catch cooked at La Mesa del Capitán or Casa Elvira (*see* Dining, *below*).

Sailing Hobie Cats and larger sailboats are available for rent at La Ropa Beach for $20–$60 per hour.

Scuba Diving **Carlos** operates day and night diving excursions on Las Gatas, and **Oliverio,** who is now over 70, runs diving excursion on Ixtapa Island. Both have kiosks on the beach. A one-tank dive with either costs about $25 to $30. The **Zihuatanejo Scuba Center,** at the foot of the Zihuatanejo pier (tel. 753/4–21–47), is operated by marine biologist Juan Barnard. The center has well-maintained equipment, including three radio-equipped boats, and offers a resort course with a morning pool orientation and an afternoon dive; a five-day certification course; tours with Sr. Barnard to any of 28 dive sites in the immediate area (about $65 for a two-tank dive); deep-water and night dives, for experienced divers only; and underwater-photography instruction. The center also sells photographs and videotapes of the day's dive.

Horseback Riding You can rent horses at La Manzanilla Ranch, near Playa La Ropa, and at Playa Linda. For $35 **Turismo Caleta** (La Puerta shopping center, tel. 753/3–04–44) picks tourists up at their hotel and transports them to La Manzanilla, where they set out on guided trail rides to Cerro de la Ropa (La Ropa hill), stopping along the way for 2½ hours of sunning and snorkeling at Las Gatas beach. There is also pickup service for 1½ hours of riding at Playa Linda, where the horses are bigger and more experienced riders can do some serious galloping along the beach; the cost is about $15.

Windsurfing This popular activity can be arranged at Las Gatas and La Ropa beaches for about $20 per hour—$30 per hour with lessons.

Parasailing You can try this scary-looking sport on the beach in the Ixtapa Hotel Zone. A 10-minute ride will cost about $12.

Golf and Tennis The **Ixtapa Golf Club** (tel. 753/3–11–63), one of the most beautiful in Mexico, is located across from the Hotel Zone in Ixtapa and is open to the public. The greens fee is $35; tennis costs $8 an hour in the daytime, $9 at night. Caddies cost $10 an hour and carts go for $26. A second 18-hole golf course is located at Marina Ixtapa.

Dining

Meals are generally less expensive in downtown Zihuatanejo than in Ixtapa or in the restaurants up in the hills, and even the most expensive ones will cost considerably less than in Acapulco. The restaurants will fall at the lower end of our price categories, verging on the category below, and casual dress is acceptable everywhere. A delicious, inexpensive snack is a *licuado*, a milkshake made with fresh fruit. It's filling and nutritious, and usually costs less than $1. You can try one in Zihuatanejo at **Jugos Michoacan** (next to the Comermex bank on Calle Vicente Guerrero, and at other locations in town) or in Ixtapa at **Nueva Zelanda.**

Ixtapa

Expensive ($30–$45) **Bogart's.** Romantic and elegant, with moorish/arabic decor and an international menu. The *Crepas Persas* filled with cheese are topped with sour cream and caviar. Or try *Suprema Casablanca*: chicken breasts stuffed with lobster, then breaded and fried. *Hotel Krystal, Playa Palmar, tel. 753/3–03–33. Reservations required. No shorts or T-shirts. AE, DC, MC, V.*

El Faro. A recent addition to Ixtapa's restaurant scene, El Faro sits atop a hill next to the funicular that goes up to the Club Pacifica complex. It has an extensive menu that includes

Dining
Bogart's, **4**
Café Onyx, **7**
Carlos 'n Charlies, **2**
Da Baffone, **6**
El Faro, **11**
El Sombrero, **8**
Las Esferas, **12**
Nueva Zelanda, **9**
Villa de la Selva, **13**

Lodging
Costa Club Ixtapa, **1**
Krystal Ixtapa, **4**
Posada Real, **3**
Sheraton Ixtapa, **10**
Stouffer Presidente, **5**
Westin Ixtapa, **12**

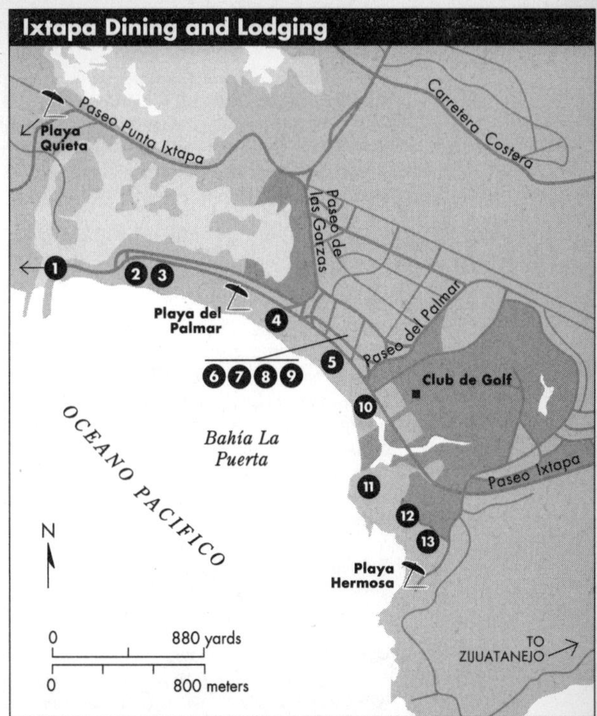

camarones en salsa de albahaca (shrimp in a basil sauce), piano music, and a spectacular view. *Playa Vista Hermosa, tel. 753/3–10–27. Reservations advised. Dress: casual. AE, MC, V.*

El Sombrero. This popular place serves Mexican food, seafood, and international dishes. The potpouri Mexicana, with chicken in mole sauce, an enchilada, and a spicy sausage, is a good introduction to real Mexican cookery. *Los Patios Shopping Center, Ixtapa, tel. 753/3–04–39. Reservations advised. Dress: casual. MC, V. Closed Sun.*

★ **Las Esferas.** This place in the Westin Ixtapa is a complex of two restaurants and a bar. **Portofino** specializes in Italian cuisine and is decorated with multicolored pastas and scenes of Italy. In **El Mexicano** the specialties are obviously Mexican, as is the decor—bright pink tablecloths, Puebla jugs, a huge tree of life, antique wood carvings, and blown glass. *Playa Vista Hermosa, tel. 753/3–21–21, ext. 3444. Reservations necessary at Portofino, advised at El Mexicano. Dress: no shorts or T-shirts. AE, DC, MC, V.*

Villa de la Selva. Just past the Hotel Camino Real, this restaurant has tables set up on multilevel terraces under the stars. Excellent international dishes and grilled steaks and seafood are served in a romantic setting, and special lighting after dark illuminates the sea and the rocks below. *Paseo de la Roca, tel. 753/3–03–62. Open daily 6–midnight. Reservations advised. Dress: casual. AE, MC, V.*

Moderate ($20–$30)

Carlos 'n Charlies. Hidden away at the end of the beach, this outpost of the famous Anderson's chain serves pork, seafood, and chicken in a Polynesian setting almost on the sand. It has a minizoo, too. *Next to Posada Real Hotel, tel. 753/3-00-35. No reservations. Dress: casual. AE, DC, MC, V.*

Da Baffone. The atmosphere is easy and informal at this well-run Italian restaurant with two dining areas; you can choose the air-conditioned dining room or the open-air porch. Try the spaghetti siubeco, prepared with cream, peppers, shrimp, and wine. *La Puerta Shopping Mall, tel. 753/3-11-22. Reservations advised. Dress: casual. AE, MC, V.*

Inexpensive (under $20)

Café Onyx. Mexican and international dishes are served under an awning at this alfresco eatery. *Across from the Holiday Inn, in the Galerías shopping mall. No phone. No reservations. Dress: casual. MC, V.*

★ **Nueva Zelanda.** This is a fast-moving cafeteria with good food that you order by numbers. Chicken enchiladas with green sauce, *sincronizadas* (flour tortillas filled with ham and cheese), and the licuados (*see above*) are all tasty. Families with young children gather here, and there is usually a line on weekends. Dinner for two can cost less than $8. *Behind the bandstand, no phone. No reservations. No credit cards.*

Zihuatanejo

Restaurants in Zihuatanejo are usually small and friendly. Talking to people can be part of the fun. If you want to find out what the town is about, go to the bar before dinner.

Expensive ($30–$45)

Coconuts. Excellent seafood and salads are served in elegant surroundings. The bar is an especially good place to find out what's going on in town. *Calle Agustin Ramírez 1, tel. 753/4-25-18. Reservations required. Dress: casual. AE, DC, MC, V. Closed Sept.–Oct.*

★ **Villa del Sol.** This restaurant, in the hotel that bears the same name, has earned a worldwide reputation for excellent quality and service. The international menu is prepared by Swiss, German, and Mexican chefs. *Hotel Villa del Sol, Playa La Ropa, tel. 753/4-22-39. Dinner reservations advised. Dress: casual. No credit cards.*

Moderate ($20–$30)

Casa Elvira. Joaquin Vasquez, the owner, claims that this is the oldest restaurant in town—it's been around since 1956. It's quaint and clean, decorated with talavera tiles from Puebla and handicrafts from Pátzcuaro, and the prices are reasonable. There's a fairly large selection of fish and seafood, including an excellent *parrillada de mariscos* (seafood grill), as well as such traditional Mexican dishes as poblano peppers stuffed with cheese and *puntas de filete albañil* (a kind of goulash). *Paseo del Pescador 16, tel. 753/4-20-61. MC, V. Open Wed.–Mon. 8 AM–10 PM.*

Chez Juan. In spite of the name, this restaurant is neither French nor Mexican but Chinese. Hot and spicy Szechuan dishes are the specialty of the house. There's also a sports bar with backgammon and checkers. *Calle Hermenegildo Galeana 4, tel. 753/4-51-55). Dress: casual. Open Sun.–Fri. 5–11. MC, V.*

El Andaluz. The name comes from a train, and that's what this place looks like, but most of the locals call it simply "the deli." On the menu are hamburgers, corned beef, pastrami, cappuccino, and eggs Benedict. *Calle Nicolás Bravo 12-A at Cuauhtémoc, tel. 753/4-38-50. No reservations. Dress: casual. Open daily for breakfast, lunch, and supper. MC, V.*

Dining
Casa Elvira, **8**
Chez Juan, **9**
Coconuts, **10**
El Andaluz, **2**
Garrabos, **3**
La Bocana, **4**
La Cabina del Capitán, **11**
La Gaviota, **23**
La Mesa del Capitán, **12**
La Perla, **26**
La Sirena Gorda, **5**
Mi Casita, **13**
Nueva Zelanda, **14**
Pepper's Garden, **15**
Puntarenas, **6**
Villa del Sol, **24**

Lodging
Avila, **7**
Bungalows las Urracas, **25**
Bungalows Pacíficos, **17**
Catalina-Sotovento, **21**
Fiesta Mexicana, **22**
Irma, **20**
Palacios, **19**
Puerto Mío, **1**
Villa del Sol, **24**
Villas Miramar, **18**
Zihuatanejo Centro, **16**

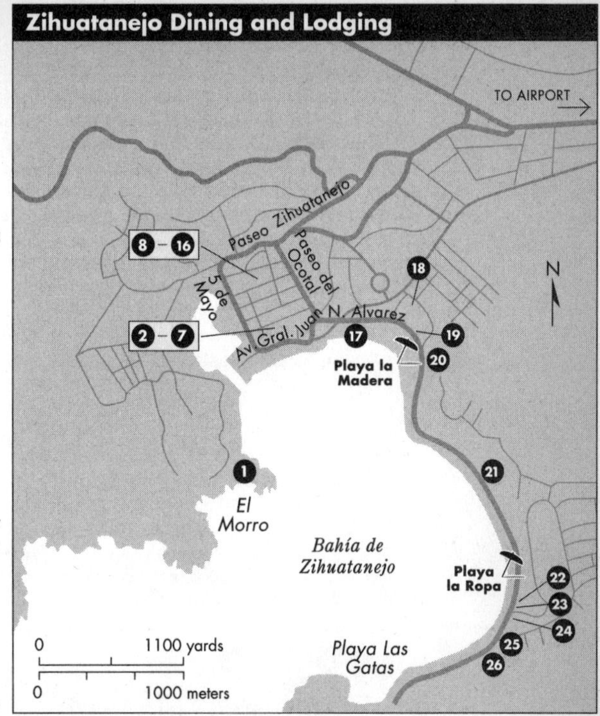

Garrabos. A delightful restaurant that specializes in seafood and Mexican cuisine. Try the seafood brochettes. *Calle Juan N. Alvarez 52, near the church and museum, tel. 753/4–29–77. Reservations advised. Dress: casual. MC, V.*

La Cabina del Capitán. A popular air-conditioned spot with a large TV screen and a parabolic antenna that attract a big crowd for major sports events. The menu is strictly hamburgers, sandwiches, and Mexican *antojitos* (tacos, enchiladas, and the like). *Calle Nicolás Bravo 18, tel. 753/4–20–27. No reservations. Dress: casual. AE, MC, V.*

La Gaviota. A mini-beach club where you can spend an afternoon swimming and sunning after having a seafood lunch. Lots of locals like this one, and the bar is pleasant. Ask the taxi driver to come back for you around 4 PM. *On Playa La Ropa, no phone. No reservations. Dress: casual. MC, V.*

★ **La Mesa del Capitán.** Now a tradition in Zihuatanejo, this restaurant has been around since 1975. The steaks, ribs, and seafood dishes are prepared under the watchful eye of the proprietor, Luz Maria. Indoor and terrace seating are available. *Calle Nicolás Bravo 18, tel. 753/4–20–27. Reservations for groups only. Dress: casual. AE, MC, V.*

Inexpensive (under $20)

La Bocana. A favorite with locals as well as visitors. The service is good and the seafood is a treat. You can eat three meals a day here. Musicians sometimes stroll through. *Calle Juan N. Alvarez 13, tel. 753/4–35–45. Dress: casual. MC, V.*

La Perla. At Doña Raquel's popular seaside restaurant and video sports bar, the hands-down favorite is *Filete La Perla,* a fish fillet baked in aluminum foil with cheese, garlic, onion, and tomato. *Playa La Ropa, tel. 753/4-27-00. Dress: casual. Open daily 9 AM-10 PM. MC, V.*

★ **La Sirena Gorda.** The specialty here is seafood tacos (try the shrimp-and-bacon combo); meals are served in rustic, yet pleasant, surroundings. *Paseo del Pescador 20-A, tel. 753/4-26-87. Dress: casual. MC, V. Open Thurs.-Tues. 7 AM-10 PM.*

Mi Casita. You can watch your meal being cooked at this clean and friendly restaurant. Try the Mexican breakfasts and affordable surf-and-turf dishes. *Calle Ejido 7, no phone. Dress: casual. AE, MC, V.*

★ **Nueva Zelanda.** From breakfast through dinner everybody drops in to this little coffee-shop-style place, which serves *tortas* (Mexican sandwiches on crusty rolls), tacos, and enchiladas. *Calle Cuauhtémoc 23, no phone. No reservations. Dress: casual. No credit cards.*

★ **Pepper's Garden.** A newcomer to Zihuatanejo, Pepper's Garden serves Mexican food. It has beautifully carved doors that lead onto the patio dining area and many picturesque colonial touches. *Calle Ignacio Altamirano 46, tel. 753/4-37-67. Reservations suggested. Dress: casual. MC, V.*

Puntarenas. This plain place serves Mexican food and great breakfasts. It's a favorite with those in the know and there's often a line, but it's worth the wait. *Across the bridge at the end of Calle Juan N. Alvarez, no phone. No reservations. Dress: casual. No credit cards. Open only in high season.*

Lodging

Ixtapa/Zihuatanejo hotel rates vary widely, and after Easter they drop 30%-40% and sometimes more. Most of the budget accommodations are in Zihuatanejo. Rooms everywhere are clean and have private baths with showers.

Ixtapa

Expensive ($100-$185)

Located at the very end of the hotel zone, on a beach protected by Ixtapa Island (which makes it good for swimming), this is the former Hotel Playa Linda, with enlarged rooms and a new restaurant, lobby, and shopping area. The rooms-each with a private terrace-are strung through one- and two-story buildings. *Carretera Escenica S/N, Municipio Teniente Azueta 40880, tel. 753/3-19-85 in Ixtapa or 5/520-6457 in Mexico City. 150 rooms with bath. Facilities: 2 tennis courts, 2 pools, 2 restaurants, outdoor disco. AE, DC, MC, V.*

★ **Krystal Ixtapa.** This attractive beachfront property is part of an excellent Mexican chain that also has hotels in Cancún, Puerta Vallarta, and Mexico City. Home to Christine's, Ixtapa's most popular disco, and Bogart's restaurant, the Krystal is one of the liveliest spots in town. *Playa Palmar, 40880, tel. 753/3-03-33. 260 rooms and suites with bath. Facilities: 2 restaurants, coffee shop, discotheque, 2 tennis courts, pool. AE, DC, MC, V.*

Sheraton Ixtapa. Large and lavish, this is the first hotel as you approach Palmar Bay, near the Palma Real golf club. Its rooms are built around an enormous atrium. *Playa Palmar, 40880, tel. 753/3-18-58. 332 rooms with bath. Facilities: pool, 4 tennis courts, 3 restaurants, coffee shop, 2 bars with live entertainment. AE, DC, MC, V.*

Stouffer Presidente. A beautifully landscaped resort that was among Ixtapa's first beachfront properties. The rooms are divided between colonial-style villas that line winding paths through the grounds and a tower with a glass elevator that provides a sensational view of Ixtapa. *Playa Palmar, 40880, tel. 753/3-00-18. 401 rooms with bath. Facilities: 3 restaurants, bar, 2 tennis courts, 2 pools, wading pool. AE, DC, MC, V.*

★ **Westin Ixtapa.** Formerly known as the Camino Real, this is a pyramid-shaped hotel whose rooms (all with private balconies) seem to cascade down the hill to secluded Vista Hermosa beach. It is one of Ixtapa's largest hotels, and is noted for excellent service. *Playa Vista Hermosa, Box 91, 40880, tel. 753/3-21-21. 428 rooms with bath. Facilities: 3 restaurants, 2 bars, 4 tennis courts, 3 pools, wading pool. AE, DC, MC, V.*

Moderate ($55–$100)

Posada Real. Smaller and more intimate than most of the Ixtapa hotels, the colonial-style Posada Real sits on Palmar Beach, has lots of charm, and offers good value. A Best Western hotel. *Playa Palmar, 40880, tel. 753/3-16-85 and 3-17-45. 108 rooms with bath. Facilities: 3 restaurants, 2 bars, disco, 2 pools, wading pool, tennis court. AE, DC, MC, V.*

Zihuatanejo

The best hotels are on La Madera or La Ropa beaches or overlooking them; the least expensive ones are downtown.

Very Expensive ($185–$285)

★ **Villa del Sol.** A small hotel with a reputation as one of the best in Mexico (its excellence has won it membership in the prestigious Relais et Château organization), the Villa del Sol is set on the best beach in Zihuatanejo. Although the hotel has all the amenities of a large resort, guests are welcome to do nothing if they so desire. *Playa La Ropa, Box 84, 40880, tel. 753/4-22-39. 21 air-conditioned suites (1 and 2 bedrooms). Facilities: restaurant, pool, beach club, tennis court. Rate includes breakfast and dinner. Children under 14 not accepted in high season. AE, MC, V.*

Expensive ($100–$185)

Puerto Mío. This small hotel overlooking Zihuatanejo Bay is part of a marina and residential development. The suites, distributed among several Mediterranean-style villas, are tastefully furnished, and the decor makes wonderful use of the bright colors always associated with Mexico. *Playa del Almacen, Bahía de Zihuatanejo, 40880, tel. 753/4-37-45, fax 753/4-20-48. 35 suites. Facilities: pool, 2 tennis courts, restaurant, bar. AE, DC, MC, V.*

Moderate ($55–$100)

Bungalows las Urracas. Each of the units has a porch in a shaded garden, a kitchen, and a stove. Bungalows las Urracas is a great bargain—and lots of people know it, which places it greatly in demand. *Playa la Ropa, Box 141, 40880, tel. 753/4-20-49. 16 bungalows. No credit cards.*

Catalina-Sotovento. Really two hotels in one, this oldie-but-goodie sits on a cliff overlooking the beach, to which you descend on stairs. The rooms are large and decorated in Mexican colonial style, with ceiling fans. *Playa La Ropa, Box 2, 40880, tel. 753/4-20-32 or 753/4-21-37. 124 rooms with bath. Facilities: 2 restaurants, 2 bars. Rate includes breakfast and lunch or dinner. AE, DC, MC, V.*

★ **Villas Miramar.** Overlooking La Madera beach, the pretty stucco rooms are nicely decorated and have tile showers, air conditioning, and ceiling fans. This all-suite hotel is an excellent value, but you need to book three months in advance and sometimes as much as two years ahead for Christmas and Easter. *Playa La Madera, Box 211, 40880, tel. 753/4-21-06. 18 suites. Facilities: restaurant, bar. AE, MC, V.*

Inexpensive (under $55)

Avila. Downtown and close to all the pier activity, the Avila has large clean rooms (some are air-conditioned), TVs, and ceiling fans. *Calle Juan N. Alvarez 8, 40880, tel. 753/4-20-10. 27 rooms with bath. AE, MC, V.*

Bungalows Pacíficos. Located on Playa La Madera but closer to downtown than the Palacios, each of these bungalows features two spacious, well-ventilated rooms (sleeping four between them), a kitchen, and a large terrace. *Playa la Madera, 40880, tel. 4-21-12. 6 bungalows. No credit cards.*

Fiesta Mexicana. The pretty Mediterranean-style rooms are surrounded by inviting palm-shaded gardens. Make reservations well in advance, especially for the winter season. *Playa la Ropa, Box 4, 40880, tel. 753/4-37-76. 63 rooms with bath. Facilities: restaurant, bar, pool. AE, DC, MC, V.*

Irma. Simple and clean, this hotel on a bluff overlooking Playa La Madera (and accessible by a stairway) gets lots of repeat visitors. Guests may use the beach club at the Fiesta Mexicana. *Playa la Madera, Box 4, 40880, tel. 753/4-20-25. 75 rooms with bath. Facilities: restaurant/bar, 2 pools, tennis. AE, DC, MC, V.*

Palacios. Some rooms in this colonial-style hotel on La Madera beach have ocean views, and all are either air-conditioned or have ceiling fans. *Playa La Madera, 40880, tel. 753/4-20-55. 24 rooms with bath. Facilities: pool, restaurant. No credit cards.*

Zihuatanejo Centro. In downtown Zihuatanejo near La Mesa del Capitán restaurant, this is a clean, commercial-type hotel. *Calle Agustín Ramírez 2, 40880, tel. 753/4-26-69. 69 rooms with bath. Facilities: pool, parking. AE, MC, V.*

The Arts and Nightlife

A good way to spend an evening is at a happy hour in one of Ixtapa's hotels. Drinks are two for the price of one, and there is no cover charge to enjoy the live music. And don't miss the sunset. **The Bay Club,** on the road to Playa La Ropa, has a marvelous ocean view. **Mariano's** bar in Zihuatanejo is where the locals hang out. The decor is nothing special, but everyone goes, especially singles. **Benji-Pio Bar,** in the El Portal shopping center, and **Le Club,** at the Westin Ixtapa, are also popular. **Christine's** at the Krystal in Ixtapa is the town's liveliest disco. **Tropicana Ixtapa,** behind Bancomer in the La Puerta Shopping Mall, is a combination restaurant, bar, and nightclub featuring live music and entertainment.

Euphoria is a spectacular new disco across from the Posada Real hotel. Every night, **Carlos 'n Charlies** has a dance party on a raised platform on the beach.

On Friday night, the **Sheraton Ixtapa** and the **Villa del Sol** hotel in Zihuatanejo stage lively Mexican Fiestas that are lots of fun.

There is a movie house with several screens, the **Multicinema Vicente Guerrero,** next to the Somex bank on Calle Vicente Guerrero. Tickets cost about $1. Movies in English generally have Spanish subtitles.

Conversion Tables

Distance

Miles/Kilometers To change miles to kilometers, multiply miles by 1.61. To obtain miles, multiply kilometers by .621. A quick conversion you can do in your head: divide the kilometers by 8, multiply by 5 to get miles; divide the miles by 5, multiply by 8 to get kilometers.

Km to Mi	Mi to Km
1 = .62	1 = 1.6
2 = 1.20	2 = 3.2
3 = 1.9	3 = 4.8
4 = 2.5	4 = 6.4
5 = 3.1	5 = 8.1
6 = 3.7	6 = 9.7
7 = 4.3	7 = 11.3
8 = 5.0	8 = 12.9

Feet/Meters To change feet to meters, multiply feet by .305. To change meters to feet, multiply meters by 3.28.

Meters to Feet	Feet to Meters
1 = 3.3	1 = .31
2 = 6.6	2 = .61
3 = 9.8	3 = .92
4 = 13.1	4 = 1.2
5 = 16.4	5 = 1.5
6 = 19.7	6 = 1.8
7 = 23.0	7 = 2.1
8 = 26.2	8 = 2.4

Liquid Volume

U.S. Gallons/Liters To change U.S. gallons to liters, multiply gallons by 3.79. To change liters to U.S. gallons, multiply liters by .264.

Liters to U.S. Gallons	U.S. Gallons to Liters
1 = .26	1 = 3.8
2 = .53	2 = 7.6
3 = .79	3 = 11.4
4 = 1.1	4 = 15.2
5 = 1.3	5 = 19.0
6 = 1.6	6 = 22.7
7 = 1.8	7 = 26.5
8 = 2.1	8 = 30.3

Spanish Vocabulary

Words and Phrases

	English	*Spanish*	*Pronunciation*
Basics	Yes/no	Sí/no	see/no
	Please	Por favor	pore fah-**vore**
	May I?	Me permite?	may pair-**mee**-tay
	Thank you (very much)	(Muchas) gracias	(**moo**-chas) **grah**-see-us
	You're welcome	De nada	day **nah**-dah
	Excuse me	Con permiso	cone pair-**me**-so
	Pardon me/what did you say?	Perdón?/Mande?	pair-**doan/ mahn**-dey
	Could you tell me?	Podría decirme?	po-**dree**-ah deh-**seer**-meh
	I'm sorry	Lo siento	lo see-**en**-toe
	Good morning!	Buenos días!	**bway**-nohs **dee**-ahs
	Good afternoon!	Buenas tardes!	**bway**-nahs **tar**-dess
	Good evening!	Buenas noches!	**bway**-nahs **no**-chess
	Goodbye!	Adiós!	ah-dee-**ohss**
	Mr./Mrs.	Señor/Señora	sen-**yore**/ sen-**yore**-ah
	Miss	Señorita	sen-yo-**ree**-tah
	Pleased to meet you	Mucho gusto	**moo**-cho **goose**-toe
	How are you?	Cómo está usted?	**ko**-mo es-**tah** oo-**sted**
	Very well, thank you.	Muy bien, gracias.	**moo**-ee bee-**en, grah**-see-us
	And you?	Y usted?	ee oos-**ted**
	Hello (on the telephone)	Bueno	**bway**-no
Numbers	one	uno	**oo**-no
	two	dos	dos
	three	tres	trace
	four	cuatro	**kwah**-tro
	five	cinco	**seen**-ko
	six	seis	sace
	seven	siete	see-**eh**-teh
	eight	ocho	**o**-cho
	nine	nueve	new-**ev**-ay
	ten	diez	dee-**es**
Days of the Week	Sunday	domingo	doe-**meen**-go
	Monday	lunes	**loo**-ness
	Tuesday	martes	**mahr**-tess
	Wednesday	miércoles	me-**air**-koh-less
	Thursday	jueves	who-**ev**-ess
	Friday	viernes	vee-**air**-ness
	Saturday	sábado	**sah**-bah-doe
Months of the Year	January	enero	eh-**neh**-ro
	February	febrero	feh-**brair**-oh
	March	marzo	**mahr**-so
	April	abril	ah-**breel**

May	mayo	**my**-oh
June	junio	**hoo**-nee-oh
July	julio	**who**-lee-yoh
August	agosto	ah-**ghos**-toe
September	septiembre	sep-tee-**em**-breh
October	octubre	oak-**too**-breh
November	noviembre	no-vee-**em**-breh
December	diciembre	dee-see-**em**-breh

Useful Phrases

Do you speak English?	¿Habla usted inglés?	**ah**-blah oos-**ted** in-**glehs**
I don't speak Spanish	No hablo español	no **ah**-blow es-pahn-**yol**
I don't understand (you)	No entiendo	no en-tee-**en**-doe
I understand (you)	Entiendo	en-tee-**en**-doe
I don't know	No sé	no **seh**
I am American/British	Soy americano(a)/ britanico(a)	soy ah-meh-ree-**kah**-no(nah)/ bree-**tah**-nee-co(cah)
What's your name?	¿Cómo se llama usted?	**koh**-mo say **yah**-mah oos-**ted**
My name is . . .	Me llamo . . .	meh **yah**-mo
What time is it?	¿Qué hora es?	keh **o**-rah es
It is one, two, three . . . o'clock.	Es la una, son las dos . . . tres	es la **oo**-nah/sone lahs dose . . . trace
Yes, please/No, thank you	Sí, por favor/No, gracias	**see,** pore fah-**vore**/no **grah**-see-us
How?	¿Cómo?	**koh**-mo
When?	¿Cuándo?	**kwahn**-doe
This/Next week	Esta semana/próxima semana	**es**-tah seh-**mah**-nah **proke**-see-mah say-**mah**-nah
This/Next month	Este mes/el próximo mes	**es**-tay mess/el **proke**-see-mo mess
This/Next year	Este año/el año que viene	**es**-tay **ahn**-yo/el **ahn**-yo kay vee-**yen**-ay
Yesterday/today/ tomorrow	Ayer/hoy/mañana	ah-**yair**/oy/mahn-**yah**-nah
This morning/ afternoon	Esta mañana/ tarde	**es**-tah mahn-**yah**-nah/ **tar**-deh
Tonight	Esta noche	**es**-tah **no**-cheh
What?	¿Qué?	kay

What is it?	¿Qué es esto?	Kay es **es**-toe
Why?	¿Por qué?	pore **kay**
Who?	¿Quién?	kee-**yen**
Where is . . .?	¿Dónde está . . . ?	**dohn**-day es-**tah**
the train station?	la estación del tren?	la es-tah-see-**on** del **trehn**
the subway station?	la estación del Metro?	la es-ta-see-**on** del **meh**-troh
the bus stop?	la parada del camión?	la pah-**rah**-duh del kah-mee-**ohn**
the post office?	el correo?	el koh-**reh**-oh
the bank?	el banco?	el **bahn**-koh
the . . . hotel?	el hotel . . . ?	el oh-**tel**
the store?	la tienda . . . ?	la tee-**en**-duh
the cashier?	la caja?	la **kah**-hah
the . . . museum?	el museo . . . ?	el moo-**seh**-oh
the hospital?	el hospital?	el ohss-pea-**tal**
the elevator?	el ascensor?	el ah-**sen**-sore
the bathroom?	el baño?	el **bahn**-yoh
Here/there	Aquí/allá	ah-**key**/ah-**yah**
Open/closed	Abierto/cerrado	ahb-**yer**-toe/ser-**ah**-doe
Left/right	Izquierda/derecha	is-key-**er**-dah/dare-**eh**-chah
Straight ahead	Derecho	deh-**reh**-cho
Is it near/far?	¿Está cerca/lejos?	es-**tah** **sair**-kah/**lay**-hohss
I'd like . . .	Quisiera . . .	kee-see-**air**-uh
a room the key a newspaper a stamp	un cuarto la llave un periódico un timbre de correo	oon **kwahr**-toe lah **yah**-veh oon pair-ee-**oh**-dee-koh oon **team**-bray day koh-**ray**-oh
to buy . . . cigarettes matches a dictionary soap a map a magazine paper envelopes a postcard	comprar . . . cigarros cerillos un diccionario jabón un mapa una revista papel sobres una tarjeta postal	kohm-**prahr** see-**gah**-rohss seh-**ree**-ohs oon deek-see-oh-**nah**-ree-oh hah-**bone** oon **mah**-pah **oo**-nah reh-**veess**-tah pah-**pel** **so**-brace **oo**-nah tar-**heh**-tuh pos-**tahl**

How much is it?	¿Cuánto cuesta?	**kwahn**-toe **kwes**-tuh
It's expensive/ cheap	Está caro/barato	es-**tah kah**-roh/ bah-**rah**-toe
A little/a lot	Un poquito/ demasiado . . .	oon poh-**kee**-toe/ day-mah-see-**ah**-doe
More/less enough/too much/too little	Más/menos Suficiente/ demasiado/ muy poco	mahss/**men**-ohss soo-fee-see-**en-tay**/ day-mah-see-**ah**-doe/ **moo**-ee **poh**-koh
Telephone	Teléfono	teh-**leh**-foh-no
Telegram	Telegrama	tay-lay-**grah**-muh
I am ill/sick	Estoy enfermo(a)	es-**toy** en-**fair**-moh(ah)
Please call a doctor	Por favor llame a un médico	pore fa-**vore ya**-may ah oon **med**-ee-koh
Help!	¡Auxilio!	ow-**zee**-lee-oh
Fire!	¡Encendio!	en-**sen**-dee-oo
Caution!/Look out!	¡Cuidado!	kwee-**dah**-doh
A bottle of . . .	Una botella de . . .	**oo**-nah bo-**tay**-yah deh
A cup of . . .	Una taza de . . .	**oo**-nah **tah**-sah deh
A glass of . . .	Un vaso de . . .	oon **vah**-so day
Ashtray	Un cenicero	oon sen-ee-**say**-roh
Bill/check	La cuenta	lah **kwen**-tah
Bread	El pan	el pahn
Breakfast	El desayuno	el day-sigh-**oon**-oh
Butter	La mantequilla	lah mahn-tay-**key**-yah
Cheers!	¡Salud!	sah-**lood**
Cocktail	Un aperitivo	oon ah-pair-ree-**tee**-voh
Dinner	La cena	lah **seh**-nah
Dish	Un plato	oon **plah**-toe
Dish of the day	El platillo de hoy	el plah-**tee**-yo day oy
Enjoy!	¡Buen provecho!	bwen pro-**veh**-cho
Fixed-price menu	La comida corrida	lah koh-**me**-dah co-**ree**-dah
Fork	El tenedor	el teh-neh-**door**
I am diabetic	Yo soy diabético(a)	yo soy dee-ah-**beh**-tee-koh(kah)
I am on a diet	Estoy a dieta	es-**toy** ah dee-**eh**-tah

I am vegetarian	Soy vegetariano(a)	soy veh-heh-tah-ree-**ah**-noh(nah)
I cannot eat . . .	No puedo comer . . .	no pweh-doe koh-**mare**
I am ready to order	Voy a ordenar	voy ah or-den-**are**
I'd like to order	Me gustaría ordenar . . .	may goose-tah-**ree**-ah or-den-**are**
I'm hungry/thirsty	Tengo hambre/sed	**ten**-go **ahm**-breh/sed
Is the tip included?	¿Está incluida la propina?	es-**tah** in-clue-**ee**-dah lah pro-**pea**-nah
It's good It's bad	Está bueno No está bueno	es-**tah** **bway**-no no es-**tah** **bway**-no
It's hot/cold	Está caliente/frío	es-**tah** kah-lee-**en**-tay/**free**-oh
Knife	El cuchillo	el koo-**chee**-yo
Lunch	La comida	lah koh-**me**-dah
Menu	La carta	lah **car**-tah
Napkin	La servilleta	lah sair-vee-**yeh**-tah
Pepper	La pimienta	lah pea-me-**en**-tah
Please give me	Por favor déme	pore fah-**vore** **day**-may
Salt	La sal	lah sahl
Spoon	Una cuchara	**oo**-nah koo-**chah**-rah
Sugar	El azúcar	el ah-**sue**-car
Waiter!/Waitress!	¡Por favor Señor/Señorita!	pore fah-**vore** sen-**yor**/sen-yor-**ee**-tah
The wine list	La lista de vinos	lah **lees**-tah deh **vee**-nos

Index

Personal Itinerary

Departure *Date*

Time

Transportation

Arrival *Date* *Time*

Departure *Date* *Time*

Transportation

Accommodations

Arrival *Date* *Time*

Departure *Date* *Time*

Transportation

Accommodations

Arrival *Date* *Time*

Departure *Date* *Time*

Transportation

Accommodations

Fodor's Travel Guides

U.S. Guides

Alaska

Arizona

Boston

California

Cape Cod, Martha's Vineyard, Nantucket

The Carolinas & the Georgia Coast

Chicago

Disney World & the Orlando Area

Florida

Hawaii

Las Vegas, Reno, Tahoe

Los Angeles

Maine, Vermont, New Hampshire

Maui

Miami & the Keys

New England

New Orleans

New York City

Pacific North Coast

Philadelphia & the Pennsylvania Dutch Country

San Diego

San Francisco

Santa Fe, Taos, Albuquerque

Seattle & Vancouver

The South

The U.S. & British Virgin Islands

The Upper Great Lakes Region

USA

Vacations in New York State

Vacations on the Jersey Shore

Virginia & Maryland

Waikiki

Washington, D.C.

Foreign Guides

Acapulco, Ixtapa, Zihuatanejo

Australia & New Zealand

Austria

The Bahamas

Baja & Mexico's Pacific Coast Resorts

Barbados

Berlin

Bermuda

Brazil

Budapest

Budget Europe

Canada

Cancun, Cozumel, Yucatan Penisula

Caribbean

Central America

China

Costa Rica, Belize, Guatemala

Czechoslovakia

Eastern Europe

Egypt

Euro Disney

Europe

Europe's Great Cities

France

Germany

Great Britain

Greece

The Himalayan Countries

Hong Kong

India

Ireland

Israel

Italy

Italy's Great Cities

Japan

Kenya & Tanzania

Korea

London

Madrid & Barcelona

Mexico

Montreal & Quebec City

Morocco

The Netherlands Belgium & Luxembourg

New Zealand

Norway

Nova Scotia, Prince Edward Island & New Brunswick

Paris

Portugal

Rome

Russia & the Baltic Countries

Scandinavia

Scotland

Singapore

South America

Southeast Asia

South Pacific

Spain

Sweden

Switzerland

Thailand

Tokyo

Toronto

Turkey

Vienna & the Danube Valley

Yugoslavia